$4.05

THE RELIGIOUS BACKGROUND
OF AMERICAN CULTURE

THE RELIGIOUS BACKGROUND
OF AMERICAN CULTURE

BY

THOMAS CUMING HALL, D.D.

Professor of English and American History and Culture,
University of Goettingen

AUTHOR OF "HISTORY OF ETHICS WITHIN ORGANIZED
CHRISTIANITY", "THE SOCIAL MEANING OF
MODERN RELIGIOUS MOVEMENTS", ETC.

BOSTON

LITTLE, BROWN, AND COMPANY

1930

To my Colleagues of the Philosophical Faculty
of the University of Goettingen
this book is dedicated in warm friendship
January, 1930

INTRODUCTORY NOTE

American history begins before America was discovered. The United States are what they are because men from England carried with them to the new land a strong tradition born of long struggle with what they thought or instinctively felt were strange and un-English ways.

The story of that tradition, especially upon its religious side, has been so misread or neglected that whole chapters of North American history are even now crying for rewriting.

A creative tradition cannot be reduced to any one simple formula. The interests of human life are too complicated to be enclosed in a phrase, and although the economic interpretation of history has thrown a flood of light upon many dark places in the study of the forms that religion, law and politics take, the word economic must be very broadly interpreted and made to include nearly all human wants and urges, in order to greatly help us. And amongst the most constant historic urges is one that is perhaps not capable of complete definition, but which under many several forms we call religion.

It is strange that in all that has been written about the United States in recent years little has been said about our religious history. We have many books more or less satisfactory about our economic history; our civilization has been well and fully treated in many books; our politics, our social structure and our literature have been amply dealt with; but an attempt to trace the course of our religious history seems to be utterly lacking. In the criticism of American civilization by thirty well-known Americans [1] no chapter is devoted to religion in any shape. In the admirable summary of our social structure by Charles A. and Mary Beard,[2] the treatment of religion is most scanty and insufficient, even though just and impartial. No recent history or textbook does the subject justice, and even in the latest edition of Channing, Hart and Turner's valuable Guide,[3] the literature on the subject of our religious development is amazingly meager.

This is the more surprising, because the early historians like George Bancroft and Palfrey have dealt with the history of New England as if it were the story of a religious experiment pure and simple, which it certainly was not. The thoughtful student of the religious streams of feeling recurrent in our history will find in them some explanation of many of our present most pressing questions. We will attempt to outline in a purely impartial way some of these currents and explain their connection with our advancing life. We take no attitude in regard to the truth or untruth of the religious positions examined; that is a personal judgment of worth with which in these pages we have no concern. We only insist that an examination of these currents and tides of religious thought and feeling cannot be passed by, without serious misinterpretation of American life.

To understand certain phases of life in America, whether on Fifth Avenue in New York or the Lake Shore Drive in Chicago, one must go back to the mists and half-lights

---

[1] "Civilization in the United States, an Inquiry by Thirty Americans." Editor, Harold E. Stearns. New York, 1922.

[2] Charles A. and Mary Beard. "The Rise of American Civilization." 2 Vols. New York, 1927.

[3] "Guide to the Study and Reading of American History." Cambridge, 1912.

of the days of King Edward III in England. The study
therefore of the English dissenting tradition should be
the first step in trying to understand the American Republic, and this fact has been forgotten or never realized;
hence the story of our relations to England has often
been clouded and rendered hazy and unsatisfactory. It
is neither helpful nor accurate to constantly speak of our
English tradition without at once asking which of several
English traditions we really mean. For English life is not
and never has been dominated by only one tradition, no
matter how much of a unit the nation may at times seem
to have been.[1] And it is the business of the thoughtful
historian to ask himself which English tradition is really
fundamental in American life.

In spite of our very conglomerate population, it is con-
fessedly an English tradition that governs the life of the
American Republic, and which has given us our speech.
French, Spanish, Dutch, Scandinavian and other elements, not to speak of the Irish and Scotch, have built
themselves into the fabric of a common American life,
but none of the fifty-two non-American varieties of national groups mentioned in the Inter-Church Commission's
Report on the steel strike of 1919 [2] has had the numbers,
unity and cohesion sufficient to seriously challenge the
supremacy of the Anglo-Saxon in North America. Although probably from sixty to seventy per cent. of the
population has non-English blood in its veins, no other
national unit has been able to force either its speech or
its tradition on even a small area of the United States.
And as a governing class rose in the colonies, it was able
to absorb even hostile elements and mold them to a

[1] *Cf.* Benjamin Disraeli's "Sybil or the Two Nations", published in 1845.
[2] *Cf.* page 133 of the Report on the Steel Strike of 1919 by the Commission of Inquiry, The Interchurch World Movement, Bishop Francis J. McConnell being Chair-
man. New York, 1920.

common will as, for instance, in Manhattan and New Jersey.

It must then be of deepest interest to ask what is this tradition; where lies the power it possesses; where and when did it arise; and what is its main content?

We hope to show that the answer of the schoolbooks and the newspapers, which is generally that it is the Puritan tradition, is both superficial and unhistorical. We will try to demonstrate that Puritanism properly understood has very little to do with marking our mentality or giving modes and patterns to our thought.

At the most English Puritanism only affected one region and that for only a very short time. We hope to prove that the real type of thought and feeling which has guided and guarded the onward march of American civilization is much older, stronger and broader in its reach than English Puritanism ever was. For the foundation of the American social structure is, we hope to show, the much older dissenting tradition of England; and that to understand our history we must free ourselves from many prejudices and cease to speak by rote the familiar phrases of the history books, and study anew the character and content of English Dissent.

We are not writing for the theological specialist, and will therefore very briefly point out what our main contention will be. We hope to show that an old, radical and hardy English Protestantism existed before the Continental type of Protestantism appeared. That this radical Protestantism it is that has dominated and to a great extent still dominates Anglo-American thinking.

Roughly we may divide Christian groups for our purposes on the basis of their estimate of the highest authority in religion. The Roman Catholic Church believes in a living organic Church as the highest authority, with the Holy

Father as its infallible mouthpiece when he speaks officially "*ex cathedra.*" The Anglo-Catholic group regards the national Church as an authoritative living organization, with an historic episcopate reaching back to the Founder of the Christian Church to guarantee the validity of orders and sacraments and the purity of the faith. The Continental type of Protestantism regards the Word of God contained in the Scriptures of the Old and New Testament as the highest authority, but looks to a pure conciliar historic Church to interpret that Word. This pure Church is easily recognized by its possession of an orderly ministry, sacraments rightly administered and a pure churchly discipline adequately maintained. The old English radical Protestantism, under the stress of persecution, poverty and cultural isolation, broke with the thought of an authoritative and interpreting Church, as well as with the conception of a priestly ministry and laid the emphasis solely upon the Bible as God's Word and as sufficient for salvation to every believing soul. Every individual was capable of being led of the Spirit to a right understanding of Scripture, and needed no historic Church and no priesthood to guide and interpret.

As a matter of fact, the thought of this old dissenting Protestantism was deeply affected by historic Christianity without always knowing whence its conceptions arose. For instance, the stern predestinarianism of Paul, Augustine and Wyclif became a common characteristic of Dissent, but so little did it know of its origin, indeed so little does it still know of it, that this is nearly always attributed to Calvin, often where Calvin was utterly unknown, or where, had he been known, he would have been regarded with deep suspicion because of his High Churchism and deeply sacramental character.

All this we hope to set forth more elaborately and yet

in terms all may understand; and hope that all who read and understand will in the future instinctively translate the term "Puritan" in ninety-nine cases out of a hundred by the more exact phrase, "the Anglo-American Dissenting Mind."

CONTENTS

PART I

PART II

xiv   *Contents*

PART ONE

THE GROWTH OF RELIGIOUS DISSENT IN
ENGLAND

CHAPTER I

THE GENESIS OF THE ENGLISH DISSENTING TRADITION

Very early in the history of the British Islands, the Roman form of Christianity came as the herald of a higher culture to a people that was evidently intellectually in advance of the outworn forms of their religious past. Into what seems to have been a sort of religious vacuum came the message of the monk Augustine in 597. Christianity seems to have been eagerly accepted and it was therefore a nominally Christian people that surrendered to the Norman conquerors in 1066. And as the Normans also held fast to the Roman Church, there was no seeming division between conquerors and conquered on the field of religion.

As a matter of fact, however, the Saxon and the Norman types of religious expression were probably more markedly different than the Church historians are generally willing to admit. The differences were obscured by the common loyalty to an historic Church and to the person of the pope as its visible head.[1] The Danish invasion made little difference, but from earliest times may be marked two streams of tendency in the churchly development. The Normans brought with them a well-developed aristocratic feudal hierarchy from Rome. Whereas the Saxon population adhered without doubt to a simpler and more primitive monastic type of Catholicism.[2] And when we

---

[1] Cf. William Stubbs. "The Constitutional History of England." 3 Vols. Oxford, 1874, especially Chaps. VIII and IX of Vol. I.
[2] Cf. Karl Mueller. "Kirchengeschichte." Bd. I. ss. 287–290.

remember that the Saxon population was relatively inarticulate, the differences were in all probability greater
than even the documents reveal them as being. In the
poem of William Langland, "Piers the Ploughman",
there are abundant evidences of the great and seemingly
widening breach between the humbler, mainly Saxon
lower clericals and the powerful, mainly Norman hierarchy. The Saxon priesthood was not so strongly tempted
to engage in political intrigue as was the ruling class, and
thus remained more purely religious and single-hearted.
Moreover, Rome made the grave mistake of filling the
higher positions in the Church with Spanish, Italian and
more especially French incumbents; many of these,
though far from all, treated England as simply a land to
exploit, and their positions as sinecures, thus widening the
gap between the classes. The *Acta Concilia* [1] are full of
complaints on this head.

It is not difficult to reconstruct a rude picture of this
more primitive monastic Catholicism, because it survived
in Ireland and Scotland long after it had seemingly disappeared in England. But for our purpose it is sufficient
to point out that the mere fact that the lower Saxon clergy
were married and had children who demanded clerical
position on the basis of their birth, and that this was
common well up to the time of the Tudors, [2] alone shows
the relative separateness and independence of the Saxon
type of Catholicism.

Thus far back in English history may be traced a line
of division between two slowly separating religious sys-
tems of thought and feeling. A conquered people made
landless and more or less economically oppressed, developed one way of thinking, while the ruling minority

---

[1] David Wilkins. "Concilia Magnæ Britanniæ et Hiberniæ." Tome. I, 465, 590, etc.
[2] John Myrck's "Instructions for Parish Priests", p. 72. Wilkins' "Concilia", II, 60.

fostered the foreign hierarchy, with its quite separate mood and pattern.

Both Roman Catholicism and feudalism are inherently cosmopolitan; for the Roman hierarchy cannot be true to itself and its history without an assertion of world-wide calling; and feudalism can hardly be content with less than imperial power moving in ever-ascending steps from higher to the highest. The feudal class in any highly organized community has more in common with the governing minorities in other lands than with the relatively uncultivated masses it rules, and feudal classes in different lands have always been ready to unite to sustain the power of a threatened ruling minority and to make common cause against the revolting masses, whether in the Middle Ages or at the time of Napoleon.

Hence it happened that the rising tide of national feeling in England, as elsewhere in the thirteenth and fourteenth centuries, met with the consistent opposition of these two great cosmopolitan forces, the Church and feudalism. Nor was it exceptional in the historical development of that day that the religious life of England soon reflected the social division; the oppressed Saxons cherished their own customs and began to resent the Norman ways. English kings were at first more often interested in their French possessions than in the welfare of their own English subjects, but the rising tide of national feeling linked itself gradually with a national language and with recognition of Saxon nationality, and carried the Throne with it.

The triumph of the English speech was only an outward and visible sign of the comparative success of the lower orders in reasserting their claim to power. It was not then and is not even now a complete triumph. In a familiar passage in Sir Walter Scott's "Ivanhoe" the differences between the speech of the Saxon serfs and the Norman lords is emphasized. The serf attended the living pig, but as soon as it was ready to be eaten it went to the lord's table and became pork, and to-day H. W. Fowler, in his dictionary of English usage, calls attention in an amusing comment upon "genteelism" to the supposed social superiority of words of French-Latin origin over the plain and downright Saxon terms.[1]

What might have happened had England remained even nominally a religious unity can only be surmised in the light of such analogies as Italy and Spain. As it happened, however, in so many cases, the great social and economic divisions in the national life received a profound and far-reaching expression in the rise of an entirely different religious outlook, which was to have momentous consequences in the life and purposes, not only of England, but of those coming colonial possessions, in which this religious outlook was to mold the thought and feelings of many then unborn generations.

The first signs of this religious division were in the field of law. The enactments known as the "Statutes of the Provisors", Edward III, in 1306 and of "*Præmunire*" in 1335 were in response to the growing demand for independence of Rome. They were the expression of a gradually forming national will. The ideal was not indeed any separation from the historic Church, but simply a demand that the national life find its expression in a national Church, and that, though the pope should remain as the central religious authority, the Church in England should have its own administration and its own higher ecclesiastics.

When, then, Richard Fitzralph of Armagh in his "de

---

[1] *Cf.* H. W. Fowler, "A Dictionary of Modern English Usage", Oxford, 1926, under the caption "Genteelisms"; see also sensible remarks under "Saxonism."

Pauperie Salvatoris" echoed the arguments of Marsiglio of Padua [1] his demand was confined to asking for a division between the temporal and the spiritual power of Rome. And this demand was being made in France and Bavaria as well as in England; for everywhere, even in Italy, the national feeling was rising.

But in England there are marked features of this struggle for nationality that separate it from the history of similar struggles in other lands. For without entering upon the vexed question of the significance of race in the rise of culture, it may be safely said that two racial traditions struggled for supremacy. The Norman nobility asserted its claim to feudal ownership of the land [2] and established an aristocratic tradition based upon land-ownership that persists in England to this day. On the other hand, a conquered Saxon population took refuge in towns and cities and established a trading tradition which has also never passed away. However alike the life of these two classes became, there remained a great difference in both thought and feeling and even manner of speech, which has never been overcome.

With the exception of the Tudors, the Throne of England has been constantly occupied by non-native houses. French, Scotch, Dutch and German houses have succeeded each other, and as a consequence of this, the aristocracy has never surrendered its soul to the Monarchy or permitted the rise of an autocratic Throne as in France or in some of the German States. One result of this has been that the Throne has often had to appeal to the populace and found in it a support against a powerful aristocracy. In the struggle between a feudal, aristocratic,

[1] About 1270 to 1336 or 1343. Main work, "Defensor Pacis seu dictiones vel libri tres adversus usurpatem Romani pontificis jurisdictionem", about 1324–1326.
[2] William Stubbs. "Constitutional History of England." Vol, I, pp. 259–280. Green's "Short History of the English People." Vol. I, pp. 151–163.

churchly tradition, and the simpler faith of the common people, the English Throne has frequently been on the side of the people as over against the hierarchy.

By quick instinct feudalism in England has often turned to the highly developed aristocratic hierarchy of Rome as to a kindred spirit, and felt keen sympathy with the æsthetically attractive culture of the priestly, sacramental system of Middle-Age Catholicism. From the beginning therefore the Norman nobility was on the side of Catholicism, even when in opposition to Rome it demanded an English Catholicism. But the struggle within Catholicism began early, and the moot question was whether Catholicism should be Roman or national. On this question the early literature leaves no room for doubt on which side the sympathies of the common people were.

The sympathy of the lower orders might not have meant much in any such internal struggle had the poorer and mainly Saxon masses remained in helpless serfdom. But the Black Death came at last also to England, about 1348. Wages rose. Serfs could seek and find freedom in the towns by relatively easy process.[1] There arose a working class of comparative independence, and on the land arose the new yeoman class. The self-consciousness of the lower orders, and especially of the yeoman class, must have been immensely raised by the victories of Crecy (1346) under Edward III, of Poitiers (1356) under the Black Prince and Agincourt (1415) under Henry V. For these victories were won by the yeomen fighting on foot against the flower of French chivalry, and once for all demonstrated that the armored knight was not invincible, and that gunpowder was to make armor useless.

---

[1] Thorold Rogers. "Six Centuries of Work and Wages." Paul Vinogradoff. "Villainage in England", Oxford, 1892, especially Chap. VI, pp. 178–210.

The population of England in the fourteenth century was between three and four millions.[1] Serfdom was rapidly breaking down for many reasons. Industry of a somewhat unorganized and primitive character was rising in economic importance, in which neither slaves nor serfs could be used with profit. The Throne of England was becoming of greater importance to the royal house than even its French possessions, and to maintain the armies needed for Continental use the English yeomen and the lower orders generally had to be humored. It was especially necessary to stand well with the tax-paying city merchants. These in turn looked up to the king, while the great land-owning aristocracy regarded the king as only *prius inter pares*, and were often very jealous of the increasing power of the Throne.

Thus it happened that the sympathies of the House of Lancaster were at first strongly with the party of the National Catholic Church, whereas the great aristocratic leaders seem generally to have been equally strong friends of Rome, as the source of all tradition and power. Norman French dominated the thought of the ruling nobility, and Latin the services of the Church, but the common man spoke Saxon and held to the simpler, less developed religion of earlier days.

In the poem of William Langland, "Piers the Ploughman",[2] and the later poems that went under his name— for our purpose, it is not necessary to distinguish between the original and the imitations—we have pictures of the increasing strain between the conceptions of the two classes. The author of "Piers the Ploughman" under-

[1] No later estimates seem to have changed substantially the estimate of Thorold Rogers in "Work and Wages", pp. 115-120.

[2] "The Vision of William concerning Piers the Ploughman." Early English Textual Society. Ed., Dr. Skeat. 1859.

stood Latin and quotes Latin in his poems, but he does not mix the two languages. His is a simple Saxon tongue, with the Saxon alliteration. His emphasis is upon conduct, and his complaints against the Church of his day are its haughty and gainful spirit. These "visions" and "dreams" are the forerunners of similar literary forms in like circles later on, as in Bunyan's "Pilgrim's Progress", nor is the outlook upon life of the two men so very different.

The absorption of the triumphant Norman population by the lower Saxon masses might have been quietly consummated, the Saxon nobility acting as a mediating element, but the feudal claim made even the Saxon nobility landless in their own country, and even if the tenure was often only changed on paper, the lower orders never having been really owners of land, yet the situation led, as it has always done in feudal countries, in Japan as in Europe, to the development of trading towns where the energetic and the restless elements could find a relative freedom for self-development. So in England, as the towns and cities grew, they formed a refuge place for the more freedom-loving elements of the Saxon people.[1] Here there arose a new life, apart in many ways from the life on the great feudal farming lands under the immediate supervision of a noble class, holding fast to the Norman language and the feudal tradition.

And it is worthy of note that in the inevitable struggle between the Throne and the higher aristocracy for supreme power, the town and the city were often to give the deciding voice, and that the Throne had often to turn to the town for its support against the claims of a jealous nobility. It is therefore significant that when Chaucer

---

[1] *Cf.* P. Kropotkin. "Mutual Aid." Chap. V. The literature is too great to quote. See Vinogradoff, "Villainage in England" for sketch, pp. 1–39.

(about 1340–1400) wrote for the rich middle-class and town population, he chose English; whereas John Gower (probably somewhat older than Chaucer, died 1408) who was the poet of the richer nobility, wrote in French at first, and only later and much more stiffly in English. Wyclif, also writing for the educated class, wrote in Latin, but when he wished to reach the people he turned like Chaucer to the speech of the common man.

But however different in color and detail the religious outlook of the Norman and Saxon populations may have been, both held fast in the earlier years to substantially one system of thought. The Normans had, undoubtedly, come to England with a much higher æsthetic development; [1] but both they and the Saxons accepted an historic Christian Church, with the pope as head and highest religious authority; an elaborate and very impressive sacramental system, entrusted by Christ himself to his authoritative Church; an historical priesthood, with the power of the keys under the pope; the duty of obedience in both faith and practice of the layman to this infallible and historic Church as represented in its priesthood. Outside of the pale of this churchly Communion there was no ordinary hope of salvation.

With regard to the contents of this faith there was general agreement. Neither the Norman nobility nor the Saxon serfs entertained any doubts as to the inherited religious tradition. But not only in England but everywhere questions were being raised in regard to the limits of the political power of the pope. There was at first no thought of any separation from the spiritual authority of Rome. It is useless to speculate upon what might have happened had a national Anglo-Catholic Church, with a

[1] But for contrary view see J. Fred. Hodgett's "The English in the Middle Ages." Lecture I, pp. 35 *ff*.

relatively widespread, accepted dogmatic theology, a fairly universally used form of worship and an efficient central episcopal administration, modeled after that of the *Curia,* sprung into being.

All the most beautiful products of the culture alike of the Anglo-Saxon monastery and of France, which the Norman nobility brought with it, were bound up with the Catholic tradition. The music of the Mass; the sculptural beauty of the rising church buildings; the order and solemnity of the daily and weekly worship; all the classic traditions of Greece and Rome, together with the wealth of Roman literature; all the sacred memories of past heroes of the faith; the very dress of the clergy and the art of the missal and the mural paintings; all these things entered into the nobler spiritual and artistic life of every worshiper. Even the yawning gap between a haughty land-owning aristocracy and the laboring serf was in a measure bridged, as both knelt before the cross on which was stretched a divine agony for the sins of the world. Separation from the Catholic tradition must have seemed to the cultivated man a deliberate going out into outer darkness, a willful rejection of all that made life beautiful and shed any light upon that unknown future that lay beyond the grave.

Not only so, but the Catholic Communion rendered a service often overlooked or ignored. Every masterful social organization must have some door through which gifted and ambitious members of the excluded classes may eventually rise to power and influence, if only to make up the wastes of war and neutralize the effects of too close intermarriage; and through the priesthood of the Catholic Church talent could and did rise to the most commanding eminence, carrying up with it many who would otherwise have remained discontented and destructive forces. The structure of the Church was not and did not pretend to be "democratic" in any sense in which one may use that appallingly abused word. It grew up with a frankly feudal society, but its ministering orders, its married and unmarried priesthood, its educational and organizing zeal made it in the eyes of thoughtful men an almost indispensable element of that society. The whole conception of culture, order and intelligence was bound up with the Catholic tradition; at the same time even the Norman nobility desired, as England became more and more its real home, and the soil of England assumed more importance than the forsaken fields of France, to feel itself master in its own house and to share in the administration of the National Church. Such a National Church might have long ministered to both the conquered and the conquerors, and in spite of inevitable small protesting minorities, supplied a national religious tradition that would have withstood for ages all storms of doubt. But this was not to be. The cleavage in the structure of English life has seldom received the proper emphasis. It is no use going into the vexed question of race and blood. The Normans were also substantially Teutonic. [1] The sources of the cleavage may have been in the beginning racial, but the broad line of an economic inferiority runs through English history, and the separation has been made plain in the rise of a form of feeling and a habit of thought that have had incalculable influence upon the whole Anglo-American development.

[1] The claims of Gobenau, Housten Stewart Chamberlin and Stoddard do not affect our argument, but must await much more investigation and discussion before they can be accepted.

CHAPTER II ·

To in any way appreciate the greatness of Wyclif, it is
first necessary to face frankly the changes he brought
about in the minds and moods of the simple folk of his
day. Happily the literature of the era gives us a fairly
full picture of the popular system of belief.[1] Naturally
the Mass stood in the foreground both of the worship and
the faith. The pope was the undisputed highest authority,
his infallibility being an article of popular faith long
before its official proclamation. The monk and the
monastery entered very largely into the picture, and the
older monastic type of Christianity was in all probability
in more or less full possession of the lower orders. Some
rivalry existed between the regular priests and these
wandering monks, as in all Catholic history. As we have
noticed, the lower orders of priests were sometimes, at
least, married. Pilgrimages to favorite shrines were a
regular means of diversion as well as of pious devotion.
Chaucer's picture of the pilgrimage to Canterbury throws
some most interesting side lights upon the social meaning
of such pilgrimages. Altars to local saints were everywhere in evidence. No healthy religious system concerns
itself only with the worship of its adherents, but enters
into all the details of the life. The Catholic Church had
taken over from paganism many of the feasts and sacred

---

[1] Bernard Lord Manning in his little essay "The People's Faith in the Time of
Wyclif" has assembled most of the material, but treats it without insight and uncritically.

days of popular opinion, and had filled them with her own special message, so that the whole Christian year rounded out symbolically the cycle of religious experience as centered about the sacrifice of the cross.

The power of the priesthood rested upon the firm faith of the people in auricular confession, in penance and the ability of the priest or confessor in the name of God and His Holy Church to forgive sin. The dogmatic refinements by which the educated were guarded against the many possible abuses of this teaching were not widely known to the common man, to whom the priest stood in the place of God's voice, and to whom the office was more than the man. This was necessary because of the exceedingly large place the saving sacraments had in the popular imagination. The administration of these sacraments was of great importance, as they had inherent magic power, imparting grace otherwise wholly beyond human reach. Thus the priest, apart from his character, was the messenger of saving grace, and in baptism, the Mass, extreme unction, confessional forgiveness, confirmation, marriage and purification the sinner must feel sure that the rite had efficacy without his having assurance of the private character of the ministering agent. It is difficult for a modern American Protestant to quite realize how complete must be the separation of the office from the man in Catholic circles in order to conserve faith in the healing possibility of a sacramental service. Here also the refinements of an elaborate and intellectually highly respectable Catholic theology save the system from many easy reproaches.

The æsthetic feeling of the people was ministered to by rich music, vocal and instrumental; the church buildings were growing in beauty and in spaciousness; priestly garments appealed to the feeling for adornment and satisfied the needs of thousands of women for self-expression in the art of embroidery; and to many men the rich adornment of missals and other sacred writings rendered the same service. Solemn processions and wonderfully well-developed ritual worship trained the Catholic mind to communal and orderly expression, and sought to lift it above the meanness and insignificance of much daily toil.

The common man was, in the worship of the Church brought as nowhere else into contact with the much higher developed culture of his Norman conquerors. Without doubt, in spite of the complaints that foreign priests exploited England, there is another side to the picture. These foreign ecclesiastics came to England bringing a culture and refinement which, if perhaps too dearly bought, were still much needed. They brought a new feeling for the art of building, and because the Sacrifice of the Mass stood in the midst of the religion of the day, no building could be too beautiful to shelter the altar upon which lay the body of the crucified Redeemer. Thus rose the village church and the stately cathedral amid a sad poverty in the ordinary home, to remind the simple worshiper of an eternal beauty into which by faith and reverence he too might enter.

Into this world of faith and habit John Wyclif was born somewhere about the year 1324. The name is written in many different ways, but gradually the simple form we have chosen seems to have won its way. Just where he was born is also a theme for academic discussion. It only interests us here to note that his home was a stronghold of sturdy Saxon thought, and that for some time the Duke of Lancaster, John of Gaunt, was his immediate overlord.

He emerges in English history as one of the foremost representatives of the critical wing of English scholasticism, and stands in direct line with William Ockham (about 1300 to 1347) and the older Duns Scotus (about 1265–1308) and along with Bradwardine and Fitzralph, the Archbishop of Armagh. In Oxford his name was powerful, and his orthodoxy beyond all question. Neither Wyclif nor any of those just named had any idea of disputing the spiritual power of the pope, even when gradually assuming a critical attitude toward the claims of political power. And Wyclif was well on in life when he at last directly attacked the political authority of the pope. It was a time of great confusion in the Roman Church, and the great Reformation of 1414, which began with the Council of Constance, was not yet even on the horizon. The successful resistance of the French king, Philip the Beautiful, to the claims of the pope, and at last the removal under Clement V of the Roman *Curia* to Avignon, and the seemingly complete submission of the pope to French demands, had weakened the influence of the pope all over Europe, but most especially was England affected. Moreover, as a result of the flight of the papal court to Avignon, and the disputes of rival claimants, the Church had lost much ground as guardian of the morals of the people and educator of the masses.

Once Wyclif had begun to question the political authority of the pope, and had defied with the help of the Duke of Gaunt the power of the archbishop, his progress toward complete separation from the thought of his time was rapid. He took part in a mission to Bruges but that part does not seem to have been very important, and we have but few details of his outward life. He is singularly reticent in regard to scenes which must have been very dramatic. His development was often seemingly a purely intellectual one, but that is only on the surface. In fact, Wyclif's real interest was ethics, and all his heresies sprang from his fierce demand for an authority on this field more trustworthy than that of the pope. In 1377 Gregory XI issued bulls against Wyclif, and cited him to appear at Rome, but from then on Wyclif's defiance of the pope, Archbishop Sudbury and Archbishop Courtenay becomes more and more pronounced, The Duke of Lancaster could not however follow him when he at last attacked the purely magic character of the Eucharist, and entered upon a controversy that was to color the religious life of England and America more deeply than even the work of Luther.

When he appeared at St. Paul's Cathedral to answer before the archbishop, John of Gaunt surrounded him with armed men, and the trial never took place. But from that on Archbishop Courtenay pushed Sudbury aside and became the outwardly successful, energetic and bitter opponent of Wyclif and his followers. In all the many descriptions of the scene, no one seems to have realized just what it meant for the history of thought in every English-speaking country; that the lines were drawn not simply between one dogmatic statement and another, but that from the entrance of William Courtenay upon the scene it became a struggle between the haughty, aristocratic, Norman tradition, with all its noble and splendid features, and a new passion filling the lives and strengthening the hands of the poorest of the poor.

Archbishop William Courtenay was a representative of the highest aristocracy of England. He was the son of Hugh, the Earl of Devon, and was through his mother related to the Throne itself; was a man of force, burned with sincere zeal for the Catholic Church, but was also a patriotic Englishman, unwilling to sacrifice any real English rights to Rome. He hated with all the force of a great soul every innovation. He felt himself quite on the

level with the king, and intensely disliked the whole policy
of Edward III. He stood for the old aristocracy, the old
Church and the old orthodoxy. His first battle was to
drive Wyclif from Oxford, and then to compel all Wyclif's
friends, one by one, to recant and desert their master.
After that he could not rest until all outward traces of
Wyclif and his Lollards were removed from the English
Catholic Church.

He it was who compelled Wyclif to appeal to the people
and to seek for them and for himself some higher authority
than either pope or Church. Wyclif seems to have been
no preacher like Luther, no organizer like Calvin, no skillful rewriter of creedal faith like Melanchthon, but he set to
work to translate the Bible and to train "Poor Preachers"
for a work that is still being carried on over the prairies of
a land Wyclif did not know existed, by men and women
speaking his tongue and holding fast to his faith. Yet
these simple folk often do not know where they got their
inspiration, and no one has yet raised a fitting monument
to the memory of the Father of Anglo-American Protestantism.

It is extremely unlikely that Wyclif himself foresaw
just what was to happen. Like his spiritual children,
Wesley and "General" Booth, he simply desired, as had
Francis of Assisi before him, to revive the spiritual life
of the Church in which he himself was to die. But from
1377 until his death in 1384 he was to work untiringly at
laying foundations that have not yet been shaken. As
he was driven from Oxford and the churches, as the powerful archbishop closed one door after another to him and his
followers, he turned ever more to the poor and lowly,
began his work in English and even more than Chaucer
is to be called the Father of the English language.

It was no light task for this old and straitened man

to take up the battle with the whole entrenched forces of Church and State; to thrust in his hand and shake the foundations of the splendid structure of an English Catholic Church, for such became the issue. If Wyclif is the Father of the dissenting mind no less is the able and devoted Archbishop Courtenay the Father of Anglo-Catholicism.

Wyclif did not attack the Mass itself; he was at Mass when the stroke came that heralded his death. He did something more dangerous: he took from it for the ordinary man all magic and external power. Preaching, he said was more important than the sacrament, and the body of Christ no longer lay upon the altar as the center of worship. The logic of his position was never more tersely expressed than by Emerson long after, who probably knew little of Wyclif, when he said the sacrament had simply ceased to interest him. The church building ceased all of a sudden to be a temple and became a conventicle. Cathedral and minster were no longer shelters for the Highest, lying in state upon the altar, but convenient places of assembly to hear preaching and to make room for prayer. For the common man Wyclif swept away even more effectually than Luther and Calvin the whole historic Church, for in its place he put the individual interpretation of the English Bible by every simple reader. The historic priesthood lost all meaning, for every Christian was a priest before God, and was under obligation so far as he had gifts and strength to proclaim the Word of God. The forgiveness of sin had nothing to do with either the magic of a sacrament or the message of a minister, but depended solely upon the calling of God to life and duty; and only in the faithful fulfillment of that duty could one make his calling and election sure. The sinner could not earn it, but he could by loving service come to realize that God had called and that he had come. Every soul could and must come into God's presence without mediation of either priest or Church. Salvation rested upon no external ceremony but solely upon a change of heart to which God called all men, and to which all the elect would respond. The pope himself could not be sure of salvation, save as he lived the life of love, and many popes had made evident by their lives that they were probably not saved.

It is hard for any one brought up in the all-pervasive atmosphere of a dissenting religiosity to realize what it must have meant for the day and generation of Wyclif to hear such teaching. With one sweep he had made the great Universal Church wholly unnecessary, for the chief meaning of such a church is to guarantee to the seeking soul the genuine character of the saving sacraments and the administering priesthood. But if the sacraments are not necessary for salvation, indeed in the extreme logic of the situation have nothing to do with salvation, and every man is a priest before God, if he is a Christian at all, then any mediating church is an insolence. Neither Luther nor Calvin went so far. Luther carefully guarded the historic Church, although he preferred to call it the Christian community; and Calvin no less carefully guarded the historic teaching ministry with its episcopal rights and duties. And for both men the sacraments were divinely appointed means of grace, which the soul neglected at its peril.

The significance of Wyclif's attitude to the sacraments has been seemingly largely overlooked, and only his work in spreading the English Bible has been emphasized. And without doubt he is the real author of that movement.[1] At the same time it was the taking away of the sacraments that made preaching and the English Bible so important if Christianity was to be preserved. The English Bible

[1] *Cf.* M. Deanesly, "The Lollard Bible." 1920. A model study of the whole subject of Wyclif's relation to the Lollard Bible.

took the place of both the pope and the historic Church as authorities in the Christian life; and the pulpit, or rather the preaching of the Bible, took the place of the sacraments as the essential means of grace. It is extremely doubtful if Wyclif himself realized as clearly as did his bitter enemies what was the reach and sweep of his teaching. Nor did he live long enough to see the movement that embodied his doctrine come to its own.

Henceforth the English Bible has taken a peculiar place in the life of England. Wyclif and the Lollards made the Bible the banner of revolt from that day on. In the long four hundred years of warfare for religious freedom and equality the English Bible has been the source of strength and comfort, whether under Wat Tyler, Oliver Cromwell, William of Orange or the Chartists. Luther's translation of the Bible has been of simply incalculable influence upon the Continent of Europe; but no land, not even any Protestant canton of Switzerland, has been a land of one book as England has been.

This place of the Bible is largely due to Wyclif's institution of the "Poor Preachers." It is no mistake, as Doctor Workman alleges, to call them lay preachers. Wyclif calls them laymen himself.[1] No doubt Wyclif used the most educated material he could get, but he is undoubtedly the Father of that lay preaching, which has marked England's Protestantism in strong contrast to the churchly Protestantism of the Continent. And this was in accordance with his well-known doctrine of the priesthood of all believers. These preachers Wyclif trained and sent out with sketches of sermons and addresses. They no doubt were suggested by the spiritual Francis-

[1] Herbert B. Workman. "John Wyclif." Vol. II, p. 202. In "Sermones", Ed. J. Loserth, Bd. II, s. 202, they are called "*idiotæ et simplices*", a quotation which Workman himself uses in another connection. See also Buddensieg, "Polemical Works in Latin", Bd. I, s. 371, where they are also called "*idiotæ*."

cans, but both the motive and the message were entirely different. It would now be hard to think of Anglo-Saxon Protestantism without this feature of its life, and it is no accident that whenever in Anglo-American life the religious impulse revives, it at once finds expression in lay preaching. Wesley's class leaders, "General" Booth's "officers", the revival preaching of Moody and his successors will at once come to mind. No similar phenomenon is found in Lutheran or Calvinistic Protestantism.

The scholastic development of Wyclif's theology is interesting but has little to do with our main discussion. It is sufficient to point out that what he handed over to his followers was the old Pauline-Augustine dogmatic system, but no longer in the name of an historic Church, but on the basis, or supposed basis, of the New Testament. Throughout the whole Lollard movement there goes a strong deterministic trend, which is often mistaken in later days for Calvinism, but has really little to do with Calvin's main emphasis upon an elect Church. It was the basis of the Lollard ethical appeal, for only by the good life could one be sure of the election.

Wyclif's whole teaching was strongly national in character, as it was born of the political movement away from Rome and her political domination. And the further Wyclif went the more bitter did he become against the pope. Not even Luther succeeded in implanting so strong and lasting a hate and fear of the pope as did Wyclif, which was naturally still further nourished by the persecutions of the succeeding years. But Wyclif also laid the foundation for a deep-rooted distrust of the organized Church, for he taught that the Church must be poor, and that it should only depend upon the free gifts of the members.[1] Wyclif is again the source for the demand for a

[1] Arnold's "Select English Works." Vol. I, p. 268 and many other places.

free Church in a free State. It is a thousand pities that his work on the Church remained unfinished, for it is not always clear just how far Wyclif was inclined to go, but his followers had less doubt, and persecution settled the matter finally for them.

Neither Luther nor Wyclif gives us full satisfaction in trying to master their thought of the relations between Church and State. One has the strong feeling that Luther was a good deal of an opportunist in the matter. Wyclif goes perhaps deeper and further, because he soon saw that the State never could really bring in the Kingdom of God, and seems to have come to the conclusion that a lasting separation was the only way open. His Lollard followers soon came to look upon the State as a necessary evil before whose power each man must bow, but as really possessing no inherent authority. Only power in the service of God's commandments had any real authority over the hearts and consciences of men. Nevertheless, when the State acted in accordance with the laws of God, its power was justified and it had authority over the elect.

Wyclif's doctrine of the Reign of God[1] has been called obscure, and no doubt the form and style are scholastic and wordy. At the same time the leading idea is plain, and has exercised an influence upon quite uneducated circles in English Dissent. God is thought of as the only supreme feudal overlord. He alone can dispose of property and power. Only the true servant of this feudal lord has a sure right to either property or power. True it is that unrighteous men are often in possession, but that is usurpation and sooner or later God's judgment will be meted out to all such usurpers. At the same time God is also the judge, and the Christian man cannot always know God's mind, and must act in conformity to the

[1] "De Dominio Divino." Ed. R. L. Poole and Losert. 1885-1904.

seeming situation and leave final judgment to God. The true servant of God has all possession and all power. Many passages distinctly remind one of Luther's later tract upon the "Freedom of the Christian Man."

Even apart from the difficulty of deciding exactly which of the writings that go under his name are genuine, there are insuperable difficulties in the way of giving anything like a unified picture of Wyclif's teaching. The time of his final development was too short. In 1374 he was still a critical yet orthodox schoolman of the realist school. In 1384 he died still in the nominal communion of the Roman Church, and as yet not convicted of heresy, though summoned to Rome to answer for his views. In this short time he laid the foundation for the most radical type of Protestantism still in existence, and taught doctrines that still control the lives of thousands and thousands of men and women in England and America.

Moreover, it lay in the very nature of his transference of authority from an external Church with a living voice to the Bible alone, that every one was entitled to find in that book what commanded his heart and conscience. The Bible is an Oriental literature stretching over at least eight hundred years. It is simply impossible to find one theological system throughout that slow development. Not even the New Testament is capable of reduction to one self-consistent system of truth without the aid of an external authority. In point of fact, Wyclif had banished all outward authority, and put in its place the individual conscience interpreting the English translation of this vast and rich Oriental literature.

Nevertheless, in its larger sense, he took his theology in reality from the historic Church. His doctrine of God, of the Trinity, of the sacrifice of Christ, of the Holy Spirit, of justification in Christ, the sacrifice of the cross, eternal life in heaven for the justified, eternal pains of hell for the damned, the resurrection from the dead and the last judgment, as well as prayer, the forgiveness of sin and the coming judgment: all conform to the historic type. It is hard to say how far Wyclif realized that his teachings were, in point of fact, very radical. Like Luther, he had no desire to leave the historic communion of the Roman Church; at the same time, by his emphasis upon the individual judgment in the reading of the Bible, he really made that historic connection quite unnecessary.

Nor is it to-day possible to say just how far Wyclif is responsible for the whole Lollard movement. The Lollards were driven at once to defend themselves and without doubt very soon went further than Wyclif had gone. The exact line between the writings of Wyclif and his immediate followers cannot now be drawn with any great certainty.[1]

[1] *Cf.* Workman, Vol. I, p. 329. In a discussion of the English works of Wyclif the author tries to separate the genuine from the later additions to the English works, but much is still unsettled. *Cf.* also Loserth. "Johann von Wiclif." Vol. II. Anhang A.

CHAPTER III

THE LOLLARD MOVEMENT

It is impossible to say what would have happened had Wyclif's teachings remained a purely academic matter. But even in Wyclif's own day his revolt against the papal authority was to become inextricably intertwined with political and social movements of great moment for all Anglo-Saxon life.

The relation of Wyclif's activity to the rebellion of the peasants in 1381 will probably never be completely cleared up. G. M. Trevelyan has summed up the matter fairly in showing that the causes of both social and religious unrest lay deeper than the expressions of them in the peasants' rising.[1] Wyclif himself never mentions it apparently. He was at work in Lutterworth, having been banished from Oxford, and was being opposed by the powerful Courtenay, although still under the protection of Lancaster. He certainly took no active part in it, and as a man of peace, hating war, he could not have much sympathy with the violence of the movement. He had no quarrel with private possession as such, but only with the corruptions he thought it brought into the Church. He was himself a lord of a manor, was of good family and had claims to social distinction apart from his being one of the most learned men of England, and having up to his death the protection if not friendship of the Duke of Lancaster.

---

[1] G. M. Trevelyan and E. Powell. "The Peasants' Rising and the Lollards." London, 1899. Cf. also Trevelyan's "England in the Age of Wycliffe." 3d Ed. London, 1904. Cf. H. B. Workman. "John Wyclif." Vol. II, Ch. VII, pp. 221–245.

The times were stirring. The yeoman class was awakening to a sense of its wrongs and its power. As it happened, however, the whole aristocratic tradition in England had become linked with the Norman conquering class. It may be somewhat exaggerated to say with Mr. Frederick Hodgetts[1] that; "The hatred to the Normans was fiercer and more settled than any national feeling that has existed in any other nation. From all the MSS. we find that the Normans were kept, not at arm's length, but at spear's length, by the people."

We must remember the power of property to bring together the possessing classes, and these comprised both Saxons and Normans. However, the intense dislike of the Normans exhibited by Mr. Hodgetts is a wholesome reminder that the fusion of the two races was not as peaceful nor as complete as has often been represented.

Whether much Norman blood flowed in English veins we cannot say. Mr. Hodgetts thinks that as the Normans did not as a rule bring their wives and families to England they were swamped by the native population.[2] There was certainly little likelihood that a proud Norman aristocracy would mingle in any legitimate way with Saxon serfs. But that the Saxon nobility was related to the Norman nobility very soon is evident.[3] Surely what happened was that the upper classes mingled to form an aristocracy deeply under the influence of what was, in spite of the assertions of Mr. Hodgetts, a really higher culture, namely that of the Norman nobility.

But the national feeling was rising, and after the home-

---

[1] J. Frederick Hodgetts. "The English in the Middle Ages." Lecture II, p. 48.

[2] *Ibid.* Page 16.

[3] *Cf.* William Stubbs' "Constitutional History of England", Vol. I, Ch. XIII, where is quoted the passage in the "Dialogus de Scaccario", I. c. 10. "*Jam cohabitantibus Anglicis et Normanis et alterutrum uxores ducentibus vel nubentibus, sic permixtæ sunt nationes ut vix discerni possit hodie, de libris loquor, quis Anglicus quis Normannus sit genere; exceptis dumtaxat ascriptitiis qui villani dicuntur.*" Select Charters, p. 193.

land of the Norman nobility had fallen back to France, the aristocracy became more completely English. Moreover, the monarchy had its battle to fight, and was everywhere engaged in a struggle for absolute power against the higher aristocracy, out of which it had itself sprung. In this struggle, as so often has happened, the Throne had to appeal to the people for support, and the people had more hope from a monarch whom they did not see or really know than from the immediate oppressing land-owning class, to which they had to pay all kinds of rent.

The rising importance of foot soldiers lent the monarch a weapon against the aristocracy, sheltered in their enclosed and fortified castles. The real feeling of any reigning house cannot fail to be at bottom aristocratic, and link itself, in any final struggle for power, with property and tradition; at the same time the Throne has in the evolutionary process to become at times the actual protector of anti-aristocratic forces, in order to maintain itself against a jealous nobility, forever plotting for its own advancement.

It was in the midst of just such a struggle that Wyclif's teaching came and set England afire. The semi-religious character of the rising under Wat Tyler and John Ball is not open to dispute. The Lollards were blamed for the bloodshed and the rioting.[1] At once the possessing classes came together to put down the rioting, and with fair and lying words the brave young king rallied enough common folk about him to divide the ranks of what threatened to be a very formidable insurrection; and once the peasants were divided the rest was easy. The bloody work of the warlike Bishop of Norwich and the death on the other hand of Archbishop Sudbury at the hands of a mob in London sowed the seeds of a bitterness between the

---

[1] *Cf.* G. M. Trevelyan. " The Peasants' Rising and the Lollards."

lower-class reformers of the Church and the upper-class sustainers of the Normanized hierarchy, which has never been sufficiently emphasized.[1]

The Lollard movement became a secret religious revolt, after its protest in 1395 it was driven more and more underground, and became increasingly not only a revolt against the Catholic Church, but against the whole life and manner of the classes still faithful to the Catholic tradition.

Even after the Norman ruling class had lost heavily in the One Hundred Years War, and especially in the desperate struggle between the houses of York and Lancaster (1459–1485) the Throne failed to gain undisputed power. The barons who forced the Magna Charta upon King John were thinking, it is true, only of the interests of their class, but they represented a force in English life that was never fully subdued. In this struggle between the Throne and the Nobility there was slowly evolved an Anglican Catholic Church, which was naturally drawn to the side that promised most power and influence to it. This Church became the religious expression of the ruling class, and as the Lollard movement was the direct denial of the Catholic tradition under the influence of Wyclif, it became increasingly Protestant and increasingly the religious expression of the lower class. This marks something in English history that has never been fully realized and which separates its religious history from that of the Continent; for Luther had the support of German princes and the aristocratic city classes. The later Continental Reformation became to a large degree a matter of geography. All classes were either Protestant or Roman Catholic. Whereas in England the oldest type of Protes-

---

[1] Not even in J. R. Green's "A Short History of the English People." Illustrated Edition. Ed. Mrs. Green. See Vol. II, pp. 470–49, where a dramatic description is given of the revolt.

tantism became the distinct possession of a lower class, and under the Lollards took on the character of a more or less class-conscious protest against the whole traditional outlook upon life of the upper classes.

It would be unhistorical to make Wyclif wholly responsible for this feature of English Protestantism. Nevertheless there lay something of this spirit of antagonism to the culture of his day in his own teaching.[1] He disliked painted church windows, elaborate church music and high ceremonial. At the same time it is surely easy to think of these dislikes as those of a man strongly touched by the teachings of the reforming orders, particularly of the Franciscans. But in his followers we see the steady growth of a deep-seated antagonism to the amusements, the forms of worship, the spirit and drift of the ruling classes more or less closely identified with the Anglican Catholic mode of thought and habit of life.

What the peasant insurrection meant to Wyclif's soul we shall never know. A year after it had been put down in fire and blood, he had the first stroke, that warned him of his approaching end. He never ceased to train his lay preachers for their task, and as his university friends fell away from him he must have turned more and more to the common people. Perhaps it would not be wholly fanciful to connect that first stroke with the battle in his own soul and the agitation of the fearful struggle going on without. With neither party can he have had much sympathy. One gets the impression in reading the work of Wyclif, that fierce and passionate as he could be at times, he was not a good party man. The individualism that has marked his movement also marked him. At a time when Oxford was battling for its freedom in his name he seems to have

---

[1] *Cf.* Herbert B. Workman. "John Wyclif." Vol. II, pp. 97-118. Also Gotthard Lechler. "Johann von Wiclif." Bd. I, ss. 564-573.

made no movement to come to its help.[1] He was seemingly a lonely man, who felt his loneliness and longed for
family ties when it was too late to form them.[2] His Poor
Preachers, however, went out to lead all sorts of movements. They in fact turned one of England's worlds
upside down. The connection, however, of the movement
with an attack upon property had the effect such an attack will always have; it united otherwise hostile classes
in a common effort to put the disturbers down.

It is astonishing nevertheless with what success these
Poor Preachers did their work. To appreciate it we must
turn back to the outlook upon life which they attacked
and destroyed for thousands and thousands to this day.
Soon the pope was more hated in these circles that even
in Germany after Luther had finished his work. The
Lollards thought of the pope as not only Antichrist, but as
an enemy of England and of their liberty. The thought of
a Universal Church, which had dominated men's minds
for a thousand years, was seemingly banished in a night. A
Universal Church had proved a tyrant and a danger, therefore English Protestantism resolved itself into unnumbered
sects and independent groups, in contented division. The
weakness of this is patent so long as one thinks of an open
fight for world supremacy by a Universal Church. But
the Protestantism of Wyclif abandoned cheerfully all such
ambition. It was content to silently permeate all society
and felt sure that the elect would hear the call. The
conventicle took the place of the historic Church. This
proved, of course, from one point of view a weakness, but
on the other hand it saved them often in the day of persecution, for their very weakness was a strength; they had

---

[1] Gotthard Lechler. "Johann von Wiclif." Bd. I. ss. 665–699.
[2] *Cf.* pathetic passages in the tract "Of widdid men and wifis", Arnold's "Select
English Works." Vol. III, p. 188.

no central authority to be attacked; they had no great property to defend; they had no visible union, so that only the really enthusiastic remained with them. The great mass of indifference and conventional attachment that has always weighed down Christianity in its organized forms from the beginning fell away.

After Sir John Oldcastle had been done to death, they had no visible leadership. They needed no priests and had no buildings; moreover, the fact that Wyclif had died in the communion of the Church enabled many with a good conscience to remain in the nominal membership of the State Church. With what effect they carried on their propaganda is seen in the estimates of their enemies. Even James Gairdner, who has little sympathy with either Wyclif or the Lollards, seems to accept the estimate of their numbers as one half of the population.[1] Careful independent examination of all the sources relied upon for any estimate of their numbers has convinced the writer that it is quite impossible to say more than that they were very numerous, and widely scattered over all Britain and southern Scotland. That they actually were a half of the population seems to the writer extremely unlikely. Certainly the open adherents of Wyclif were never so much as a third of the population, although there may have been many who secretly sympathized with this or that side of the movement. One thing we may assume: that the Lollards had the sympathy, secret or open, of the poorer classes, although even here the very lowest classes were often their bitterest foes, on account of the Lollard attitude toward sport and amusements generally.

True this attitude was far more a class dislike of the expensive ways of life of an oppressing class than even the Lollards themselves knew. The very lowest class

[1] Doctor James Gairdner. "Lollardy and the Reformation in England." Vol. I, p. 13.

however was dependent upon the upper aristocracy, and rejoiced in the shows, the dances, the tournaments and display from which they in a small way often profited. It was the serious-minded and upward-struggling class that adopted Lollardy, and thus it became ever more the schoolmaster to train a people for struggle and to nerve its most energetic and independent members for a contest for power.

There remains no doubt what class the Lollards reached. Persecution was soon successful in driving away all the educated and the aristocratic from its ranks. As Doctor Gairdner says about it later on: "Instead of half the population being Wycliffite in the beginning of Henry VIII.'s reign, cases of heresy were at that time comparatively rare, and such heretics as there were met with very little sympathy from men of good education or of any social standing."[1] And this was no doubt true from the beginning. In other words, the classes the Lollards appealed to with success were just the classes that made early Christianity strong. It was the small, hard-working, rising, poor, dispossessed class, instinctively feeling its way to greater power and influence, imbued with the faith that a righteous God had called it to duty and life eternal, and full of the sense of the futility of a life of mere pleasure.

The reformed Roman Catholic Church after the Council of Constance in 1414 set itself to root out the hated heresy, but before that Archbishop Courtenay, who died in 1396, had given himself to its suppression and gave the pronounced lower-class character to the movement, which it was from this time on to bear. The line was soon drawn. The Anglican Catholic Church was not long in capturing the universities, the old nobility, the richer classes in the towns, the Crown and the proletariat—so far as such a

[1] Gairdner. "Lollardy and the Reformation in England." Vol. I, p. 14.

class was present—with the dependent household-service class. The lists of the martyrs give us a fairly accurate picture of the classes that accepted Lollard doctrine. But the Lollards in their turn sought to separate themselves and their worship and their lives as far as possible from the hated, oppressing State Church. They visited no shrines, worshiped no images, kneeled to no cross, went no longer to confession. They needed no Gothic church buildings. Where two or three were gathered together, there was a church. They needed no papist priest, for the preaching of the Word of God was for them more than sacrament and the hearing better than confession. Indeed, the sacrament was either neglected altogether, it seems, or simply regarded as a sweet reminder of the death of the Saviour. All sacred days were swept away save the one day of rest, on which the Lord rose. All the æsthetic elements of the highly developed Catholic worship became for them heathen idolatry, and stained glass, church organs, paintings in churches were all heathenish and unbiblical.

We have abundant testimony in the trials and petitions to the character of Lollard doctrine. We must remember, of course, that we are dealing with a very humble and obscure element of the people. Poor and hard-working, and evidently soon cherishing the one desire to read, so that the Bible would be intelligible, the Lollard adherent gave up all that marked the life of the prosperous class. He went to no Morris dances, he played no cards, he thought maypoles wicked and the festivals of the Church heathenish. Sports he abhorred, and fine clothes and luxury were the signs of Satan. All that made life joyous to his oppressors was to him an evidence of sin and led to eternal damnation.

The old Pauline-Augustine system he took over from

Wyclif without any question. He found it all, he thought, in Paul. Much that a later ignorance has called Calvinism is far older than Calvin, and has had nothing to do with Calvinism. On the whole, however, the Englishman, at least the lower-class Englishman, is not greatly interested in theology. In this the Lollards were typical English-men; they were interested in conduct. The conventicle watched over the details of the conduct of the members, though of course they had their quarrels about dogma; but even here, if we are to judge of the early Lollards by the later ones, the question was always simply one of in-terpretation of Scripture, and rarely if ever of logical or theological precision.

It was in this age of suppression and struggle that that element of somber other-worldliness came into English re-ligious life which has been wrongly ascribed to much later Puritanism, and which bears quite another character. But more than that, English Protestantism became linked with an actual antagonism to art, and even with a certain type of literature, as stage plays, and later to novels, because these things were linked in its thought with the habits and manners of a hated class. Puritan-ism, as we shall see later, never could have taken this attitude.

Thus in the age between Chaucer and Shakespeare, there was growing up a class destined to take a foremost place in the development of the resources of England, but still wholly outside the influences which made Chaucer, Gower and Occleve as well as Shakespeare, Ben Jonson and Marlowe possible. That this was possible is due on the one hand to the genius of Wyclif, and on the other to the insistent persecution of the State Church and the equally insistent resistance of the stubborn Anglo-Saxon workingman.

The underestimate of the Lollard movement by even its latest historians[1] is due to the fact that it was driven under the surface of English life, and has relatively little place in England's literature, and we who deal with books and records think nothing of much importance that is not in records and literature. But only a very small part of life gets into books, and the Lollard movement belongs to that great part of a national life which is under the surface, but which gives tone and color to the whole. For it was the rising class which was under Lollard influence. What would we know of Christianity if all we knew came from classic literature? What, as a matter of fact, do we know of Mithraism, Christianity's greatest rival, simply because it failed and Christianity did not?

But if we can show, as we hope to do, that Lollardism survived until the time of the later Reformation so called under Henry VIII; that it deliberately rejected nearly all that characterized the later Protestantism; that it has remained true to its essential character in England and even still more in America; that it is still influencing thousands of Protestants of the Wyclif type in direct contrast to the Protestantism of Continental type; and that in its struggle for supremacy, it has large chance of relative success: then surely we are not entitled to speak, as Doctor Workman often does, of "the failure" or "the relative failure" of a "premature Reformation."

In going over all the evidences of the teaching of the Lollards[2] one may readily accept nearly all the assertions of their enemies with regard to the great diversity of their

---

[1] James Gairdner. "Lollardy and the Reformation in England." 2 Vols. 1908. This author wholly misjudges them in many places.

[2] The chief sources are; Canon Shirley's ed. of "Fasciculi Zizaniorum Magister Johannis Wyclif cum Tritico." (Rolls Series) London, 1858. *Cf.* especially "Lollard Conclusions", pp. 360, in which most critics see the substance of the Protest to Parliament of 1395. *Cf.* also Wilkins. "Concilia Mag. Brit." Vol. III, pp. 116 *ff.* (Literæ Gregorii XI) 157 *ff.* pp. 170, 208–211. Especially 221 (Conclusiones Lollardorum), etc.

heresies. When an illiterate but earnest group of Occidental people accepted a rich Oriental literature as inspired directly from God and given as the sole rule of faith and conduct, the wonder is not that many heresies were soon evolved, but that they kept so much of the traditional content of historical Christianity intact. Through all the trials and accusations runs the general complaint that they denied the historic Church and its authority; that they rejected the Mass; that they had no priests and no churches; that they listened to untrained and unauthorized preachers; that they met secretly and refused the ministrations of the authorized clergy, and so on. They are also definitely accused of Arianism, denying the deity of Jesus, the worship of saints and the abuse of the pope. In nearly all cases it would be possible to quote something from Wyclif in seeming support of even extreme positions, or at least from writings that up to recent date have been accepted as from Wyclif; but we find the accused themselves seemingly seldom quoting Wyclif; it is always the Bible.

The name Lollard was given as a term of reproach and was used very early,[1] and like all such names was used to cover every divergence from the established type of church belief. Moreover, as there was no central organization, and the quarrels between various groups were often very bitter, it was impossible for any outsider to describe accurately by any term the many dissenting religious meetings that had no connection with the State religion, so that in all the trials up to a very late date they are all called indiscriminately Lollards, or simply heretics. But the writer cannot find much evidence of any even informal organization of the various groups. However, the absence

---

[1] Probably from "lollen" "lallen" to sing softly, mumble. *Cf.* Oxford Dictionary. The word is older than Wyclif and came from the Continent.

of evidence does not prove that some such simple organization did not exist. It may have done so, but the danger such organization would involve and the secrecy necessary to avoid it; the illiterate character of the groups and the changing character of the little congregations, due to poverty and oppression, may easily have made it impossible to follow it up. Moreover, it lay in the very nature of the new character of the Lollard tradition to maintain the independence of each individual congregation.

CHAPTER IV

LOLLARDISM UP TO THE TIME OF HENRY VIII

The estimate to which reference has already been made, that the Lollards formed a half of the English population in the beginning of the fifteenth century rests upon the statement of Henry Knighton of Leicestershire in his "Chronicle."[1] He gives no reason for his belief that a half of the population were followers of Wyclif,[2] but says the sect of Wyclifites "is held in such great honor in these days and has so multiplied, that you can hardly see two men passing in the road, but one of them shall be a disciple of Wyclif."[3] Such estimates are always open to suspicion, but surely point to a very wide spread of Lollard doctrine. And in 1428, although a fierce persecution had set in and had already robbed Lollardism of its chief academic supporters, Archbishop Chichele writes, "the Lollards are as numerous as ever." He was a constant and vigilant persecutor of the sect, and in 1416 issued a pastoral letter requiring careful inquiry whether persons were suspected of heresy, of holding secret conventicles, or possessing books written in English or receiving persons favoring heresy.[4] The prohibition of books written in English points both to a wide spread of the English writings of Wyclif and of the Anglo-Saxon character of the movement.

By this time all the influential adherents of Wyclif in

[1] Ed. by J. R. Lunley. 2 Vols. 1889.
[2] Chronicle Collectiones 1664.
[3] *Ibid.* 2666.
[4] Wilkins. Acta Concilia Britanniæ. Vol. III, p. 378.

Oxford had submitted, and some of them had been well rewarded for their submission. Rigg, Repington, Hereford, Purvey, Aston and many more had gone over to the State Church, and soon Sir John Oldcastle was the only leader of any social standing. In a poem of Thomas Occleve's[1] he laments the conduct of Oldcastle, not seemingly because he thus risked his immortal soul, but because he stains his knightly honor, and that the cause was unpopular in good society.

> "And no man with thee holdeth
> Sauf cursid caitifs, heirs of dirknesse."

In other words Lollardism had been driven underground, and the aristocratic classes adhered to the Anglo-Catholic State Church.

History deals with ruling classes and with State documents. It can hardly do otherwise, because these constitute almost the entire material at hand. At the same time it must ever be borne in mind that ruling classes never in any land or at any time represent more than a small percentage of the actual population, and that great forces are ever at work unseen and unrecorded. We have no means of knowing, for instance, what proportion of the population at this time really understood the language of the Norman aristocracy. But it is evidently quite possible that Knighton's estimate of the numbers of the Lollards might be right, and that they would nevertheless be ignored save in the records of their trials for heresy. And once the universities and good society had been cleared of heresy, it was hardly worth while to spend time and money hunting down "consecrated cobblers", as Sydney Smith contemptuously called the Lollards of his day.[2]

And yet we have abundant evidence that not only was

[1] Anglia. Vol. V, pp. 23–37.
[2] *Cf.* Collected Works. Vol. I, p. 185.

Lollardism not suppressed by the Church, but that at times at least it flamed up in a threatening way. In 1449 Bishop Reginald Pecock wrote a curious book that needs careful reading[1] for in it he reveals the fact that the Lollard criticism of the Church had a wide hearing, and that some apology was necessary. It is for him "the lay party" or the "Bible men." The errors of the Lollards are those we have become familiar with; the sole authority of the letter of Scripture; the futility, to say the least, of sacraments; lay preaching; inward illumination; the unbiblical character of the hierarchy, of images, processions, paintings in the churches, etc. That Pecock was himself adjudged a heretic and had to abjure his errors is one of the ironies of ecclesiastical history.

In Pecock's work we see how fully established certain lines of thought were that have never since passed out of English history, and that all the consequences of this way of thinking had already begun to reveal themselves. The Lollards were already split into sects and small groups. At the same time they were united in bonds of a common faith in the individual and in his right to judge of Scripture and to form his own creed.

That Lollardism had not died out from the effects of the persecution we see in the long lists of martyrs from 1430 to 1466. But even more striking is the fact that even in Oxford, in spite of all the seeming victory and the fierce suppression, there was waged a fierce war for Wyclif's teaching from 1485 to 1495. And in spite of the fact that we have records of the burning of heretics in 1506, the "Concilia magnæ Britanniæ" are full of the complaints of the Church authorities that the State is not severe enough, and that heresy is more widely diffused than

[1] Reginald Pecock. "The Repressor of Over Much Blaming of the Clergy." Ed. by C. Babington, Rolls Series. 2 Vols., 1858.

ever. As late as 1528, Convocation as the highest Church court, complains that heresy is everywhere spread abroad in Canterbury itself. And if it was abroad in Canterbury, we may assume with confidence that it was not suppressed elsewhere.

The constant assumption that Lollardy had been much weakened or even suppressed by persecution, which we find in all the accounts of it, rests upon the fact that the influential classes were driven from it, but when the question is faced: "When was it suppressed?", there is no answer. The fact is that the persecution was far too spasmodic and far too superficial to affect anything probably, save the reviving of the fires of fanaticism, and keeping the movement freed from half-hearted followers. The wars for the throne of England prevented any such persistent and thorough-going persecution as enabled the Roman Church to stamp out all heresy in Spain and Italy.

In the "Concilia magnæ Britanniæ" we have the records of trials for heresy in practically every quarter of England, but everywhere the same complaint: heresy is gaining. Where then did it even numerically lose? And everywhere the same type of Protestantism emerges. The English Bible is the sole authority, the sacraments are denied, the priesthood is spurned. There is always some divergence in the things emphasized; now it is the denial of image worship, now it is refusal to have the children baptized, now it is unauthorized preaching and meeting in secret conventicles. But the type remains the same, and bears on its face the stamp of Wyclif. The name Lollard covers all heresy and is used until at last other nicknames take its place.

But above all, that which seemingly prevented a really successful persecution of the Lollards was the fact that the struggle between the National Catholic Church and the demands of Rome never really ceased. Even the most powerful archbishops had to keep national feeling in mind, and even so earnest a Catholic as Archbishop Courtenay had to fight for the rights of the English Church. Under these circumstances the Lollards, who were intensely national as over against Rome, were evidently often left entirely alone. What part the Lollards played in the struggle of the House of Lancaster is uncertain, and when peace was made with Rome it was at the expense of the Lollards; at the same time there is no evidence of any very bloody or widespread outrooting of the sect. If then, as we have seen, all accounts agree that up to 1461 heresy, that is Lollardism, was widespread, and was still increasing, there is no chance that between 1461 and 1485 any very serious State action against them was possible. Then under Henry VII there was no inclination to persecute any section of a people that needed more than anything else rest and peace. And in 1531–1532 came the final break with Rome, and never again was the Church of England strong enough to effectively persecute to the death heresy within the realm.

In 1525 Bishop Tunstal remarked of Luther's teachings "that there was nothing new in them, but that they simply put new weapons in the hands of already existing bands of Wyclif heretics."[1] It is certain that under different names, and with very different degrees of divergence from the Anglo-Catholic Church, large numbers of the followers of Wyclif, as "Bible Men" or the "Lay Party" were scattered all over England and the southern portion of Scotland; that they were especially strong in the towns seems from the later history likely. They were composed of the lower elements of the population as re-

[1] In a letter to Erasmus. 1525.

gards wealth and station, but were not without some
education, for manuscripts of Wyclif's translation of the
Bible are even now turning up.[1] When we remember what
havoc the printing press played with the preservation of
handwritten documents, we must infer that the class that
used these translations possessed many more of them, and
could read them. Moreover, they were a class that was
rising in economic importance as England became more
and more a shipping and exporting nation, for they were,
as one sees from the trades they give as their occupations
when arraigned for heresy, mainly small handworkers and
tradespeople.

We must then conclude that Doctor Gairdner greatly
understates the case when he says as the outcome of his
work: "Lollardy teaching remained a latent power in the
community. . . . Its teachings, for good or evil, have
influenced human thought and action more or less all the
succeeding centuries. They mingled with and domineered
over the Reformation, though they did not bring it on."[2]
Wyclif and his Lollards have given the world a type of
Protestantism that survives until our day, and still forms
the thoughts and feelings of thousands. It is a type that
must be most carefully distinguished from the Continental
type on the one hand and the Catholic (Anglican) type
on the other. It was no premature Reformation, as Doctor
Workman calls it, but a steady and growing revolt, that
was indeed greatly affected by the Continental Reformation, but was exceedingly independent of it, and in the
long run flung it off, to take on its own specific type again,
and again to emphasize the teachings of the real Father of
English Protestantism, John Wyclif.

---

[1] Miss M. Deanesly could use 170 such in 1920, when writing her admirable volume
on "The Lollard Bible", and more have turned up since.
[2] "Lollardy and the Reformation in England." Vol. I, p. 100.

This type of Protestantism became for many reasons a tradition rather than an organization, but a tradition that was strong enough to call into being many organizations, and flexible enough to give these a common outlook upon life, while at the same time allowing so much freedom that it is sometimes difficult to trace the tradition.

One of these reasons for the wide divergence has been pointed out. The dissenting tradition, which rose out of Lollardism, has from the beginning been a battling movement of a class rising up to power. Some of the elements of this class struggle may have existed even in Wyclif himself, for although a lord of a manor, and with good family connections, there is in him a bitter earnestness in fighting for the rights of the English under classes that suggests the old struggle against Norman tyranny. However this may be, in his followers we see the whole effect of the fact that Archbishop Courtenay forced the movement to become a struggle of a class, at first for mere existence, and then for power and recognition. As one reads the accounts of the persecutions of the Lollards in the "Concilia magnæ Britanniæ" and elsewhere, one is more and more impressed with the fact that it was often quite as much a political demand for national unity of faith as religious conviction that led to the persecutions. It was the political bishop that most hated and feared Lollardism.

Wat Tyler and John Ball were, no doubt, also responsible for this class character, which attaches to the English dissenting tradition, but that might have been changed, had Oxford University happened to be under less firm and able leadership. As it happened, men like the Bishop of Norwich and the Archbishop of Canterbury drew the lines which have persisted throughout all English history. They not only made the dissenting tradition a class struggle, but forced it underground, and compelled it to seek other than purely political means for the realization of its ends. Dissent was outlawed, and even as it slowly spread, its conquests were confined to the relatively lowly and unknown.

This explains also why the teachings of Wyclif were steadily rendered more radical in their transmission from group to group. The papal Church for Wyclif needed reformation, but was still a Church of Christ, even if the pope was condemned; for his followers, the Church was antichristian, and no words were coarse enough to describe the pope. Wyclif as a good schoolman could not cut himself off from the historic Church. His followers saw in the historic Church only the home of oppression and the continuation of heathenism. Wyclif rejected transubstantiation and all magical salvation in a mechanical sense from the Mass. At the same time, he saw in the Mass some sort of real presence, though the bread remained bread and the wine remained wine. For his followers the Mass was a heathen idolatry, and even when they kept the Lord's Supper it was only because it was given as a sign of a covenant relationship, was not necessary to salvation, and could be dispensed with. Priests became simply preachers, and for priests and bishops who did not preach the Lollards had unbounded contempt, as we see in the pages of Bishop Pecock's defense of them. They were "dumb dogs."

On the side of conduct we see even more plainly the effects of the persecution of an upper class. All that marks the life, especially the lighter side of that life, of the ruling class, becomes "worldly" and evil. Here again the emphasis varies according to the level of culture of the period. But actors, stage plays, public dances, cards, all games of chance, even the seemingly harmless maypoles come, as already noted, at one time or another under the general condemnation. For most of these reactions it would only be possible to quote general utterances of Wyclif, or exceedingly forced constructions of Bible texts. But every little conventicle had its own conception of what should be called "worldly", drawn from the experiences of an economically weak class in its contacts with luxury and wealth.

CHAPTER V

CONTINENTAL PROTESTANTISM AND THE DISSENTING
TRADITION IN ENGLAND

The plan of this book excludes the entrance upon
theological details, especially upon those where differences
of opinion still exist. But to bring out the fact that Anglo-
American Protestantism is something distinctly independent in spirit and history from the Continental type,
we must very briefly sum up the generally accepted outlines of Continental Protestantism.

One of the first things that strikes the student is the
fact of the geographical separation of Roman Catholicism
from Protestantism in Middle Europe. The Peace of
Westphalia (1648) could not, it is true, really establish
the religion of the reigning prince as the religion of the
people. Nevertheless, in the division of Europe between
Catholicism and Protestantism, all classes were either for
the most part Catholic or for the most part Protestant.
The division was not one of education, or of wealth, or
of social standing. There were Protestant and Roman
Catholic princes and Reigning Houses. In science, art and
literature both confessions had their part.

Any faithful study of Luther and Calvin and the
Continental reformers reveals the fact that they were all
profoundly desirous of keeping in close touch with the
historic Church. Only gradually did they grow away
from the Mother Church and claim for themselves and
their followers their share in early Christianity. The old
fundamental, so-called ecumenical creeds were for Luther

and Calvin of great authority, and though both pope and Church Council could and did err, yet historical Christianity was fundamental and even essential to a right understanding of the Bible.

Accordingly then, both the Lutheran and the Calvinistic types of Protestantism regarded the Church as established by Christ himself and furnished from the beginning with an historic ministry, to be the ordinary guardian of the grace-imparting sacraments. Luther did not use the word "Church" freely, seemingly for fear of misunderstanding, but he speaks of the historic Christian communion, under various terms. Nor is any one safe outside the visible communion of the Christian Church.

The grace-imparting sacraments were of vital importance to the thinking of both Luther and Calvin and all the Continental reformers. They devoted whole volumes and an enormous amount of learning in trying to exactly define the two especially important sacraments, the Lord's Supper and baptism. They kept confirmation, confession and marriage but relegated them to a lower plane; however, that was in line with some of the best Roman Catholic scholastic opinion. And in order to insure the right administration of these sacraments it was vitally necessary that the ministry set apart by Christ himself be maintained in full vigor and authority. For Calvin the marks of a true Church were simple; the pure preaching of the Word of God, the properly ordained ministry and the right administration of the sacraments. Nor would Luther have seriously differed with him at this point. For both types of Continental Protestantism, bishop and presbyter meant the same thing, and neither of these terms is unchristian, only the word "bishop" should not imply a separate and higher work.

To this ministry is entrusted the defense of the faith,

and the administration of the sacraments. The reformers disliked indeed the word "priest" because it had been abused, but the Church remains a sacrificial institution, and even the church building has a special significance because Christ is really present in the bread and wine of the sacramental feast, although any reservation of the elements is to be condemned as leading the ignorant to worship the elements instead of the spiritual presence. Into the details of the discussion of the nature of the real presence we need not go; it is as complicated as any medieval discussion could be. It only should be remembered that the mystical, magical and superrational in the sacramental system is retained, and that therefore there is still room for the Gothic church and the spacious home for the altar, because from time to time God is in a special manner present on the altar to the believer.

It is therefore a striking feature of the Continental type of reformation that all that can be kept of the older cultural life is still retained. True it is that anything which the reformers thought conflicted with the word of Scripture, or was so connected with abuses in the past as to render it a menace to the spiritual life was omitted, but there was no hostility to the culture embodied in the Catholic tradition as such. Such class hostility was indeed present in Middle Europe at the time of the Reformation, and the uprising of the peasants and the destruction of the images on the Continent seemed at one time to be gaining headway, but the leaders of the Reformation sternly set themselves against these excesses, and with the support of the princes and wealthy classes suppressed the movement.

Some of the Roman Catholic art was banished, but there rose in its place a Protestant art, somewhat severer in type, and lacking some of the pagan freedom that had given the art of the Renaissance its charm; nevertheless a

very high art. The music of the churches received a new
and valuable impulse. The architecture lacked indeed
warmth and life, for the sense of the real presence of God
in the building was confined to a few stated occasions and
was wrapped up in dimly understood metaphysical distinctions, but there was no seeking of bareness for the
sake of bareness. Moreover, Protestantism continued to
build great church buildings dedicated to worship.

This type of Protestantism had no fundamental objection to the classical culture as seen in France and Italy,
and indeed recognized the Humanistic revival as a welcome ally, opening as it did the pages of the Old and New
Testaments in the original languages for all men to study.
It retained the old universities within its borders and
established new ones modeled after the older ones. Theology retained its place at the head of the lists of the
sciences, and stands there still to-day. It favored education and culture as in themselves good, and if it is true
that the type of culture was very greatly influenced by the
free city and the great rising middle and trading classes,
nevertheless kings and princes, wealth and station all had
their part in the development of the type.

When now we turn from this picture to that of the
sturdy dissenting tradition of England, the contrast is
startling, and we have only been blinded in the past to the
difference by the fact that an established State Church
has occupied the foreground and hidden the divergence.
Moreover the dissenting tradition has been often lost in
the many organizations it has called into being, for the
seeds of division lie in the very nature of the tradition
itself. When we think of Protestant England we naturally
think of the Continental High-Church type of Protestantism, forgetting that the State Church of England has
never called itself Protestant. But we remember that it

has severed itself from Rome, that its services are in English, that it has generally abandoned auricular confession, and speaks of the Communion service or Eucharist and not of Mass, and that the elements of the Communion service are not reserved for adoration.

The old English dissenting tradition has however abandoned all High-Church claims. The church is the number of the elect, and only God knows His own. It has abandoned all claims to an historic priesthood or even ministry. Every man or even woman is capable of the call to preach and teach. It needs no House of God, for every room can be a meeting place; hence in England there are no dissenting "churches" but only "meetinghouses", "chapels" or "tabernacles." When it keeps the sacrament it is only as a "sign" of the covenant, or in obedience to God's command, but it has no magic power and no special grace-imparting efficacy. It has no special interest in the historic Church, for the Bible is all the individual believer needs, and in it he has enough. He has also the promise that inward enlightenment will attend the study of it and direct him to the truth. Hence also the dissenting tradition is exceedingly individualistic. Every man and woman stands alone before God without any need of a mediating priesthood or a protecting and interceding Church. The sermon has taken the place of the sacrament, the pulpit of the altar.

In no Continental country is the Bible looked at in the way it is in England. It has become, in the course of the long struggle with Rome, the flag of revolt, and in the struggle of Dissent with the Establishment it has been arsenal and bulwark. Everything which the struggling dissenting class disliked in the conduct and mode of life of the ruling class was naturally found to be forbidden by the Bible, for it would be difficult to find anything one could not prove out of the pages of that picturesque literature.

The persecution of Dissent by the State, even weak and spasmodic as it was, only served to harden all these traits in the tradition. The conventicle was secret and so to many much more attractive. To starved social life it ministered with redoubled power. The very danger, no doubt, increased the warmth and intimacy of the fellowship. The more the State Church persecuted, the more it became to the dissenters the very image of the Anti-Christ and its ways the ways of the Evil One. The identification of the Establishment with the wealthy and the powerful made the dissenting tradition a part of the class struggle, even if this element was seldom recognized, and would probably have been repudiated by at least the more responsible members. The struggle strengthened the will, and educated the ignorant, and added to the power of the group by frightening the weak away; but on the other hand it brought into the life a certain narrowness and sometimes even a bitterness and censoriousness that led to constant splits and divisions.

Yet these very divisions contributed to the spread of the tradition, for group rivaled group in missionary activity, and thus there was built up a great English dissenting body, whose numbers and influence are even now vastly underestimated both in England and America. Dissent dissolves easily into smaller bodies, holding often absurdly fantastic notions as seen from the outside, and yet holding firmly in an astonishing way to a few central principles. There is in the accounts of the trials of the Lollards for heresy hardly any opinion so absurd that it is not attributed to this or that one of the accused, and often, no doubt, with a measure of justice.

The entire lack of any central organization in the early history, as well as the absence of all corporate property rendered English conventicle Dissent at one point very weak. Whereas the Continental and English High-Church bodies, whether Roman or Anglican, had great central places of worship with a well-preserved cult that ministered to æsthetic and social wants even when the religious impulse was very low, the poor dissenters had nothing to rely upon save the steady enthusiasm of the scattered groups. When then the religious impulse sank in power, Dissent must have lost enormously. Its inherent rationalism and individualism had no counterpoise in any developed ecclesiasticism or cult. In the great awakening of England to a new artistic and intellectual life that began with Henry VII and reached its climax under Elizabeth, their part is overshadowed both by Humanism and by Continental Protestantism, though we shall have occasion to examine a little more fully later on (Chapter VII) what was their probable influence.

Throughout the history of English Dissent there runs a strong primitive Christian strain, and for the simple reason that the Bible was constantly cited as supposedly the only authority; and in point of fact the orthodox theology of the Roman Catholic and creedal Protestant Churches cannot be indisputably traced to the New Testament without the help of a traditional interpretation. In this orthodoxy Oriental, Grecian and Roman elements, as well as primitive pagan features, are present, but an authoritative and historic Church was steadily at work rounding all out to an intellectually tenable system. For such authoritative interpretation, English conventicle Protestantism had no place. Each individual was therefore inclined to slough off such of these accretions to the body of Christian doctrine as he or she did not find congenial or consonant with the letter of the Bible uncritically accepted in an English translation.

CHAPTER VI

HENRY VIII AND ANGLO-CATHOLICISM

No State Church can afford to exclude too many elements of the national life from its communion. It must always represent a compromise between conflicting views of life and religion. The Establishment in England has always borne this character in a marked degree. As Macaulay says: "To this day the constitution, the doctrines, and the services of the Church, retain the visible marks of the compromise from which she sprang. She occupies a middle position between the Churches of Rome and Geneva."[1] This has often been made a reason of reproach by its critics, but if a State Church is to maintain itself it is hard to see how it can be otherwise.

The relations of King Henry VIII to the English Reformation are not generally matters of pride to Protestants, but on the other hand the leaders of the High-Church movement in England under men like Ward, Pusey and Newman refused with a great measure of historic justice to think of Henry VIII as the Father of the Anglo-Catholic Church. In educated circles in England both Humanism and the Continental type of Protestantism had made a deep impression, and Henry VIII had written a reply to Luther for which he had received the proud title of "defender of the faith", given by Leo X in 1521. His ultimate quarrel with the pope was but the continuation of the age-long struggle of England for independence in the management of her own affairs, and the divorce was

[1] Macaulay. "History of England." Vol. I, Chap. I, p. 56.

only the outward occasion for the separation, which would surely have come in any event.

Nor could Henry VIII, with all his power, have made such a complete break with Rome had not England long before had a great body of Protestant opinion in her midst. It is truly astonishing how easily the change was made, and when we read of ministers who were priests under Henry VIII and then his Protestant ministers, then once more Roman Catholic under Mary, only to conform again to the Anglican Church under Elizabeth, it must not be forgotten that the lines were often not so sharply drawn as the names Roman Catholic and Protestant would now imply. There were all sorts of shadings between Roman Catholicism and High-Church Anglicanism. The nearest approach of the English State Church to the Protestant type as evolving on the Continent was under Edward VI, but never again did the Anglican Church follow up that line of development, and while she did not purge herself completely of the Continental type of Protestantism on the one hand or of Catholicism on the other, she remained ever more firmly attached to that Anglo-Catholicism which has battled ever since with the more Protestant elements in her constitution.

It was often assumed then, and is still assumed, that Geneva represented the extreme type of Protestantism. But in point of fact neither Lutheranism nor Calvinism represented anything nearly as radical as the type of Protestantism represented by the dissenting tradition at work in England at this time. How large the numbers were no one can say, but judging from what soon took place under Elizabeth it is fair to say that, however humble and obscure the Lollard type of dissent may have been, it was everywhere represented in England and Scotland, and must have had some significance even for the political life, for laws against it were reversed under Edward VI.[1] Many a good English churchman could at that time worship with equal comfort in Rome or Westminster, and so long as he had an historic Church, an historic episcopate to guarantee to him the right administration of the sacraments, and liberty to interpret the articles and rubrics in what he regarded as their historic sense, he could leave the question of the administrative rights of the pope to the ecclesiastical lawyers. He might or might not look up privately to the pope as the supreme authority in religion, but the age-long struggle against the administrative powers of the pope had made all well-informed Englishmen ready for Henry's refusal to submit to the pope in reversing the law of *præmunire*, or even referring the question of the divorce to a foreign court.

There is every reason for thinking that on the whole the Anglican Church as constructed by Archbishop Cranmer was as skillful a compromise as could then have been made. It represented a very High-Church type of Protestantism, or rather Anglicanism, for though it emphasized the reading of the Bible and prayers in English, it made at the same time no claims to any personal right of private judgment, but rather established the outward authority of the State to enforce religion even by the death penalty. But then the State was for Cranmer no secular power, but embraced the convocation and a parliament, in which the archbishop and the bishops sat. This religious State thus took the place of the pope.

No doubt the obscure dissenters saw with hope the opening of the Bible, the Englishing of the services, the separation from Rome, the repudiation of the adoration

[1] Green's "Short History of the English People." Vol. II, p. 711. Ed. 1872. John Knox considered the Lollards in Ayrshire as his forerunners.

of the Eucharist, the acceptance of the homilies, and many other changes that marked the drift from Rome. At the same time they could not possibly hope either from Henry VIII or even Edward VI any fulfillment of their desires for the reformation of England's religious life. They could no more accept the outward authority of even a professedly Christian State than they could the authority of the pope.

We enter with the time of Henry VIII upon a period when the press and the gradually extended freedom of worship permitted more open expression on the part of this radical Lollard type of Protestantism, and thanks to the careful work of Doctor Champlin Burrage we have collected for us many of the most interesting documents referring to this type of Dissent,[1] although the writer must often widely differ from him in his interpretation of the material. Burrage, for instance, calls attention to a letter of Bishop Horne, written in 1571, in which he describes the numerous groups of small sects. According to this letter, they were "poor people" who were "entirely ignorant and unknown." They "worked out their own laws and regulations" and "despised the Eucharist"; they would also like to "destroy all churches because they are dedicated to the pope." They despised not only the "ministry of the Church (*i.e.* the Protestant State Church under Elizabeth) but even the office itself."[2] No description of the Lollards could be more exact. And in the same year Bishop Cox writes to Rudolf Gualter (February) complaining of sects "whose members will not enter our churches, will not baptise their children, do not come to the Lord's Supper, will not listen to our preaching. These people remain separate from us, go

[1] Champlin Burrage. "The Early English Dissenters." 2 Vols.
[2] *Ibid.* Vol. I, p. 89.

their own ways, practise a private religion and meet
together in private houses."[1] And these are only a few
of the complaints that demonstrate the fact that this
type of Protestantism was widely distributed over England. If now early in the reign of Queen Elizabeth we find
these groups widely spread, we may rest assured that they
were scarcely less numerous under Henry VIII. Two
things are especially noteworthy: the fact that they
condemned church buildings as dedicated to popery,
revealing that old antagonism to the expressions of culture
linked in their minds with the aristocratic tradition, and
that they are all "poor and unknown" people.

Such Lollard groups would hardly be affected by the
short but severe persecution under Queen Mary. It lasted
only three and a half years, and cost only about three
hundred martyrs,[2] and these were for the most part well-
known supporters of the Anglican type of Reformation.
The obscure sects were by this time evidently adepts in
hiding themselves before the storms of persecution. On
the other hand, the loss of some of the most Protestant-
thinking of the leaders of the Anglo-Catholic Reformation
left the State Church even further removed from the world
of the dissenting tradition than it might have been had
the Continental type of Protestantism embraced by
Archbishop Cranmer had greater weight. Like all the
Tudors, Queen Elizabeth was far more a Humanist than
either a Protestant or a Catholic, but just for that reason
she liked all that recalled the æsthetic side of the Roman
Catholic tradition; she liked candles on the altar, churchly
vestments for the clergy, favored an unmarried clergy,
petted the hierarchy as long as it remained a submissive
adornment of her absolutism. Thus the State Church

[1] Burrage. "The Early English Dissenters." Vol. I, p. 90.
[2] See James Gairdner. "Lollardy and the Reformation." Vol. I, p. 327.

became the Church of the court and of society, and the breach between the religion of the poor and that of the ruling class was widened and deepened.

This breach between the religious thinking of the two classes has been obscured in English history by a variety of circumstances, and would be even now often emphatically repudiated in good faith by many otherwise well-informed persons. It remains however a demonstrable fact.[1] The immediate dependents upon wealth and station were then and are now compelled to outward conformity. Moreover, the antagonism of the dissenting tradition to the amusements and luxury of the upper classes keeps all those poorer persons who minister to the amusement of the rich away from the conventicle. State players and all who had to do with the theater were, of course, excluded from any dissenting company. Tavern keepers and the thousand and one hangers-on of the hunting countryside, of sport and amusement at country fairs, etc., were all more or less taboo for the seriously minded dissenter. It remained nevertheless a poor but a tremendously serious element in the life of England, and affected the thinking of circles very far removed from its immediate influence.

[1] In 1923 appeared the "Herald Book of Labor Members" of the English House of Commons. In it are given lives of the members of the party that under J. Ramsay MacDonald held office from January, 1924, to November, 1924. There are listed 139 names. Of these it says of MacDonald: "The village dominie, discerning his genius, gave him special aid in his studies, and made him pupil teacher." Only two names are given as having any connection with the State Established Church, and these seemingly with the "evangelical" wing of it, while thirty of the members are listed as preachers, lay workers, teachers and officers in the governing bodies of various dissenting sects, and practically all who have given any religious indications are in sympathy by birth or circumstance with Dissent. Unfortunately the Labor Yearbooks that have been since issued do not give the religious affiliations of the party membership, but it is not too much to assert that the Dissenting Chapel and the Bible have given the training to the Labor members, which has made their eloquence in the rather fastidious House of Commons a matter of amazement. Their speech has no sonorous Ciceronian impressiveness, but rings with the Saxon rhythms of Defoe, Cobbett, Cobden and John Bright. And none of these had a "flair" for that dreadful word "problem", or found the misuse of "optimism" and "pessimism" so "intriguing" that these corruptions of our speech dot their pages like fly-spots on an old mirror.

The name Lollard disappears, but from the time of
Elizabeth on we hear increasingly of "Anabaptists",
"sectaries", "heretics", "Brownists" (later on) and
even "atheists." The evidence for the hostile attitude of
the lower English classes to the Roman Catholic Church
appears when we read the accounts of the confiscation of
the monasteries and abbeys. When they are dispossessed,
the mob is described as wanting to destroy all altars and
all the altar pictures. This was not the attitude of the
Anglo-Catholic Church nor even of the High-Church type
of Continental Protestantism. If the monasteries and
abbeys were as popular as some High-Church writers
would seem to maintain, why were the mobs so rabid and
why was the destruction so complete? There is no doubt
that they did much to relieve poverty and suffering, they
formed often the only refuge where misery had a place to
hide its head, and yet the opposition to their confiscation
was either entirely lacking, or very slight. Only when we
duly appreciate the work that Lollardism had been doing
for some one hundred and thirty years are we prepared
for such an attitude on the part of the poor.

We read of how wonder-working images were exposed
on the market place as an object of scoff and laughter,
then to be burnt. No half-hearted reform movement
under Henry VIII or Archbishop Cranmer accounts for
this dislike and contempt. The destruction of the monasteries took place under Thomas Cromwell in the years
1530–1540 and can hardly be connected with the icono-
clastic movement on the Continent, for although this
began in 1522, yet there was surely no such intimate
connection between the poor of England and the destructive mobs of Switzerland and Germany that they can be
thought of as influencing each other.

It is probable that only a part of the English people

were really so madly opposed to Catholicism that the destruction of the beautiful churches and chapels connected with the religious houses was hailed with satisfaction, but it must have been a very considerable part of the population. The king and his advisors did not confiscate the religious houses primarily as a Protestant movement, but simply as a fiscal and legal measure and as a demonstration against the pope. But the confiscation was greeted with intense satisfaction by certainly some classes in the community. Who were these? Not those who had hitherto been such loyal friends of Rome. The fact seems to be that a bitterly anti-Romish fraction of the English people rejoiced at last to see what it regarded as idolatry destroyed, and the power of the priesthood broken.

Nor are we left in doubt as to the movement having some connection with Wyclif. One of the first tracts issued from the press of William Tyndale was "The Examination of William Thorpe",[1] one of the many circulated forbidden books relating to Wyclif by one of his followers,[2] and there is no doubt as to which type of Protestantism William Tyndale belonged, in spite of his sojourn with Luther. He rejected transubstantiation in favor of the later Lollard interpretation of Wyclif's use of the word "signum" to describe the Eucharist. His notes show the extreme radicalism of his views, both as regards the priesthood and the Church.[3] He is the Father of the movement within the Anglican Church, which from the beginning sought a more radical reform of the Church than the ruling class, and especially the king, was ready

---

[1] One of Wyclif's early and devoted followers, whose notes of his examination before Arundel was a classic of Lollard literature.

[2] "Concilia magnæ Britanniæ", Vol. III, p. 739. "The Acts and Monuments of John Foxe." 1844. Vol. III, p. 256.

[3] For this reason Doctor James Gairdner has no love for Tyndale. *Cf.* his account of him in "Lollardy and the Reformation." Vol. II especially.

to undertake. The wide acceptance of Tyndale's New Testament, which Coverdale's version never superseded, in these more Protestant circles, testifies to the preparedness of men's minds for a wider departure from Rome than even the stricter types of High-Church Continental Protestantism contemplated.

The influence of the Continental type of Protestantism, with its emphasis upon the mystic presence of Christ in the bread and wine; its very strong insistence upon the outward authority of an historic Church; and its maintenance of an ordained ministry of historic claims to special power and interpretative privilege had naturally very great influence upon the educated class, and in the universities under Henry VIII there was much restlessness and heresy. The Tudor demand was always for religious unity, and up to 1531 the persecutions for heresy were often severe but at the same time evidently so spasmodic and ill-advised that they often did more harm to the persecutors than to the cause of complaint. In the "Acts and Monuments" collected by John Foxe it is not always easy to separate the two types of Protestantism that now appear: the old English, native Lollard type, with the characteristics now familiar to us, and the High-Church type as seen in Luther and Calvin. A common opposition to Rome brought all shades and types of Protestantism together. All alike fought the Roman Catholic doctrine of transubstantiation, the final authority of the pope, auricular confession and the power of the priest to forgive sin. All were brought together in a common suffering, and a common dislike of the outward "trappings", as they were often called, of the stately worship of the Established Church. Whether under Henry VIII or Queen Elizabeth, the demand for national unity had, no doubt, strong support from all who had political insight. To a very large number of even religious persons moreover, it was of more importance that England should exhibit a united front to Spain, France and the Empire, in order to be sought as an ally by these, than that points of ritual and doctrine be thoroughly discussed and understood by the man on the street.

To a very great number of the leading minds of the day Humanism had taken the place of dogmatic religion, and the study of Aristotle in the original Greek and the revival of Platonism were not likely to breed any fanatic hate either of Roman Catholic culture or of the æsthetic elements of its service still retained in Anglican Catholicism. The censorship may in part account for the astonishingly small part religious strife plays in the stage plays of those days. But this silence emphasizes the fact that the scorn which the Restoration stage poured out upon Dissent was most strikingly absent from the Elizabethan literature. If, which is very doubtful, Sir John Oldcastle is the figure made fun of in Shakespeare's Falstaff, there is no hint in Shakespeare of any contempt for the content of the Lollard faith. In no sense can Falstaff be called a religious hypocrite, and when he says,

"I would I were a weaver, I could sing psalms,"

he only marks the class out of which the psalm-singing groups came, and it can hardly be called mockery of them.

There was, however, a movement on the horizon with which the world was yet to reckon, and with that we now must deal.

CHAPTER VII

THE ELIZABETHAN PURITANISM

Calvinism may be called an intrusion upon the religious life of England and has never really taken root there. Much that is called Calvinism has no real relation to Calvin's system and is simply the predestinarianism that underlies so much Christian thinking, Catholic as well as Protestant. It must be remembered that Calvin's contribution to Protestantism was not primarily theological but ecclesiastical. More particularly did Calvin make no pretense of an advance over the familiar Pauline-Augustinian doctrine of election.

At the same time, at this point Calvin stood nearer Wyclif than did Luther, and in relation to reform of the Church life he was more radical and therefore more in sympathy with the radical type of Protestantism, now struggling for wider expression in England, than Luther would have been. As it happened, groups of English men and women had fled from the persecutions of Mary and had taken refuge in various places on the Continent, more particularly in Frankfort-on-the-Main, and had come strongly under the influence of the Continental type of Protestantism. To judge by their occupations and their interests, the laymen among these refugees were from the class that mostly favored Dissent, but the ministers were seemingly educated members of the State Establishment.

The first feeling of the returned refugees was evidently one of great disappointment.[1] The State Church under

[1] Daniel Neal's "History of the Puritans." Parson's Abridged Ed. Vol. I, p. 89.

Elizabeth looked very unlike the dissenting conventicle. The Queen was greatly superior to her father as a ruler, and had surrounded herself with a most notable group of advisers, but her personal character was not on a much higher level, and the Church was for her chiefly a valuable political instrument. She was still playing with both Roman Catholic Spain and with the Protestant princes, so she did not care to have the State Church look either too Protestant or too Roman. As was the case with so many of her educated subjects, Humanism had taken the place in her life that the Church once had occupied. She was highly educated, delighted in translating from the classic languages into English, and prided herself on her taste and judgment.

She was, however, above all a politician and a stateswoman and insisted on the outward unity of the State Church. She looked upon the Church as a sure support for the Throne, and as such it must have the appearance at least of commanding the assent of all her subjects. All she seems to have demanded was an outward conformity, nor did this seem to most men in those days unreasonable. At first she favored the small number of Puritans who desired to take over in large part the Continental type of Protestantism as they had seen it in Geneva, or learned it from Calvin and Beza. But the Calvinistic thinking was soon seen to be far too theocratic for the purposes of the English Throne. Partly perhaps from æsthetic reasons and partly not to offend the Roman Catholic sentiment in England and still more in Spain and France, Elizabeth wanted to retain as much of the outward cult as she could.

It is quite pitiable to see how small was the horizon of the poor little groups that had settled down in the Netherlands, in Switzerland and on the Rhine. They were

intensely interested in the place of the communion table
in church buildings, in the garments in which the preacher
appeared, in the outward adornment of the place of
worship and such external matters. They had fierce
quarrels among themselves about matters that seemed
to the Continental reformers quite secondary. Nevertheless, there arose in England out of them a Puritan party,
whose main interest was something more intelligently
chosen than the clothes of the preacher.

The word "Puritan" will be used henceforth in these
pages to cover a distinct type of religious tradition. It
is true that the name has been very loosely used, and that
within certain bounds every one has a right to make his
own definition, if he then abides by it. But it is just, to
avoid a very great and troublesome confusion, that one
should distinguish sharply between the Separatist and
the Puritan.[1] Historically the Puritan party played a
special part, and as a political party had a separate
background from English Dissent; Scotland and Geneva
gave to Puritanism both a different outlook on life, and a
fighting character that made it a power out of all proportion to its numbers. Puritanism as it rose in England was
essentially Presbyterian in character. It was always under
the influence of the great Calvinistic divines and was
furnished by them with a State policy as well as a theology.
In Scotland was found substantially an almost complete
expression of Puritanism, and although it is often difficult
to say such and such a man was a "Puritan", the party as
such had distinct notes. In fact, Puritanism should not
be confused with the sects, for which it had almost as
profound a dislike as had the Anglican and Roman tradition. Nor was it cowardice or love of ease that kept the

[1] Champlin Burrage. "The Early English Dissenters in the Light of Recent
Research." 1912. Vol. I, pp. 84, 93, *et seq.*

great body of the Puritans within the State Church, as Mr. James Truslow Adams seems to think.[1] Often secession would have been an easy way out of difficulty. But the real Puritan was bound to claim the State Church for his own purposes as the divine organization which was a sacramental, historic and ministerial reality, founded by Christ and against which the gates of hell should not prevail. So long as the Word of God was preached, the sacraments rightly administered and a duly ordained ministry acknowledged, he had no business to leave the historic Church but must remain within and protest with all his might against all abuses.

The Lollard sectarian might or might not conform according to his conscience. He had no respect for the historic Church and no need of an ordained ministry. He had no need for church buildings and no especial reverence for the sacraments, save as they were commanded signs of fellowship.

Were the difference merely theological, it might be left to the doctors of divinity. But the difference was far more radical. The bare outlines of a theology were held in common. All thought about alike on God, the Trinity, the deity of Christ, the atonement, revelation, resurrection, heaven and hell, and the main historic dogmas. They differed in their notions of the State, the Church, history, authority, priesthood, the content of the religious life and the relations of the Christian man to his fellows in Church and State. Both had a history of struggle and partial success behind them, but the history was very different in each case. As we have tried to show, Wyclif is the Father of the English dissenting type, and Puritanism goes to the Continent of Europe for its essential characteristics.

[1] *Cf.* James Truslow Adams. "The Founding of New England." Chap. IV, p. 68.

To properly appreciate the greatness as well as the weakness of the English Puritans, it must be remembered that they represented the High-Church wing of the English Protestant movement. They intelligently took over from Calvin not simply his theology—that they had already to a great extent—but his High-Church views, both with regard to the place and office of the Church, as also in regard to the ordained ministry and the historic creeds. They were to form in England as well as in Scotland, and as the Calvinists were to do in the Netherlands and in France, a fighting edge for the anti-Roman forces.

This Puritan party has been so ignorantly praised and so equally ignorantly blamed, that although some of the facts are quite easily obtained few take the trouble to review them. The very name Puritan has become almost meaningless because used to describe movements and types of thought wholly different from it. It would be well if possible to limit the term to the small but exceedingly powerful political party that rose in the time of Queen Elizabeth and which then disappeared as a political force in 1660 at the Restoration.

But above all else one should carefully distinguish between the High-Church, highly organized and historically orthodox Puritans and the Low-Church, radical, scattered and often very unorthodox dissenters. It is not a matter of theology in which only theologians may be interested; it is a matter of entirely different outlook on life. The Puritans were not only *not* "Separatists" but demanded the right to establish a State Church and to control it. Their ideal was a theocracy on the lines of the Old Testament. They had no objection to the historic episcopacy, on the contrary, if only all presbyters were accounted alike in dignity; a bishopric for the sake of administrative order was unobjectionable. Calvin himself was not opposed to episcopacy as such, if thought of only as a matter of order and arrangement. At the same time the ministry, and this included the ruling eldership, was ordained of God, as an historic and priestly ministry, with all the power of the keys, as seen in the power of excommunication. And according to Calvin, the State was ordained of God to carry out the judgments of the Church. Thus the trial and burning of Servetus was not a chance judgment, but the sober outcome of the theory of the power of the Church and the duty of the State.

The stronger the influence of Calvin, Beza and Bullinger was on the Puritan party, the stronger was the sentiment for a State Church, but it was bound to bear the marks of the true Church. With all this the children of the Lollards could not agree. They hated a State Church from which they had experienced only persecution and arrogance. In various degrees they did without a stated ministry, and lay preachers were everywhere welcome. Even more than the Continental type of Protestantism they emphasized the bare letter of Scripture, and the faith that the humblest could receive enlightenment so as to understand the Bible.

Naturally the Separatists had much in common with the Puritans; more particularly in the struggle to break the power of a High-Church party in England, so nearly like the Roman Church that it seemed to both Separatists and Puritans only another form of the same idolatry, as they considered it. Moreover, both Separatists and Puritans accepted broadly a system of dogmatic faith that was supposed by the Separatists to have come wholly from the Bible, but which the Puritans defended as, indeed, consonant with the Word of God, as they would have put it, but which rested upon the findings of the primitive Church, and whose formulation was the work of acknowledged Fathers of the Church. This was part of that marked attitude toward the whole historical development of doctrine. It was not that the Separatists denied history, but their interest in it was distinctly limited by the fact that the inner light of the Holy Spirit was sufficient in the present day to guide the sincere soul away from error.

To the Puritan, the unity of the Church was a matter of great importance. He demanded that the State should step in and compel conformity. For only in the communion of the historic, visible Church had the soul assurance of ultimate salvation. And this Church had teaching power, and the right of deciding what was truth, and of defense by trials for heresy of the truth. The Separatist, when logical, could only claim for the conventicle the right of giving the right hand of fellowship to kindred spirits, and each small group was the judge of the limits of tolerance.

Up to the time of Queen Elizabeth, the picture of the Separatist conventicle must be drawn almost wholly from the complaints against it in the trials contained in the accounts of the Bishops' Courts and the "Concilia magnæ Britanniæ." But from 1600 on we have increasing literature on the subject of the differences both between the Puritans and the Separatists, and the State Church and the reforming Puritans within the Establishment. It is often dreary reading. The questions seem to us now so secondary in view of the pressing political and religious decisions upon which England's future depended. Into these quarrels we happily do not need to go, for the details of vestments, the position of the altar, the exact definition of the real presence of Christ in the Eucharist, or the limits of free will, do not really touch the questions that interest us in trying to grasp the tradition that lies at the basis of Anglo-American culture.

It was in the early years of Elizabeth's reign that English colonists first began unsuccessful attempts at establishing settlements in the New World. It was not to escape persecution that John Smith led his rather forlorn following under King James' government to Virginia, but rather in the spirit of adventure and of acquisition. Supporting all the various enterprises that mark this period are the new city aristocrats, men who were making the English trading tradition a step to political power, and wealth and credit a substitute for the possession of land and dependent tenants. In the lists of those who went first to Virginia we find many ranked as "gentlemen", but the really effective colonists were evidently small tradespeople, workmen and the lower town population. From the beginning there were all manner of colonists. The second supply ship to Virginia brought "eight Germans and Poles" to start infant industries.[1] John Smith makes a pathetic plea for competent workmen. He asks for "30 carpenters, husbandmen, gardeners, fishermen, blacksmiths, masons, and diggers up of tree's roots, well provided, (rather than the 1000 of such as we have."[2] Behind all the settlements were corporations, with charters making various more or less effective attempts to regulate the conduct of the new colonists. But far from these being religious refugees, they were, John Smith says in his "History of Virginia", for the most part "poor gentlemen, tradesmen, servingmen, libertines, and such like, ten times more fit to spoil a commonwealth than either to begin or maintain one."[3]

[1] John Fiske. "Old Virginia and Her Neighbours." Vol. I, p. 123.
[2] Captain John Smith's "Works", pp. 442–443, quoted by Fiske.
[3] John Smith's "History of Virginia", p. 90.

And when under a second charter a larger company came, he further describes them as:

> To a thousand mischiefs those lewd Captaines led this lewd company, wherein were many unruly gallants packed thither by their friends to escape ill destinies, and those would dispose and determine of the government, sometimes to one, the next day to another; to-day the old commission must rule, to-morrow the new, the next day neither, in fine they would rule all or ruine all; yet in charatie we must endure them thus to destroy us, or by correcting their follies, have brought the world's censure upon us to be guiltie of their blouds. Happie had we beene had they never arrived, and we forever abandoned, as we were left to our fortunes; for on earth for the number, was never more confusion, or misery than their factions occasioned.

Only the firm and stern despotism of Lord Delaware saved the situation, but he soon had to return on account of ill health. Again and again and from all sources we read of the "shiftless and graceless set of ne'er-do-weels" that come out to the colony.

There is no hint that the Virginia colony was in any sense a "Puritan" colony, but we find exactly the same laws, nominally at least, in force as later in New England, and generally regarded as the result of Puritanism. A code of laws sanctioned by the Company in London made it a capital crime not to attend church services, or to blaspheme God's name, or speak "against the known articles of the Christian faith." (Under Dale in 1611.)[1] And later in 1662,

> Enachted that the Lord's Day be kept holy, and no journeys be made on that day unless upon necessity. And all persons inhabiting in this country having no lawful excuse, shall every

[1] John Fiske, "Old Virginia and Her Neighbours." Vol. I, p. 164.

sunday resort to the parish church or chappel (sic) and there orderly during the common prayer, preaching and divine service, upon penalty of being fined 50 pounds of Tobacco by the County Court. This act shall not extend to Quakers, or other Recusants, who totally absent themselves, but they shall be liable to the penalty imposed by the Stat. 23. Eliz. viz. £20 sterling for every months absence, &c. and all Quakers assembling in unlawful conventicles, shall be fined every man so taken 200 pounds of Tobacco for every time of such meeting.

What interests us is the fact that such enactments have nothing to do with Puritanism, but are simply the expression of the demand, made in that day by almost every State, for outward religious uniformity. Of course these laws were incapable of effective enforcement in the scattered and far from orderly settlements up and down the James River. They were naturally never really enforced save against especially obnoxious persons, but served, as do thousands of similar laws in our own day, as now and again legal excuses for the suppression of those who in moments of excitement incurred the wrath or the suspicion of the community. There were probably laws on the statute book of Virginia in the time of the Georges, against blasphemy and swearing, when George Washington used the free language of every gentleman of his day and generation.

When therefore we ask ourselves what was the religious tradition of the earliest English colonists that was really governing the lives of any such as were under the influence of religion at all, it is not to the statute book we must turn. How large the proportion was of persons who went to Virginia who may be fairly said to have gone for any other reason than acquisition or adventure we cannot say, but to judge from the testimony of the appeals for colonists made by the trading companies it was not large. The great companies that backed up the Virginia adventure were all frankly acquisitive. Spain had grown rich from the spoils of South America, and now since the defeat of the Armada, England hoped for gold and a passage to the East for her trade. According to Fiske, the second charter for Virginia had behind it 659 persons. Of these 21 were peers, 96 were knights, 11 were clergymen and physicians, 53 are described as captains, 28 as engineers, 58 as gentlemen, 110 as merchants, while the remaining 282 are variously designated or only the names given. But most significant of all is the fact that the list includes the Companies of the City of London, 56 in all, Mercers, Grocers, Drapers, Fishmongers, Vintners, Brewers, etc. The Corporation was frankly a company of "Adventurers and Planters." Nor can it be truly said that Puritanism had anything to do with the establishment of the first popular General Assembly in America, when the Governor issued writs for an elective legislative body in July, 1619. The Virginia House of Burgesses had not unchecked authority, but it was a long step toward self-government. There was no thought in any one's mind of anything that we would now call democracy, and if there had been it would have been rudely crushed by three changes in the character of the colony. First, tobacco became the staple crop and demanded large plantations as the essential basis of cheap and wide cultivation; secondly, cheap labor was needed and could be used on plantations so that the coming of Negro slaves, brought by the Dutch in 1619, met a signal need; and third, about the same time King James ordered the transportation of one hundred "idle and dissolute persons" to be sent to Virginia to be bound over to be servants to the colonists, thus introducing that system of temporary white slavery into colonial life that left its marks on America long after the system had fallen into abeyance.[1]

If Puritanism had anything to do with the fundamental thought of Virginia, now would have been the time to realize the theocracy, which is the fundamental note of any truly Calvinistic Puritanism. But if any such aspiration was anywhere present, the writer has failed to find it after most diligent search. The State Establishment as it stood in England under James I was taken over bodily to Virginia, and in fact remained about on the somewhat Low-Church level apparently fashionable in London at that time. Nor had the Company in London any leanings toward a Puritan theocracy. Nicholas Ferrar was, if anything, rather a High-Church Anglican, with leanings toward the æsthetic side of Roman Catholic culture, even if politically opposed to a Stuart tyranny, and up to the fall of the Company in London (in 1624), Ferrar and Sandys, together with the Earl of Southampton, were the leading spirits of the whole enterprise. Sandys was the pupil and lifelong friend of Richard Hooker, the famous author of "Laws of Ecclesiastical Polity", and the opponent of the well-known Presbyterian preacher Travers; while Shakespeare's friend, the Earl of Southampton, was no Puritan.

All this time Puritanism was growing stronger and more definite in its aims in England and Scotland, but it had no part in molding the life and feeling of the first English colony in Virginia. Yet it was in Virginia that we see the first local Assembly, and the sturdiest expression of that spirit of self-help and self-government, that rather intense individualism which marks American life, and which is so often linked with what is called Puritanism. In the enactments of the Assembly we see exactly the same

[1] John Howard Hinton. "History of the United States." Vol. I, p. 37.

interference with the individual conduct,—laws against drunkenness, swearing, enactments to discourage luxury in clothes. In 1662 we read: "Every person who refuses to have his child Baptized by a lawful Minister, shall be amerced 2000 pounds of Tobacco; half to the Parish, half to the informer." In the same year we read: "The Man and Woman committing fornication shall pay each 500 pounds of Tobacco and to be bound to their good behaviour."

Nor is it possible to show any great difference in the class of persons that went to make up the population of the colony. From all the lists and names coming down to us we see that an upper class soon came into power, and that a few well-known English families were represented, but the population as a whole was mixed. Servants were freely brought into the colony. Indentured servants became the rule in the Southern colonies, and "decayed" gentlemen are constantly mentioned, but Germans, Poles, Frenchmen and workmen from Flanders were among the colonists. In spite of all laws it was naturally impossible to enforce uniformity of thought, and that the religious regulations were more than enactments upon paper we seriously doubt; at least the cases tried before the courts do not suggest more than a very spasmodic attempt to really enforce them.

Not more seriously can we take the enactments in regard to the education of the Indians. In England the Company granted ten thousand acres of land for a university to be built at Henrico, and the bishops in response to letters from King James collected fifteen hundred pounds to this same end, it being understood that the university was also to be a foundation for white education.[1] But the intentions were better than the fulfillment. Yet here again we see exactly the same respect

---

[1] John Hinton's "History", Vol. I, p. 37.

for education, and the professions of idealism in regard to the conversion of the Indians as elsewhere, and, alas, the same real indifference to any actual attempt at accomplishment.

When we ask the more difficult question: What English religious tradition controlled the beginnings of the colony in Virginia, the answer must be that neither any very High-Church Anglicanism is in evidence, nor any very pronounced radical Protestantism; but that the great body of those going out as colonists were of the class from which Dissent drew its members.[1]

[1] These lines were written before the writer had an opportunity to examine the more detailed and exhaustive studies of Professor Thomas Jefferson Wertenbacher on this field, but he sees no reason to modify his views formed on his own more limited investigations.

PART TWO

THE SPREAD AND TRIUMPH OF THE DISSENTING
TRADITION IN NORTH AMERICA

CHAPTER VIII

NEW ENGLAND AND ITS RELIGIOUS TRADITION IN NORTH AMERICA

The destruction of the Spanish Armada has often been sung as a great Protestant victory, and indirectly that was the case. At the same time directly it was the victory of nationalism over religious international imperialism, and of Humanism over revealed religion. The guiding forces of English life were at that time in no sense to be called truly Protestant. Elizabeth was a Humanist, her advisers were almost to a man either Humanists or under the influence of the Anglo-Catholic tradition. The Puritans were only very tentatively influential in the beginning of her reign and soon gave way to more amenable opportunists. Humanism was neither Protestant nor Catholic, although, no doubt, fitting better into a radical Protestantism than into the Catholic tradition, yet in a sense destructive of both. So far as the Roman tradition had preserved æsthetic values, Humanism was on the side of Catholicism as over against any religious tradition hostile to classic culture; but so far as Catholicism was in the way of the submission of all questions to the tribunal of informed human reason, Humanism was against it and on the side of Protestantism.[1]

The victory over Spain gave North America over to England and France, and as it happened among the religious traditions struggling for England's soul it was Protestantism that took up the task of making North

[1] *Cf.* Ueberweg. "Geschichte der Philosophie." Bd. III, ss. 5–23. Auf. 1901.

America Anglo-Saxon instead of French. The question that interests us now is which Protestant tradition really mastered the American continent. For as we have seen, not only was England divided between an Anglo-Catholic party and a Protestant party, but two well-defined types of Protestantism were also contending for victory,— on the one hand a Continental type, with Calvin as its chief inspiration, and an older primitive English Protestant type of which Wyclif and the Lollards were the main teachers.

The question is a broader and more important one than that discussed so interestingly by Mr. James Truslow Adams [1] in his recent work. It is not simply a question of names, but of great contending types of thought, marking and modifying as well as being molded by contending social forces. Nor is it a merely interesting historical question, but one that thrusts itself upon us to-day in our endeavor to discover the underlying streams of social movement in Anglo-American life. That there was a difference between Separatism and Puritanism can hardly be doubted in the light of the work of John A. Goodwin [2] and the better ordered and more recent work of Doctor Burrage.[3] It is, however, most important to examine more carefully than has been done which type of religious thought has been really influential in forming American life as far as any religious tradition has guided it. And in the very outset of our inquiry it is well to remind ourselves of the fact that it is easy to overestimate the influence of religion, for religion itself is, in its forms at least, the child of intellectual and economic forces that lie outside it.

[1] *Cf.* James Truslow Adams. "The Founding of New England." Boston, 1921. Chap. IV.
[2] John A. Goodwin. "The Pilgrim Republic." Boston, 1899.
[3] Champlin Burrage. "The Church Covenant Idea", 1904; "The Early English Dissenters", 1912, etc.

We do not need to repeat the story which has now been told so well of the landing of the little band of Pilgrims on that winter day on Plymouth Rock. They came in part from Holland, where a little colony of refugees had found temporary shelter. It is well to remember that they themselves placed the economic motive in the foreground. William Bradford says in his "History of Plymouth Plantation":

And first, they saw & found by experience the hardnes of ye place (Leyden) & countrie to be such, as few in comparison would come to them, and fewer would that would bide it out, and continew with them. For many that came to them, and many more that desired to be with them, could not endure the great labor and hard fare, with other inconveniences which they underwent & were contented with.

And again, "But it was thought that if a better and easier place of living could be had, it would draw many & take away these discouragements."[1] Beyond question nearly all that came to the New World came either to better their fortunes or from sheer love of adventure. But along with these fundamental motives were mingled many others, and religious freedom, not in the abstract, but the freedom each one required for his own need, played of course a part.

The Pilgrims in their pact speak of "a civill bodie politick" and the motives set forth are the glory of God, the advancement of Christianity, and the honor of the king. There is no thought of a theocracy; and there was no limiting the franchise to church members. Myles Standish was, seemingly, never a member of the Plymouth church. The question then arises: What was the fundamental religious tradition of the little settlement? That they were in spirit Separatists is beyond dispute. But both Robinson

[1] William Bradford. "History of Plymouth Plantation." Chap. IV, pp. 22–23.

and Brewster regarded themselves as in accordance with the French Reformed churches in point of Church government. In their "first breefe note" they say:

Touching the Ecclesiasticall ministrie, namly of pastores for teaching, elders for ruling, & deacons for distributing the churches contribution, as allso for the too Sacraments, baptisme, and the Lords supper, we doe wholy and in all points agree with the French reformed churches, according to their publick confession of faith. The oath of Supremacie we shall willingly take if it be required of us, and that conveniente satisfaction be not given by our taking the oath of Alleagence.[1]

It is none the less true that these Pilgrims differed sharply from the French Reformed churches, which could hardly be thought of as being for years content with lay preaching, for Brewster was not only simply a deacon, but so regarded himself, and did not administer the sacraments. Nor is it thinkable that a French Presbyterian church would be content without the regular administration of the sacraments for seemingly nearly seven years. In 1629 the Pilgrims had at last a regularly ordained minister, the Reverend Ralph Smith. Brewster himself regretted the fact that the sacraments were not administered,[2] and laid it to the absence of their pastor John Robinson, but surely had they really had churchly feeling for the Sacramental grace they could easily have supplied the need.

They needed a sacred building as little as they needed a stated ministry. "Upon the hill they had (have) a large square house, with a flat roof, made of thick-sawn planks, stayed with oak beams, upon the top of which they have six cannons, which shoot iron balls of four and five pounds, and command the surrounding country. The lower part they use for their church, where they preach

---

1 William Bradford. "History of Plymouth Plantation", p. 34. Ed. Boston, 1856.
2 *Ibid*. P. 161.

on Sundays and the usual hollidays."[1] They had no need of any church building, for the conventicle could meet anywhere. It is not known whether they had a church building in Leyden or not. They owned a "large building opposite St. Peter's Church" (Winslow) but there is no record of any church building, nor could the writer find any evidence in Leyden of their being known to have used any Dutch church for worship.

This attitude both toward the sacraments and the church building is so exactly the attitude of the Lollard conventicle, and so exactly the opposite of the attitude of Calvinistic Puritanism that it forms a most striking contrast between the conventicle and the Puritan type of Protestantism. It is not an attitude of rejection but of indifference.

Not only so but they seemingly had no stated creed. Historical systematic theology has never been the central interest of English Dissent. As later on the congregation separated, and different churches formed, each congregation could form its own creed just as the Lollard conventicles are accused of doing in past history.[2] They had no central authority, nor did they need any such, for the Bible, together with the Holy Spirit to interpret it, was all they really needed.

The whole attitude of Plymouth to the later Puritan settlements is also characteristic of the atmosphere out of which English Dissent came. The very spirit of comparative tolerance reflects that attitude of occasional conformity that marked much Separatism. They could point to the fact that John Robinson and his following were ready to submit to the English bishops as servants of the king in all outward things. They only asked to have their

[1] A letter of De Rasieres, of Fort Amsterdam, in 1627. Quoted by Walker. "History of the Congregational Churches in America", p. 73.
[2] Wilkins. "Consilia magnæ Britanniæ." Tome III, p. 378 and other passages.

own worship also, and to be let alone. Their appeal to King James through their friends in London when they sought a charter is almost pathetic at this point. Later Defoe was very impatient at this characteristic of his fellow dissenters, but Lollardism would not perhaps have so strongly survived but for it. They lived two lives, one of apparent conformity and the other of secret worship. The old Lollards could point to the fact that Wyclif had died in the communion of the Roman Catholic Church and that Paul frequented the Jewish synagogues.

Nothing is more striking in the accounts of Bradford and Winslow of the early Pilgrims than the simplicity and naïveté of their theory of Church government and of theological orthodoxy. This is characteristic of any faith built up, or supposed to be built up, on the Bible alone. Such faith must be primitive, for neither a developed ecclesiastical system nor a self-consistent theology can be deduced without the help of tradition, from the New Testament alone.

The insistence of Wyclif and the early Lollards upon the sole authority of the Bible cut off lower-class English Protestantism from the traditional creeds and from the historical development, and the naïve faith that every unlettered man by the help of the Holy Spirit was in a position to understand and expound an elaborate Oriental literature is reflected in the faith of men who, like Robinson and Brewster, were not unlettered. The theory of Church government as elaborated by Deacon Fuller convinced Endicott that it was in accordance with the Scriptures, which it no doubt was, because there is no very elaborate system of Church government set forth in the New Testament.

With the New Testament alone in hand men went back naturally to the very primitive autonomous government of early Christianity.[1] And this simple form suited the hunted conventicle as it had suited the early persecuted Christians. Thus we find the congregational form of government the natural one to mark the simple attitude of men dependent wholly upon the New Testament. The real father of the Congregational Church is not the erratic Brown, nor even the brave and able Barrow, but John Wyclif and the early Lollards, as they are the Fathers of all the congregational types of Church government which we will see developing in various dissenting sects.

But it is not only in Church government that the outlook of these early Pilgrim Fathers reminds us of Lollard conventicle Protestantism, but in their insistence upon morals rather than pure doctrine, and upon the careful watch over the conduct of the individual member. Men like John Robinson knew Calvin and found in him a genial formulator of much that they believed, but all the essential teachings upon which they laid emphasis are older than Calvin, and even in the form in which they were taught bear more the stamp of Paul and Wyclif than of Geneva. True, they knew nothing at first hand of Wyclif, unless some scattered translations of the Bible may have come into their hands, but the persistence of a religious tradition cannot be overestimated, and any one who studies the outcome of the Reformation in England must satisfy himself that streams of tradition wholly independent and even contradictory of Continental Protestantism appear in the reigns of Henry VIII and Queen Elizabeth.

The bare plainness of the meetinghouse, the rejection of all the amusements of the relatively leisure class, as seen in the attitude of the Plymouth Colony to Morton and Merrie Mount, where a maypole and dancing gave especial offense, is not to be traced to Puritanism, but to

[1] *Cf.* Mueller. "Kirchengeschichte." Bd. I, p. 42 *ff.*

the very natural and primitive instincts that made the conventicle type of Protestantism suspicious of all that marked the ruling class and their way of life. It seemed "worldly" and therefore irreligious to the simple, hard-working and very serious English dissenting lower orders to spend time and money upon such amusements, nor was it difficult to find some passage in the Bible that ignorance could construe as prohibition of the thing disliked. This is a common feature of the ethics of all fighting lower-class morality.

The formation of a church at Salem was not only characteristic of the method of the conventicle type of Protestantism, but proved decisive in regard to the future of church life in New England. In a letter of Charles Gott quoted by Bradford [1] we find the characteristic two-fold call to the ministry, one an inward call, and the other the outward call, "when a company of beleevers are joyned togither in covenante, to walke togither in all the ways of God, and every member (being men) are to have a free voyce in the choyce of their officers &c."; and the ordaining is by the individual church and for the individual church. The suspicion and dislike of the State Church appears in the secularization of marriage and burial, to which a minister was not invited, and which were long considered purely secular affairs. All that reminded them of the Christian year was forbidden, and only the Sabbath or Lord's Day was kept.

Characteristic of the life of the Plymouth Colony was the fact that the main interest was not theological dispute, but moral discipline. As Bradford remarks: ". . . . hear (as I am verily perswaded) is not more evills in this kind, nor nothing nere so many by proportion, as in other places; but they are here more discoverd and seen, and

[1] William Bradford. "History of Plymouth Plantation", pp. 265–266. Ed. 1856.

made publick by due serch, inquisition, and due punish-
ment; for the churches looke narrowly to their members,
and the magistrates over all, more strictly then in other
places."[1] Whether the moral life was either higher or lower
than in a similar community elsewhere cannot now be
determined. It was not a company of saints. Drunkenness, uncleanness, fornication and theft, murder and
blasphemy, all came before courts of the little community
as well as sins not easily discussed now in public. The
horizon was narrow, and even the strong common sense
of a man like Bradford did not save him from the absurd-
ity of putting to death a youth of seventeen or eighteen
years of age for offenses that would now result in the
doubtfully healing process of a reform school, and the
sentence was carried out with superstitious attention to
the law of Leviticus 20:15.[2] At the same time, it is
doubtful if the attention to sexual questions so often
noticed in Bradford and Winthrop is not more a mark of
class morality than of religious trend. This phenomenon
may be marked wherever a rising class has to protect its
women from the seductions of a powerful and attractive
aristocracy, and the best protection is the stressing of the
purity of the woman and the self-control of the male in
sexual relations. We see the same thing in early Christianity, as a freedman class struggled up out of slavery conditions; and under similiar circumstances in England, under
the Norman and Normanized landed aristocracy, arose
the well-known prudery of English middle-class life. The
seduction of the lower-class woman by members of the
landed aristocracy in whose power she is, forms the favorite
theme of the English novel from Richardson to George
Eliot. Nowhere has the religious taboo in the interests of

---

[1] William Bradford. "History of Plymouth Plantation", p. 386.
[2] *Ibid.* P. 398. Ed. 1856.

class morality had such scope as in the field of the sexual relations.

Very striking is the attention to trading that marks all the records of the early Pilgrim life. If one goes to Bradford's History or his letter-book, expecting to find much light upon the shades of religious belief of the Pilgrim Fathers he will be very much disappointed. For one page upon such themes he will find by actual computation some twenty-five pages on trading conditions, on the relations to the English Company and the commercial needs of the little colony. This is natural, of course, but in spite of the frequent references to the goodness or the severity of God the whole tone is frankly secular. It is also characteristic that although small farming was a necessity, and all had to engage in it more or less, very little can be gleaned of the actual processes of the farming from the literature at our disposal. In point of fact it was a population that at first was evidently very helpless on the land. That the Indians had to teach the colonists how to grow Indian corn was perhaps very natural, but they had also to learn, so far as they did learn, how to hunt and fish; nor do they seem to have taken very kindly to a farming life, and at first at least depended much upon trade with the Indians for their supply of food. All who came from Leyden were small craftsmen, and the others as far as we can judge came from the cities and small towns of England, with the morality and outlook of the lower middle-class townsman. The contrast with the French colonists as Francis Parkman so graphically and ably describes them to us [1] is very great. The adventurous younger sons of the French nobility and the servant class they imported

---

[1] Francis Parkman. New Library Ed. Little, Brown and Company, Boston. 12 Vols. 1914. Especially "Pioneers of France in the New World" and "A Half-Century of Conflict."

got on in many ways better with the Indians than the unimaginative lower-class English; they were also more at home in the woods and wilds of America, but they did not come to found French families, and they dreamt of Paris and France even in the arms of their Indian squaws. And while the Protestant pastors raised up prodigious numbers of children to the glory of God and the further settlement of New England, the Jesuit priests remained sterile and unfruitful trees. Bradford points out the great advantage the French had in warfare, as they lay behind their fortified trading-posts and harassed the English colonists spread for agricultural purposes over an open country. But in the end the English middle-class home was bound to win out over Jesuit priest and French adventurer.

The greater toleration of the Plymouth Colony in contrast to Massachusetts can be too greatly stressed. Naturally the dissenting circles had to learn a certain toleration of one another for they were continually splitting up into small bodies, largely on questions of personal conduct or cult, and they had more in common with each other than with the State Church, in spite of all differences, and intolerant betrayal of each other would have meant the extermination of them all. But the toleration had its limitations. Even when the Welshman Roger Williams and later John Locke, the typical Whig, tried to formulate the dissenting faith in religious tolerance, they left out Jews and Catholics as well as all atheists and agnostics. The conventicle autonomy of the individual religious group made for toleration, for when any one was persecuted in one group he had only to flee into another. Then, too, the striking indifference to any abstract theology made for a certain type of toleration. Bradford, in a dignified defense of the Plymouth Colony, already quoted, against attacks stresses the fact that religious dissension was unknown in Plymouth. On the other hand, in regard to the outward conduct of the colonists, the Pilgrims were as intolerant as any of their neighbors and rather proud of this fact.

In the early Plymouth Colony we see more plainly than later the conventicle attitude toward a stated ministry. The utterly worthless Reverend John Lyford, whom we have already mentioned, is not a trustworthy witness when unsupported by other evidence, but in a letter to London, dated August 22, 1624, he says, with a great measure of truth: "houlding this principle, that the Lord hath not appointed any ordinariy ministrie for the conversion of those that are without"; and again: "Though in truth they have had no ministrie here since they came, but such as may be performed by any of you, by their owne possition, what soever great pretences they make; but herin they equivocate, as in many other things they doe." The charge of equivocation is, of course, absurd. The attitude toward a stated ministry is exactly that characteristic of conventicle history from Wyclif on. Where a properly qualified minister is to be had, each individual group is not only free to sustain him, but generally seems to have done so. The most of Wyclif's "Poor Preachers" seem undoubtedly to have been "clerks" and at least students at Oxford, but the later Lollard preachers had no such qualification, and as we have seen, Wyclif calls his own Poor Preachers "laymen." Each little group had some more or less formally acknowledged leader to whom it turned, and if he was a trained teacher so much the better. One may see exactly this attitude in existing English dissenting groups, like the so-called "Plymouth Brethren", or in Quaker meetings or some Baptist groups. It is the historic attitude toward a ministry which reflects the older and primitive attitude of early Christianity.

To sum up what we may observe in the character of the Plymouth Colony, we find there an unconscious reproduction of the religious life of the obscure "heretical" sects that in greater or less number made England ready for the so-called Reformation of Henry VIII. These sects had a common character underlying the great divergence of name and cult, due to the entire lack of any central organization and of any attention to historic tradition or to a priestly ministry. The little Plymouth group bears also all the marks of the sturdy, poorer, landless class that was rising to importance as English industry and English trade slowly either transcended in importance or absorbed the landowning interest. This English Protestant tradition can better be observed in its outworking upon English and Anglo-American life than even in its literature, for the historian must remember that unwritten traditions from the time of children's games to the usages of the funeral form much more than half of human life. With the Bible in their hands and interpreting it in the light of this unwritten tradition, the Pilgrim Fathers reproduced with wonderful accuracy a type of Protestantism quite different from anything to be found outside of Anglican and Anglo-American circles. The æsthetic bareness of its life and the colorless severity of its codes gave perhaps added intensity to this type of Protestantism, and made it the fitting mode of religious thought for the rapid political and economic advance of the class that gave it birth.

CHAPTER IX

THE RELIGIOUS TRADITION OF MASSACHUSETTS BAY COLONY

In John Goodwin's "Pilgrim Republic" the attempt is made to represent the Massachusetts Bay Colony as a more or less deliberate attack upon the Separatism of Plymouth. In a comment upon John Robinson's letter to Bradford, Goodwin writes: "in fact, though he (Robinson) did not say so, a plot was already in progress for wresting the colony from Congregational rule, and establishing there the Church of England after the Puritan forms.[1] The evidence is certainly not contained in either of the two letters of Robinson's which we have in full. It is true he speaks of five or six of the Company in London as being warmly for the sending of Robinson and the remaining members of his flock to New England, and of five or six being "our bitter professed adversaries", but no definite reason is given for the opposition. The passage reads as follows:

Besids, howsoever for the presente the adventurers aledg nothing but want of money, which is an invincible dificulty, yet if that be taken away by you, others will witout doubte be found. For the better clearing of this we must dispose the adventures into 3. parts; and of them some 5 or 6. (as I conceive) are absolutely bent for us, above any others. Other 5 or 6 are our bitter professed adversaries. The rest, being the body, I conceive to be honestly minded, & loveingly also toward us; yet such as have others (namly the forward preachers) nerer unto them, then us, and whose course so farr as ther is

[1] John Goodwin. "The Pilgrim Republic", p. 256.

any difference, they would advance then ours. Now what a hanck (hold) these men have over the professors, you know. And I persuade myselfe, that for me, they of all others are unwilling I should be transported, espetially such of them as have an eye that way themselves; as thinking if I come ther, ther market will be mard in many regards.[1]

Knowing as we do that there were internal disputes within the Company that had nothing to do with religious debate, and that faction and political, especially Court, influence were playing their part in the division of opinion, it is hard to believe that the opposition to transplanting the rest of the Leyden congregation together with their pastor was solely a Puritan move against Separatism. In fact, the lines between the two contending Protestant traditions that seem to us from a distance sharp and easily drawn were at that time blurred by many circumstances.

The four thousand or more emigrants that came over to form the Massachusetts Bay Colony from 1628 on were not in any sense of the word Puritans. The historian must free himself from the atmosphere created by Palfrey, Bancroft, Thanksgiving Day sermons and New England dinners. The Massachusetts Bay Colony was a commercial and political undertaking with a small Puritanized leadership, but the ease with which all episcopacy was soon stripped from the Church life is significant. The Puritans hated separation from the State Establishment, and so far as they really had come to comprehend and admire the Calvinistic system they were from the Continental point of view right. The establishment of a theocracy on the basis of the Old Testament was, no doubt, in the minds of many who came over, but England was neither Scotland nor Geneva. When James I wanted to

[1] William Bradford. "History of Plymouth Plantation", p. 166. Ed. 1856.

purge the English Church of all nonconformist elements
he found only about three hundred who were not ready
to accept his tests of conformity; nor should one be led
astray by the taunts that those Puritans who stayed in
the Church did so only for the bread and butter of the
Establishment. Some were, without question, merely
time-servers, but the great majority cherished the old
Catholic Tradition that Church and State were but two
sides of the one divinely appointed authority that guided
the life of man and could not think of a Church separate
from the State. Lollards, Brownists, Barrowists, Anabaptists, and sects with which the educated and power-
possessing class had as little to do as possible, could alone
think of a Church thus separated.

When we study the names of those in England who were
interested in the plantations in North America, we have
always to do with about the same small group. Virginia,
Plymouth and Massachusetts were all backed by far-
sighted enemies of Spain, to many of whom Protestantism was, no doubt, a very real thing; to others the English
national Catholic tradition was equally precious; others
were frankly Humanists. The same Earl of Warwick who
signed the patent (1629–1630) for Plymouth was the
instrument for getting the charter for Massachusetts.[1]

It is hard to believe that even so able a man as the
good Deacon Fuller, who came as physician to the help
of Endicott and the Massachusetts Colony, was able to
upset any very fixed principles held by Endicott. Indeed
he himself says that the Independency Fuller stood for
had been his own opinion since he had seen the light.[2]

"It is as farr as I can yet gather, no other then is
warrented by the evidence of truth, and the same which

---

[1] Justin Winsor. "History of America." Vol. III, p. 308.
[2] William Bradford. "History of Plymouth Plantation", p. 265. Ed. 1856.

I have professed and maintained ever since the Lord in mercie revealed him selfe unto me."

Let any instructed Calvinist contemplate Calvin's feelings viewing the Congregational Independency of New England! Where purity of doctrine is of more importance than the good life, a group of conventicles, with no central power to enforce purity of teaching upon all the associated churches, would be to Calvin the denial of all semblance of the One Church of Christ, founded by Him especially to guarantee truth and the right administration of the sacraments, and in spite of abuses, continuous throughout the ages. Puritanism survived in New England only in the broad sense that the State supported as the official form of church organization an increasing number of independent churches, which never were able to agree either upon a common creed or even upon a very effective administrative machinery. Neither the "Cambridge Platform" of 1648 nor the "Saybrook Platform" of Connecticut in 1708 was successful in really uniting the churches of even the States that gave them birth, Massachusetts and Connecticut. The vague general approval of the Westminster Confession of Faith had no binding force upon any individual church, and the autonomy of the separate church was always admitted. Puritanism was a party within the State Episcopal Church; and uniformity of worship and ritual with bishops or presbyters to enforce the uniformity, if need be by the power of the State, which according to Calvinistic Puritanism should always be at the disposal of the true Church, formed the life of their contention. Puritanism demanded the purification of the State Church from the Roman abuses, and if any large body of Puritans had ever come to Massachusetts they could have as easily established their Presbyterian ideal as did John Knox in

Scotland. For New England was just as divided as was Scotland and a small determined body of intelligent Puritans could have forced their ideal upon Maine, Massachusetts, Connecticut and probably even upon Plymouth. But no such attempt was ever made.

The so-called Synod of Cambridge was meeting in 1648 just as Independency was sweeping the last traces of Puritanism out of Westminster to establish in its place the indigenous English religious tradition of conventicle Independency. Cromwell had been forced by the folly of an arrogant Scottish Presbyterianism to take the side of the Independents, although as a soldier he would have been far more at home in a Presbyterian atmosphere, with its central authority and its firmer discipline. But Calvinistic Puritanism was a foreign growth in England, whereas the independent conventicle could look back, and did look back, to over two hundred and fifty years of honorable struggle and suffering.[1] Scottish Presbyterian Puritanism could make no stand against English Independency so long as this had leadership and was united, but it lies in the very nature of the conventicle, with its autonomy of the individual group, to fly apart, and when Cromwell disappeared Presbyterianism betrayed Independency and was itself then betrayed.

The defeat of Puritanism in England gave to Independency in New England complete freedom to develop itself as the native and natural Protestant type. Thus arose the Congregational Church as the complete demonstration in New England that the same religious tradition that governed the class from which the colonies all drew their support was at work in the New World.

It is common to call attention to the superior class of

---

[1] Th Leevellers were fully conscious of their ancestry. *Cf.* Carlyle on this point. "Cromwell's Letters and Speeches." Vol. II, pp. 22 *ff.* London Ed. 1858.

28582

the Massachusetts Bay colonists, but this apparently applied only to the leaders.[1] If between 1630 and 1640 actually twenty thousand persons came to the shores of New England as has been estimated[2] we may be sure not only that they were not all Puritans, but that religion played a very small part in their coming, and that if Lechford's estimate is sound, most of them were exceedingly indifferent to religion.[3] Although the right of voting was tied up with church membership, and all social recognition was linked with it, only about a third of the population were members of the church. But the influence of a religious tradition is not to be judged by any such formal test. What seems to have been decisive is the common class feeling that lent itself readily to the leadership of those who were in point of fact the educated members of the same class, with all the characteristics of that class. The Reverend John Cotton, who boasted of his dislike of Separatism, was at the same time the stern opponent of Episcopacy, of the established ritual of the Church of England, and of all that really marked and gave character to the old Anglo-Catholic tradition. Former membership in the State Church and education were not sufficient to wipe out the prejudices embodied in lower-class English Protestantism. In spite of the aristocratic support in England the actual population of New England seems to have been singularly homogeneous, as seen in the common character of the law-giving, the common speech, the common type of developed Church government.

In spite of bitter persecution at first, the Quakers really soon won their battle for recognition as a branch of the great English dissenting tree. The Baptists could not be

---

[1] *Cf.* James Truslow Adams. "The Founding of New England", pp. 124 *ff.*
[2] "A Century of Population Growth." 1909.
[3] Thomas Lechford. "Plain Dealing; or News from New England." Boston, 1867.

suppressed, because of the autonomy of the individual groups, and as intellectual Arianism came, it too had to be at first fought, then tolerated, then embraced.

That the richer, more powerful and better backed Massachusetts Bay Colony looked down a little upon Plymouth may be admitted; that in the matter of the disputed territory in Connecticut, Massachusetts behaved badly is also seemingly certain, but in spite of some grumbling criticism, all the leaders—Bradford, Brewster, Winthrop, Winslow, Myles Standish and the others—lived on good terms with each other, had the same prejudices, the same general faith, the same general outlook upon life, the same subservient respect for success and social station. Nor does it seem at all evident that Plymouth was more "democratic" save that it did not link the franchise with church membership. And even here we must inquire closely into the motives of this limitation.

Very early in the history of the colonies the question arose as to the right of voting and the question of the position of baptised persons, who however had never made claim to a personal experience of religion, and were therefore according to the dissenting type of Protestantism not "members" of the Church. The Continental type of Protestantism, both in its Calvinistic and its Lutheran forms, retains confirmation, and, as in the Catholic tradition, the child automatically comes into the communion of the Church after almost nominal instruction at a certain age. The English dissenting type was so strongly individualistic and personal emotional reactions instead of cult and organization formed so strongly the basis of the religious tradition, that confirmation was dropped. The logic of the dissenting type would of course lead also to adult baptism, and to this many therefore turned, but probably the family urge was too strong, and infant baptism was very generally retained. This lack of logical coherence revenged itself in almost innumerable disputes about the character of the baptised person who is without any claim to emotional religious experience. Between 1640 and 1650 there was being waged a fierce fight in England between the divided and distracted forces of English Protestantism and the Continental compromise with the Catholic tradition, which had in its Calvinistic form captured Scotland and aimed at the capture of England. Had Westminster Presbyterianism captured England it would have forced itself, if necessary, by fire and sword upon the American colonies. The English Parliament had already handed over to a commission all the power previously held by the king. A little party in Massachusetts demanded the right of suffrage simply on the basis of baptism and appealed to the English Parliament, which was at that time strongly under the influence of Presbyterian Puritanism. Now it is worth noting that nowhere was seemingly the dread of Puritan influence in the colonial management greater than in Massachusetts, and accordingly it was Edward Winslow of Plymouth who was sent to defend Massachusetts before Parliament, and his success was made possible in all probability by the complete overthrow of the Parliament by Cromwell and the Independent army, to the great rejoicing of both Massachusetts and Plymouth.

These instinctive reactions of the New England colonies mark better than anything else the type of religious tradition that lies at the basis of the life of New England. It was not only strongly hostile to the old Anglo-Catholic tradition, but was also very suspicious of even the Continental type of churchly Protestantism. It esteemed a teaching ministry highly, but was suspicious of all attempts at establishing a hierarchy. The minister had only character in connection with an individual church and its activities. Again and again attempts were made by a more or less Puritanized clergy to break down this distinctive feature of the English dissenting tradition, but always without success. In this respect Massachusetts was as stubborn as Plymouth. On this basis a theocracy is impossible, and the Old Testament model quite out of all question. The attitude of Massachusetts toward the Old Testament is not essentially Puritan, for the Lollards read and revered as the Word of God both Old Testament and New, and the Plymouth Colony made the laws of Leviticus a part of the code of the colony. It was the work of Wyclif that made the reading of the whole Bible obligatory upon all Christian men and women, and made it an authority over the lives of all, apart from churchly tradition and authority. But that very fact also excluded any theocracy, for every man and woman was responsible only to Christ as head of the invisible Church. Not even the conventicle group which grew into the Congregational Church of New England had power over the individual conscience, save only as it could give or withhold the right hand of fellowship.

According to the stern teaching of Wyclif, not even the pope could be saved if not predestinate. The assurance of salvation came only as a gift of God's grace as a personal experience. This teaching underlies all later dissenting emphasis upon the individual church being a group of those who had thus won a knowledge of God and salvation. Quite different was the Calvinistic Puritan's attitude: for him every man was bound within the communion of the Church to make his calling and election sure in the fulfillment of all duty, by obedience to God's laws and the partaking of all the ordinary means of grace, including the sacrament. Neither Independent nor Puritan thought that man could be saved by works, but for the Calvinist the historic Church as a guarantee of the pure preaching of the Word and right administration of the sacrament had a meaning it never had or could have for the Congregationalist. It was simply ignorance of history and theology that led many to confuse the traditional conventicle doctrine of predestination with that of Calvin. Quite properly, and from an historical point of view justifiably, all mention of Calvin was dropped at the Congregational Synod of Boston in 1865. On the other hand, it was almost inevitable that the clear formulation of a theological system by Calvin, that had much more in common with Independency than with Lutheranism, should have blinded men's eyes to the radical difference in the attitude of the two toward history and the traditional Church.

The rejection of Puritanism at the Synod of Cambridge in 1648 was deliberate and the endorsement of the Westminster Confession of Faith was not made binding on the individual churches. As in England so also in New England the older and native tradition proved stronger than the Continental Puritan type. For a little while Presbyterianism held its own in Connecticut, but here also the character of Presbyterianism changed and was gradually brought into line with the traditional dissenting type. The impossibility of making the State the servant of several hundred independent churches made connection with the State relatively unimportant from the point of view of those who otherwise would have much dreaded any such menace to the freedom they needed.

The Congregational churches of Massachusetts, Connecticut, Maine and Plymouth had the seemingly almost undivided support of the population, even where that population was deprived of the franchise so far as it did not belong to the church. But to call this population Puritan, even in the widest sense of that term, would compel us to find some other name to designate that which the same population deliberately rejected and evidently more or less secretly feared. True, they did not themselves probably realize how old and honorable was their history, for the lack of historic feeling that attended the whole development revenged itself at this point. Every conventicle had in the Bible and the Holy Spirit enough to make historic Christianity superfluous, but there were in Massachusetts a few, mostly ministers, who were real Puritans, and to these the thought of a theocracy was inspiration, and led to constant attempts to give Congregationalism a united creed and a form of government strong enough to coerce the recalcitrant and make due use of the communal power. It is an evidence of the strength of the dissenting mind that all such attempts failed. The traditionalism that Puritanism valued so highly had seemingly no meaning for Dissent; as individuals, the ministers had a very high place in the social and intellectual life of New England, but they were never permitted to form a hierarchy apart from the individual churches to which they belonged. Many of the so-called marks of Puritanism have nothing to do with Puritanism, and some are far older than Puritanism, as we have before noted; for instance, compulsory church attendance. This was enforced by the State Church in the days of Elizabeth by the law of 1593, aimed rather at Roman and Puritan Recusants before Puritanism had gained any headway, and by those who were bitterly opposed to Puritanism as it arose.[1] Plainness of dress was a mark of Dissent, as seen in the Quaker dress, in the dress

[1] *Cf.* W. P. M. Kennedy. "Elizabethan Episcopal Administration." Vol. I, p. 166 and many other passages. Palfrey. "History of New England." Vol. I, p. 122.

of the Lollard preachers, and dislike of all display. The dislike of stage plays, of maypoles, of dancing and card playing was widespread in England long before Puritanism came. Dicing and card playing were forbidden the Anglo-Catholic clergy before ever Puritanism had any hold upon English life. When Puritanism came to Massachusetts it found there a population that already had its own life and its own prejudices, and although it controlled a small but very powerful minority it was far more influenced by Dissent than Dissent was by Puritanism. They had many prejudices and opinions in common; so far as Dissent had a theology it was congenial for the most part to the Puritans. Outwardly the sacrament did not divide them; for both the sermon was most important; in strictness of life both held substantially the same ideals; yet a great gulf separated the world of Independency from the world of Puritanism, and as the strain in England increased between these two worlds it is perfectly plain on which side the sympathies of the New England population were. The non-sacramental, unchurchly, unpriestly Congregationalism could have brooked no High-Church Presbyterianism as its master, and had Presbyterianism won out in England it might have given rise to much trouble, for any attempt to enforce Puritan-Presbyterian standards upon New England would have been fiercely resisted.

The Continental Presbyterian-Puritan type of Protestantism was felt instinctively, it would seem, both in England and New England to be foreign, and un-English. This is seen in the attitude of the Pilgrims to Dutch Protestantism, and in the later attitude of New England as a whole to Presbyterianism in Connecticut. In spite of all they had in common, and in spite of a steadily growing intimacy between the two types, the English dissenting type never really understood the cardinal principles of Calvinistic Puritanism, and what has always happened when the two types met for coöperation has been a more or less pronounced weakening of the Presbyterian-Puritan demands. Congregationalism has never especially emphasized purity of doctrine, and has been hospitable to all shades of Arianism and Unitarianism. Sacramental questions it leaves to the individual groups to settle in their own way. The purely voluntary character of the central Synod or Association has always been jealously guarded, and in spite of the fact that in accordance with the tradition of their history the sermon has always been in the center of the church life, in no denomination has the energetic layman played a greater part. The "deacon" of Congregational history is a more characteristic figure than even the "preacher." In its theory Presbyterian-Puritanism, as we have more than once emphasized, knows no laymen in its government. In American practice the dissenting tradition won its way in New England and thence over the country. In Massachusetts and Connecticut the union of the State with the Church was Puritan in principle, but in point of fact all that Presbyterian-Puritanism values in that union, namely the power to maintain pure doctrine, was at the very beginning sacrificed by the admission that the individual church was autonomous.

The settlement of Connecticut furnishes another example of the drift away from the theocratic idea of the Puritan type, when under the influence of Thomas Hooker (1586–1647) a civil government was established with no provision for membership in any church organization. In a sermon on Deuteronomy 1:13, Hooker set forth three principles: "1. The choice of public magistrates belongs unto the people, by God's own allowance. 2. The privilege of election which belongs to the people must not be exercised according to their humors, but according to the blessed will of God. 3. They who have power to appoint officers and magistrates, it is in their power also to set the bounds and limits of the power and place unto which they call them." [1] Let any impartial reader go straight from the reading of Calvin's Fourth Book of Institutes, more particularly the first and the twentieth chapters, to the work of Thomas Hooker on "Survey of the Summe of Church Discipline" (1648) and he will at once mark the entire difference in point of view, even when the appeal is made to the same passages of Scripture. Calvin's defense of the monarchy and an aristocracy as against the fury of the Anabaptists (*contre la fureur des Anabaptistes*) and his denunciation of Anarchy [2] reflect the essentially aristocratic, or perhaps better, essentially theocratic attitude of Puritanism in its Calvinistic moods. The Church is to be nourished by good kings, who in their turn are to do the bidding of the Church, which as Calvin carefully points out is not in the hands of the people but of pastors and doctors, to whom God has entrusted the pure preaching of the Word of God.[3] In Geneva and Scotland, Calvinism developed as the religious expression of a triumphant ruling class, at a time when Dissent was still the faith of a relatively humble and struggling lower class. But in New England the Calvinistic Puritanism was the attitude of too small a class to overcome the resistance of the great body of the colonists and to control their religious life.

---

[1] Palfrey. "History of New England." Vol. I, p. 537 (Note).

[2] "*Au-contraire l'Histoire sainte nous raconte, qu'entre les inconveniens qu'apporte l'Anarchie, les superstitions avoyent la vogue en Israel, parce que ce Peuple n'avoit point de Roy, & que chacun faisoit ce qui sembloit estre droit.*" "Institution Chréstienne." Livr. IV, Chap. XX, 9.

[3] "*Il a mis ce divin tresor comme en dépost entre les mains de son Église, ou. il a établi des Pasteurs & des Docteurs, etc.*" "Institution Chréstienne." Livr. IV, Chap. I, 1.

CHAPTER X

THE RELIGIOUS TRADITION OF THE COLONY OF VIRGINIA

To some it may seem superfluous to inquire about the religious tradition of an English colony supposedly settled by Cavaliers and where the State Church of England was recognized as the Established Church of the settlers. Happily we possess now an ample and accessible mass of documents setting forth in great detail the actions and motives of those in England who promoted the enterprise.[1]

So far as we know, no one has ever claimed that Virginia was a "Puritan" colony. Nor can any one rise from the study of the material collected by Mr. Brown without realizing that substantially the same motives as well as the same set of men backed both Virginia and Massachusetts. Some color has been lent to the popular tradition that Virginia was settled by Cavaliers by the fact that after the collapse of the House of Stuart a number of the followers of the king fled to Virginia.[2] Some three hundred and thirty came in one ship alone. The colony had to surrender to the Commonwealth, but when Charles II came to the throne it officially expressed its regrets and pleaded force as the ground of the surrender. Officially the colony remained true to the House of Stuart, and rejoiced at the restoration to the throne of Charles II.

In 1710 Governor Spottswood wrote to the Bishop of London to whom the colonies were somewhat vaguely

[1] Alexander Brown. "The Genesis of the United States." A Series of Historical Manuscripts, Collected and Edited by . . . ." 2 Vols. London, 1890.
[2] Justin Winsor. "Narrative and Critical History of America." Vol. III, p. 148.

assigned, that "it is a peculiar blessing to this country to have few of any kind of Dissenters", and in the same year to the Council of Trade: "That happy Establishment of the Church of England which the Colony enjoys with less mixture of Dissenters than any other of her Majesties Plantations." In 1642 three Congregational ministers came to the colony to expound their views of Church government, but they were not long in the country, for by enactment of the Assembly all ministers except those of the Church of England were obliged to leave the colony.

Laws as strict as those of Massachusetts regulated churchgoing, and clergy were regularly sent over from England to minister to the spiritual wants of the colonists. As in New England prayers and sermons marked the coming and going of the governors, and Alexander Whitaker's "Good News" from Virginia is written in the same pious tone as the Puritan histories. It was written to prove: "that the finger of God hath been the only true worker here; that God first showed us the place, God called us hither, and here God by his special providence hath maintained us." (1613) In 1631 the Virginia Assembly passed a Law of Uniformity, and made the English canons and constitution the norm. It was this law whose enforcement by Governor Berkeley in 1641 made it impossible for the Congregational ministers, whom by the way Virginia had sent for, to stay in the colony. In the struggle between King Charles I and the Parliament, Virginia was officially with the king, and in 1649 the Puritan section of the State Church was practically driven from Virginia into Maryland, and the coming of the Cavaliers, estimated at eight hundred to one thousand seemed to draw a new sharp line between a Roman-Catholic Maryland sheltering a Puritan colony on the one side and a loyal Virginia on the other.

Nor was this loyal Virginia a bit behind Massachusetts in trying by law to see that men and women behaved themselves as the ministers directed. Sabbath breaking was punished, and no one might take a voyage save to go to church. All oaths were fined, the ministry was protected by a law "that no man shall disparage a minister whereby the minds of his parishoners may be alienated from him and his ministry prove less effectuall, upon pain of severe censure of the governor and council." Churchgoing was enforced and the sexual relations looked after in the spirit of New England.

After the Restoration, Virginia was again the loyal colony of the king, and the State Church was again supreme.

But in spite of all appearances, it may be safely stated that the actual Anglo-Catholic religious tradition never had any real hold upon even official Virginia. It is an evidence of the vitality and strength of the Anglo-Catholic tradition that it survived the overlordship of Queen Elizabeth and the Stuarts. The foundations, moreover, which Courtenay, Cranmer, Laud and others had laid have survived to our own day. But the days that followed upon the death of Elizabeth were too full of turmoil and confusion in the homeland for that tradition to transplant itself to the New World.

In the first place no bishop was sent, and the nominally State Church of the colonies was ruled by a commissary of the Bishop of London. No doubt one can point to good individual ministers like the Reverend Alexander Whitaker, whom we have quoted, but almost in proportion as these were really effective did they lean toward the Protestant outlook, usually of the Continental type. The actual missionary work in the New World was done either by Roman Catholics or by the pronouncedly Protestant type of preacher. Nearly all that has given the Anglo-Catholic type its hold over the ruling-class mind in England seems singularly lacking in the colonial State Church. The church buildings were seemingly as bare as in New England, and the services as depressing. Those æsthetic values that still make a powerful appeal in England to-day were quite as neglected as in New England. Nor do we have to search very far to find the reason: exactly the same class settled Virginia and Maryland as settled Massachusetts and Connecticut. The "Cavalier Virginia" is a myth.

True that after the beheading of Charles I many Cavaliers fled to Virginia. But even supposing that over one thousand, as has been supposed, came, one must remember that with the very much poorer Pilgrim colonists there came fourteen servants in a group of one hundred and two, and we have no means of knowing how many servants belonging to quite another class than the Cavaliers came with them, nor do we know just how many returned as soon as Charles II came to the Throne; only it is certain that many did at once return to bask in the favor of the new Court. As Virginia and Maryland could and did use indentured servants far more profitably than they could be used in New England, the proportion of these was very much greater than in the more northerly colonies, and the social level of the population correspondingly lower. The fact that tobacco, indigo, rice and at last cotton gave rise to great plantations later on should not blind us to the fact that the aristocracy that arose with these plantations and the slave service that made them profitable were of later date, and that this aristocracy was small and indigenous to the soil. We have no means of knowing just how much English upper-class blood flowed in the veins of the American colonists. Only

three families in Virginia were known to be connected
with historic families in England.[1] But younger sons of
historic families may have settled in the colonies under
names not used by the heads of aristocratic families. But
it still remains true that the great mass of the population
was of lower-class origin. Neither Lord Fairfield nor
Lord Baltimore were really settlers in America, and were
not typical even of those who took interest in the development of the country.

It is misleading to identify the English Establishment
in Virginia with the old Anglo-Catholic religious tradition.
One thing the records make perfectly plain is that Anglo-
Catholicism in its power and beauty never had the least
influence upon the religious life of the colony; up at least
to the time of Queen Anne. The government of the
churches was divided between the governor of the colony
at the time being and the vestries of the individual
churches, who often failed entirely to present the in-
cumbent, and so had him completely in their power.
There were no bishops to properly organize and supervise
the work of the Church. The condition of the Establishment in England from 1660 up to 1702 was bad enough,
and the struggles that led up to the second Revolution in
1688 left little time for colonial expansion.[2]

From 1701 on the Episcopal churches in the colonies
were largely supported by the Society for the Propagation
of the Gospel in Foreign Parts.[3] But from any Catholic
point of view there was the same chaos. The clergy were
judged by laymen, and the churches were in the hands

[1] Thomas J. Wertenbacher. Quoted by Charles A. Beard. "The Rise of American Civilization." Vol. I, p. 128.

[2] *Cf.* for fuller discussion and ample details, Arthur Lyon Cross. "The Anglican Episcopate and the American Colonies." London, 1902. (Harvard Historical Studies. Vol. IX.)

[3] Charter granted by William III in June, 1701.

practically of the vestries. There were excellent individual clergymen, but on the whole the standard was low, and some of the clergy were even drunken and dissolute. Many were not bad men, but were of the "sporting parson" type common enough also in England.

John Howard Hinton, writing about 1832, says:

Equally adverse to true godliness has been found the secular endowment and nomination of the ministers of religion. In no section of the republic was this system more deeply rooted or more fondly clung to, than in Virginia, where Episcopacy had been established as the state religion from the first. After it had been abandoned everywhere else it was acted upon here, conjoined with a legal prohibition of a different worship. According to the wisdom of some persons in the old world, Virginia, under this treatment, ought to have been a religious paradise: unhappily, however, it was a religious desert, the ecclesiastical revenues of which were absorbed by a tribe of irreligious clergymen, and the people abandoned to neglect and impiety, while neighbouring states were enjoying the benefits of a disinterested and devoted ministry.[1]

John A. Doyle, in the "Cambridge Modern History" series says:

The weakness of Anglicanism in the American colonies has been attributed to lack of organization and controlling machinery. The appointment of commissaries by the Bishop of London, to whose diocese the colonies in theory pertained, was no doubt an inadequate substitute for direct episcopal control. The establishment of an American Episcopate was urgently advocated by Bishop Berkeley. The attempt nearly succeeded, and was only frustrated at the last moment by the imperfectly concealed hostility of Walpole. Yet one may doubt whether any machinery could have done much for a Church which was clearly felt by the majority of the settlers, and

[1] John Howard Hinton. "History of the United States." Vol. II, p. 373.

especially by the most earnest and spiritually minded section of them, to be an exotic, which could appeal to no inspiring associations in the past, and which had done little for the mental and spiritual life of the colonies since they had become separate communities.[1]

But the subsequent history of the colonies shows that had any attempt been made to really establish a bishopric and a real Anglo-Catholic tradition of power and influence, it would have been driven off because so nearly approaching Rome and so dangerous to the liberties of the settlements as to warrant violence. Episcopacy only survived in Virginia, and later in Maryland and the Carolinas, and only received a half-hearted support in New York and New Jersey because it was too indifferent and too unaggressive to really count in the life. The real explanation of its curious position can be best given when we remember that the mass of the English settlers came from a class that, as far as it had a religious tradition, was trained in Dissent. This class asked generally only to be let alone, and it was so accustomed in England to pay for an Establishment it never used, that it was ready to do the same in the new country, on condition, however, that in spite of all regulations it was let alone. The attempt in Virginia to take the Establishment seriously led, as we have seen, to a wholesale exodus from the settlement, and that no colony could in the end economically endure. England had been "Lollardized" too thoroughly in its lower classes to submit in the New World to any Anglo-Catholic tradition that approached such reality as Laud, for instance, sought to give it.

This class was not only willing but eager to submit to moral regulations such as have been falsely called Puritan;

---

[1] John A. Doyle, M. A. "The Cambridge Modern History." Vol. VII, p. 58.

not only were they accustomed to such regulations but approved them. We have seen how exactly they reproduced the regulations of the Plymouth and Massachusetts settlements. The dissenting elements formed probably more than a half of the whole population, and were also the rather more serious half of that population. As far as the writer has been able to trace the culture of Virginia in those early days, allowing for differences in climate and gradually increasing differences in production, we see exactly the same culture as in the Northern settlements. Neither in the North nor in the South was the population quite homogeneous. There was everywhere, even in Plymouth, a well-to-do aristocracy, to which the poorer class paid often an almost servile deference. It had everywhere the political power in its hands, even where, as in Plymouth, the vote was not attached to such conditions as church membership or the holding of property. To this small aristocracy the minister always belonged, rather however by virtue of his supposed education than because of his cloth. At the same time he does not seem to have been readily taken up into the actual governing body, which, indeed, "asked the advice" of the clergy, but kept the power in hands of the lay body.

Thus the Establishment in Virginia was almost nominal, and had seemingly almost no religious influence outside a very small range of colonial life.

The noiseless way in which the Revolution of 1688 passed over all the colonies points to the lifelessness of the Stuart and Anglo-Catholic party in the New World. Nowhere was religion a very vital issue, for even in New England Puritanism had been swallowed up in the Congregational Church and all thought of establishing a Calvinistic theocracy had passed away; and in Virginia as well as in Maryland there was growing up a generation in respectful but skeptical indifference to all religious disputes.

The period from about the New England Synod of 1637 to the agitation over independence has been characterized by Mr. Charles Francis Adams as a period "at once provincial and glacial." This he attributes to the triumph of what he calls "Puritan orthodoxy." But in Virginia the sleep was if possible even profounder. New England had at least Cotton Mather and Jonathan Edwards, but Virginia had absolutely no one to rival these. England was rejoicing in the works of Milton, Clarendon, Burnet, Dryden, Pope, Goldsmith, Bunyan, Defoe, Newton and Locke. But no one rises up to attribute this colonial barrenness to Puritan orthodoxy in Virginia and Maryland. Moreover, the population of Virginia, Maryland, Georgia and the two Carolinas was much greater than that of New England. Was not this artistic barrenness due to the training of that dissenting class in England, to whom the æsthetic values of the ruling class had become abhorrent as the wordly and vain pursuits of the wicked? The Puritans were not mainly responsible for this; they came from a rather higher level of social estimate. It was the poor and despised conventicle that had at last not only triumphed over both Roman-Catholic and Anglo-Catholic tradition, but had also pushed aside the compromise Puritans, who still grasped political power, but were daily falling behind in the race for leadership in the colonial life. This dissenting mass came to America not to write books but to better themselves in an economic sense, and they were succeeding wonderfully in doing this. They were building ships in New England that were soon to outstrip England's fleetest vessels; they were making a rum that was to make the American trade in slaves the envy of Europe, they were organizing a system of breaking England's laws that was piling up money with its promise of independence and future power. They were slowly evolving an aristocracy of their own; an aristocracy of great plantation owners in the South, of trade and ship-building and smuggling in the North and of finance and commerce in the Middle States. Until America had given the dissenting masses money and possession, literature and art had little place in their rather starved imaginations. This was not the fault of either Puritanism or of America, but of the long and bitter struggle with a Normanized upper class in England, separated by both religious tradition and the possession of political power from the great body of the plain people.

The hatred of the Anglo-Catholic tradition is writ large over all colonial life, both in New England and in Virginia. One only needs to recall the friction the rather miserable payment to the ministers of the Establishment always caused, ending in the celebrated case in which Patrick Henry won his first honors as a leader of the people against attempted tyranny. One does not take as sober evidence the attacks of a popular jury lawyer, and his denunciations of the Virginia ministry may be properly discounted, but the fact that such an attack upon a whole class was popular and won his case for him speaks volumes for the place Episcopacy had in the minds of the inhabitants of the only State that had really remained seemingly true to the Catholic tradition in the troubled years of Cromwell's Rebellion.

The fact is that the conventicle type of Protestantism is certain in the long run to produce a high individualism, and that sooner or later a rationalistic wing is sure to form, for deep in the heart of this type is the faith in the ability of each individual to think out his own salvation; true he holds to the Bible and feels that he is being moved by the Holy Spirit, but in moments of spiritual and intellectual excitement it is not always easy to know just when the Holy Spirit speaks and when common sense. Nor was it otherwise in America. In the new surroundings it was doubly easy to shake off the remains of old traditions, and as the dissenting conventicle has never laid great stress upon history, here then was soon an atmosphere in which a respectful skepticism and a quiet but steady rationalism had abundant opportunity to flourish. The coldly indifferent Establishment gave plenty of room for those who were satisfied with an outward conformity while cherishing their own opinions. As far as one can judge, the educated members of the Virginia generation that later fought the war for independence were all more or less Deists and skeptics like Washington, Jefferson, Randolph of Roanoke, Madison and most of the leaders of thought. But with the exception of Jefferson, who belonged to no Christian body, nearly all seem to have gone to the Established Church and most of the leaders seem to have been members in good standing.

With the religious leanings of the poorer and the middle classes a later chapter will deal. Sufficient it is now to point out that even on those who from all classes waited in good faith upon the ministry of the Episcopal Church, and who had the good fortune to find earnest and faithful pastors, and such undoubtedly were to be found, the actual life and influence of the Anglo-Catholic tradition could not have its full chance to operate, for the colonial Church was cut off from all the national sources of power that long age, a highly developed ritual, a cathedral service, an elaborate machinery, high social station for the leaders lent it. From all accounts, as before noted, its services were almost as bare and forbidding as those of its conventicle rivals. No cathedral service presented a model of dignity and æsthetic effectiveness, nor could commissaries command the respect and obedience that bishops of high social standing could easily obtain. When to all this is added the fact that, making allowances for prejudices and overstatement, it still remains true that the average clergyman was not much if at all above the rather boisterous and riotous moral level of the owners of the plantations round about, we see that the Established Church of Virginia fell far below its opportunities as a factor in culture.

It seems hardly likely that the relative spiritual and intellectual poverty of the American colonies had much to do either with the political dependence or the religious faith of the population. We see the same artistic poverty in South Africa, in Australia and South America. Colonizing populations are not drawn from the most successful circles of the homeland; they have overwhelming tasks on their hands for a generation or two merely to construct the material basis of a national life; literature and art demand a class for their support which has at least comparative leisure at its disposal, and such a class, even as it comes into being, must be slowly trained to need and enjoy the fruits of the higher life. The higher life cannot be led alone, and the great centers of older civilizations were wholly lacking; there were but few inspirational institutions, such as museums, art galleries, music centers, and similar institutions.

Indeed the frictions resulting from political dependence seem to have been the first incentives to an examination of classic literature. It is amazing what a place the rather crude conceptions of Greece and Rome and their later democracies take in the political discussions of the opening years of struggle with England. In the Southern colonies at least a classic paganism seems quite as much to be the basis of the cultural life as any Christian tradition, but even in New England the colonial house shows the influence of the pagan classic culture.

It is impossible to pass over a religious type of thought, which has more claim to be called really Puritan than most of the groups so designated. The movement of the Scotch and the Scotch-Irish from the old home to the New World was connected not only with economic pressure but with the demand for a religious freedom they could not find at home. The type is the Continental Protestantism of Calvinistic complexion. John Knox came to Scotland at a time of almost endless confusion, and established with the help of a small band of highborn leaders a theocracy more nearly approaching Calvin's conception than even Calvin himself was able to secure in Geneva. After desperate struggle the Church of Scotland actually became the organizing principle of the nation's life. Calvin's demands were accepted as the notes of a true Church, namely the "pure preaching of the Word" by a duly accredited ordained ministry, to whom alone the administration of the grace-imparting sacraments was entrusted. This type places great emphasis upon the interpretative mission of the early creeds, and upon the importance of historic continuity. It has many points of contact with the Catholic tradition, which, however, it fiercely denounces, and regards the whole old Catholic development as an antichristian betrayal of the truth. The Church is for those of this way of thinking a divine institution, to which is promised the ultimate government of the world. In theory, the Church is wholly in the hands of ordained men, and no laymen have part in its rule; and this must be so, for the historic Church is the judge of pure doctrine, and only ordained men are competent judges of orthodoxy. Pure doctrine is also more important than conduct, for, as we have seen, Calvin taught that out of pure doctrine alone could proceed right conduct. The strong points of this type of faith are its sense of order, discipline and feeling for group action. It shares with the sects a great devotion to the letter of the Bible, and lays great emphasis upon education and reading. More particularly, and in contrast to the dissenting sects, it demands a trained and educated ministry; it is, like Calvin, aristocratic in feeling and temper. Its weaknesses are a certain narrowness of vision, lack of all sympathy with the softer types of Southern Catholicism, and even some antagonism to religious artistic expression. It is often hard and even arrogant. Its history is one of battles and conflict, in which the stern stories of the Old Testament have had as much weight as the gentler teaching of the New. Its tone has often been the tone of the old desert Prophetism, and it is almost as much a fighting type of religion as Islam.

Very early in the history of the colonies this type appeared, but it was usually swallowed up, as in Connecticut, by the greater numerical mass of Dissenters, or it was weakened in its influence by the Continental forms it found in New York under the Dutch, and which, holding in theory the same line of teaching, really had much softened and modified it under the influence of Dutch Humanism and the resulting Arminianism. But in Pennsylvania it found a home and from there made its way into Virginia, Maryland and the Southern colonies. It succeeded in preserving its peculiar color and spirit in a quite wonderful way, and it was foremost in the fighting lines against the French, not because these Puritan Protestants loved England, but because they hated Roman-Catholic France. Successive waves of immigration from Scotland but still more from the North of Ireland kept the numbers and the spirit up, and as a frontier population they were only surpassed by the Germans. This Scotch-Irish population had nothing in theory against the slavery that was gradually evolving a new and unique culture in the South; indeed, many of them became most successful plantation owners, but they could not easily accept the conditions that a slaveowning culture imposed upon the white laboring class, and so they followed the drift away from the coast to the West and the mountains.

Whereas in New England they had easily mingled with and then been absorbed by the dissenting tradition, in Virginia, Maryland and the later Southern colonies they hated all that reminded them of Catholicism, and held firmly to a very strict though often legal type of Calvinism. Indeed, in the history of these Presbyterian settlers we see often a deep-seated misunderstanding of the lines that separated them from the Dissenters. The very stern doctrine of predestination taught by Wyclif and his Lollards was strength to little feeble bodies who were thus assured of their ultimate triumph as the elect of God. This doctrine of election was mistaken for or identified with Calvinism, and the grave differences in regard to the church, ministry and the sacraments were either ignored or brushed aside. Thus, in the New England States, the Congregational bodies absorbed the Presbyterians where they were most numerous, whereas in Northern New York the Presbyterians, by superior organization, often absorbed the Congregationalists. This could not happen in Virginia, where the Episcopal Church was established, and both race and religious tradition tended to maintain sharp lines of division. Moreover, the coldness and indifference of the Established Church repelled these rugged but sincere and within their limits intelligent Scotch-Irish with a fighting faith in their hearts, and a sharp and clear-cut theology in their heads.

It has often seemed strange that the States that fought most fiercely to free the West from the influences of France, and to make the Mississippi Valley English, should thirteen years later have been not one bit behind New England in fighting England. The reasons lie largely in the influence of this Scotch-Irish group. When in 1719 the Scotch-Irish began to come to America they were the bitter enemies of England, and particularly of the Anglo-Catholic tradition of England as established in Ireland. It was French Catholicism that they fought in America, and when that battle was over they were as eager as any to fight the English; especially when the threat of a bishop and a really active Anglo-Catholicism seemed to be on the horizon. For the Scotch-Irish grew up in bitter opposition to all Catholicism, in both its Roman and Anglican forms. Its hatred of the papacy and of Episcopal Catholicism amounted to a passion. In its extreme reaction from all æsthetic ritual it banished organs, hymn-singing, set prayers of all sorts; even the ritual recitation of the Lord's Prayer was disliked. It condemned all religious days save the Lord's Day, which was identified with the Jewish Sabbath and began on Saturday evening. The congregation stood up to pray and sat to sing. Its outlook upon life was harsh, honest, God-fearing and sincere, tremendously self-respecting and independent. The blood of the race was lowland Scotch and therefore not really different from that of the North of England. At the time of the greatest inflow to America, the Scotch-Irish were probably the most literate population of the British Isles.

At the same time, their influence upon the religious

thinking of the rest of the population was probably limited by the extreme attitude their struggle with Catholicism had forced upon them. But on the political field they avenged themselves upon their former oppressors by making possible the War of Independence, and mightily aiding in carrying it to a successful conclusion. The bare and almost forbidding character of their worship should not blind us to the very High-Church character of their thinking. Outside the Church there was no reasonable hope of salvation, and the notes of the true Church were the familiar Calvinistic demands; the pure Word of God, the rightly ordained ministry, and the due administration of the sacraments. The Lord's Supper was approached with almost superstitious reverence, with undue emphasis upon Paul's word in I Cor. 11:29 about eating and drinking unworthily. Churchgoing was a universal obligation and the ministry possessed priestly authority in the community. Their sins and weaknesses were those of a high-spirited and struggling race marked often by the hard fierceness such a struggle involves. In the next chapter we will see them again and have occasion to note their influence upon other religious traditions with which they came in contact.

CHAPTER XI

RELIGIOUS TOLERATION AND COLONIAL CULTURE

Religious toleration was not a virtue especially emphasized in early Christian history. True it is that both Tertullian and Lactantius made pleas for the kind of religious freedom the early Christians needed, but when the Church got into power it had learned nothing from its own hard experience and at once began to persecute. In this respect, the record of historic Christianity is a good deal worse than that of Islam. Even if Count de Gobineau's judgment is perhaps a little too sweeping,[1] and local persecution has not always been absent from Mohammedan history.

At the same time must be remembered that unity within the empire was one of the elements of the unwritten agreement with the Christian bishops, and that this unity had a political bearing. Constantine had personally, probably, very little understanding of just what Christianity pretended to be. But, like Elizabeth of England, he needed the support of the churchly organization, and could only get that by enforcing legally the demands of a State Church. Nor is it easy to defend toleration, if one assumes a divinely infallibly guided Church interpreting a message of salvation and a system of sacramental grace without which the world is lost in eternal pains of hell forever, and the least distortion of which message may mean the loss of countless millions of souls. The heretic

---

[1] Count Joseph A. de Gobineau. "Les Religions et les Philosophies dans l'Asia Central." 1865. Pp. 24 *ff*.

is guilty of high treason to his kind, no matter how well meaning he may be. From this point of view, it was the duty of the Church as soon as it had the power to direct the equally divinely instituted State, to enforce the truth committed once for all to its hands. To act otherwise would have been to surrender faith in infallible religious guidance.

The Anglo-Catholic tradition and the Continental type of Protestantism in both its Lutheran and Calvinistic forms, took over this reasoning from Roman Catholicism. Individuals like the Frenchman Castilio or the Swiss reformer Zwingli were inclined to toleration, but no reformer of note took exception to Calvin's having the State burn Servetus. Everywhere the State was freely invoked to suppress heresy and maintain what the reformers regarded as the truth.

Nor is there in either the writings of Wyclif or in the accusations against the Lollards any indication that they had come to any demand for toleration beyond that which they needed for the spreading of their message. But the logic of Wyclif's attitude toward the use of force and violence by the Roman Church might have led him sooner or later to demand spiritual freedom. Certainly the Lollards went further than did even Wyclif in their denunciation of all war.[1] And if war and violence were

---

[1] The twelve conclusions of the Lollards in the year 1394 are a most useful summary of their teaching. The tenth conclusion is so interesting that it is here given in full from Wilkins. "Concilia magnæ Britanniæ", Tome III, p. 222.

Decima conclusio, quod homocidium per bellum vel prætensam legem justitiæ pro temporali causa sine spirituali revelatione, est expresse contrarium Novo Testamento, quod quidem est lex gratiæ et plena misericordiarium. Ista conclusio est aperte probata per exempla prædicationis Christi hic in terra, qui maxime docuit hominem ad diligendum inimicos, et ad miserandum eis, et non accidendum eos. Ratio est hæc, quod pro majore parte, ubi homines pugnant, post primum ictum charitas rumpitur; et quisquis moritur extra charitatem, vadit rectam viam ad infernum. Et ultra hoc nos bene cognoscimus, quod nullus clericus scit liberare per scripturam, vel per rationem legitimam, punitionem mortis pro uno peccato mortali, et non pro alio; sed lex misericordiæ, quæ est Novum Testamentum, inhebet omnimodum homicidium; nam in evangelio dictum est antiquis "Non occides."

all evil, then surely the persecution of even the heretic
was made difficult, for burning men in love is difficult.
But the main reasons for any persecution were also absent, for there was no property to protect and no sacred
ministry among the poor, hunted Lollards. Their weakness was such that they had no temptation to persecute.
Yet they were not really tolerant, for the constant splitting up of the conventicle was due to the intolerant
insistence upon small points, mainly of conduct, dress,
habit or strange opinions of one sort or another.

The logical outcome of the Lollard teaching that the
Holy Spirit would guide each individual in the reading of
Scripture should surely make all persecution for opinion
impossible. Moreover, Wyclif's conception of the relations between the State and the Church would forbid any
such misuse of the State by the Church as Christian
history demanded.

To two children of the dissenting type of Protestantism
belongs then the credit of developing a doctrine of religious
toleration; these two are the Baptists and the Quakers.
Both represent very pronounced types of conventicle
Protestantism. For both the Bible is the sole authority;
the Quakers do without any sacraments, and the Baptists
treat them as signs of a covenant simply, without magic
grace-imparting power. Both recognize the autonomy of
the individual group of worshipers, and in both there is
no historic priestly ministry. The lay preacher has played
a large part in the development of both connections. The
Quakers owe their inspiration and organization to George

*Corollarium est, quod sane est expoliatio pauperis populi, quando domini adquirunt
indulgentias a poena et culpa illis, qui juvant exercitum eorum ad interficiendum populum
christianum in longinquis terris, pro temporali lucro, sicut et nos vidimus milites, qui
currunt ad ethnicos, id est, in toto "Hethenes" ad quærendum eis nomen in occisione
hominum, multo magis malas merentur grates de rege pacis, quia per humilitatem et
patientiam nostram fides fuit multiplicata, et pugnatores ac interfectores Christus Jesus
odit ac minatur, dicens: "Qui gladio percutit, gladio peribit."*

Fox (1624-1690), Robert Barclay (1648-1690) and William Penn (1644-1718). The most noteworthy feature of their teaching is simply a decisive emphasis upon the inner light which all conventicle Protestantism has to assume in the reading of the Bible to save the common man from error. The faith that the Holy Spirit will guide even the ignorant into all truth, if truly converted, makes, of course, all outward authority apart from the Bible unnecessary. It is impossible to establish any literary connection between the Quakers and the older forms of conventicle Protestantism. But the fact that older conventicle sects like the "Seekers" and some Anabaptists at once recognized the spiritual relationship points to those unwritten traditions that kept English Dissent alive.[1]

The coming of Quakers to Massachusetts in 1656 produced a storm of opposition, which was not always the fault of the colony, for it must be confessed that the extravagances of some of the Quakers were very obnoxious, and the language used was often provocative. On the other hand many were called Quakers who were really only deluded and weak-minded persons carried away by religious excitement. Laws were passed by which in the four New England colonies of Massachusetts, Connecticut, Plymouth and New Haven all Quakers were to be whipped, imprisoned and banished, and in Massachusetts a Quaker who returned after banishment was to be punished with death; as a matter of fact four—one woman and three men—did suffer this penalty. But popular feeling was evidently against the ruling class in this matter, and the same feeling that had led to the toleration of Baptists in Boston in 1665 led soon to the toleration of Quakers. The last actual whipping of a Quaker was in

[1] *Cf.* Theodor Sippell. "Zur Vorgeschichte des Quäkertums." 1920. Giessen.

1677.[1] Quakers spread over all the colonies, and at first were persecuted in nearly all.

One honorable exception was the Providence Plantation or what is now Rhode Island. Here Roger Williams (1604–1684) had developed a theory of toleration that was as far-going as at that time was possible. In his "Bloudy Tenent of Persecution for the Cause of Conscience", Roger Williams asserts the broad principle that religious freedom was the only really Christian way. And when driven from Massachusetts in 1636 he founded the town of Providence on a basis of religious freedom. For a little he was attracted to the Anabaptists, probably by the fact that they were the forerunners in the matter of religious tolerance, but his restless mind led him from question to question, and no one of the sects can absolutely claim him. He was the incarnation of one pronounced side of conventicle Protestantism, namely, overweening identification of personal opinion with the revealed will of God. In his controversy with the Reverend Mr. Cotton in which he wrote "The Bloudy Tenent yet more Bloudy", the modern man is instinctively on the side of Roger Williams. But that is because the modern man has lost the ecclesiastical sense that pervades any real Puritanism, and Cotton was one of the last of the Puritans. Conventicle Protestantism still clung to the infallibility of the Bible, and while asserting the right of every man to read and interpret it for himself was still bound to an external code of regulations.

When we read such a work as Roger Williams's intemperate and ill-informed attack upon George Fox [2] we realize that the whole question of the reasons for and the

[1] American Church History Series. Vol. XII, 206–210. Where also a good bibliography is given.
[2] "George Fox Digged out of his Burrows." 1676. Narragansett Club Ed. 6 Vols.

extent of religious tolerance has not even yet been fairly faced.

Very enlightening is the way in which toleration of the Quakers in New York was brought about. Old Peter Stuyvesant was not a bigot, but when women started praying and preaching in the open streets he had them arrested and with their friend and helper Robert Hodgson they were put into prison. Then when another Quaker John Bowne was banished to Holland, the directors of the colony at Amsterdam sent him back with a letter to Stuyvesant saying:

We very much doubt if vigorous proceedings against them (the Quakers) ought not to be discontinued except you intend to check and destroy your population, which, however, in the youth at least of your existence ought rather to be encouraged by all possible means. . . . The consciences of men, at least, ought ever to remain free and unshackled. Let every one be unmolested as long as he is modest; as long as his conduct in a political sense is irreproachable; as long as he does not disturb others or oppose the government. This maxim of moderation has always been the guide of the magistrates of this city, and the consequence has been that, from every land, people have flocked to this asylum. Tread thus in their steps, and, we doubt not you will be blessed.[1]

This was in the year 1663.

Waning faith in infallible ecclesiasticism and the need of increasing population have had quite as much to do with religious toleration in the colonial history as any theoretical conviction. At the same time the very intense individualism characteristic of the dissenting mentality, combined with the training they had received through their history of peaceful separation in case of disagreement

[1] Quoted from Bowden by Professor Thomas in his "History of the Friends." American Church History Series. Vol. XII, pp. 215–216.

among themselves, made the dissenters and their type of Protestantism the steady bearers of a gospel of toleration in the New World. Had Puritanism really been the spirit of American history it could not have yielded its ground so readily. A Church that really believes with all its heart that it has an errorless message without which countless thousands will go to everlasting pains of hell forever, and whose distortion endangers the social structure and leads perhaps to hopeless ruin, cannot afford to dally with sentimental tolerance of even well-meant heresy. Real religion when alive and self-conscious is seldom tolerant.

At the same time Wyclif and history are responsible in large measure for such tolerance as the colonial culture knew. Wyclif had insisted upon a poor and possessionless Church, and the persecutors of the Lollards saw to it that they remained poor, for Archbishop Courtenay soon drove all the higher clergy and the possessing class out of the movement. When therefore Dissent blossomed out again it was as a mass of separate little autonomous, possessionless groups. And when transplanted to North America neither the Congregationalists, nor the Baptists, and still less the Quakers, had any ecclesiastical property to be jeopardized by divisions, and no central organization to be imperilled, and no priestly ministry with a vested interest in orthodoxy to guard the gates. Men are never really tolerant of an attack upon what they regard as vital values, but scattered and individualistic Separatism had a more vital interest in the freedom it needed for its life than even the assertion by force of religious opinion.

These things, rather than any abstract reasoning, made also the experiment of William Penn in New Jersey and Pennsylvania a great success. And when in 1681 two shiploads of emigrants landed to found a new commonwealth it was to be on the broadest lines of religious tolerance then known. In less than three years it had a population generally estimated at seven thousand. Now population in those days in America meant wealth, safety and power. From Germany came also converts as well as the group of kindred spirits known as Mennonites, a German sect (Simons Menno was born in Friesland, 1492) that was deeply influenced by the Quaker teaching, and in turn profoundly influenced the Quaker type of piety. With such an example of the success of toleration in attracting population, no colony could well afford to draw again the lines of orthodoxy so sharply as to drive away the much needed increase of population. Moreover, a profound religious indifference was gradually creeping over the educated classes. The Peace of Westphalia in Middle Europe, and the close of the era of Cromwell in England left men's minds weary of religious struggle and all ecclesiastical machinery most desperately weakened and impoverished. This was reflected, as were all European movements and moods, in the thinking and conduct of the colonies.

Another attempt at tolerance not so wide as in Pennsylvania, but some years earlier (1633-1634) had been made in Maryland where the second Lord Baltimore, Cecilius Calvert, had been given a large grant of land by Charles I, the first Lord Baltimore (George Calvert) having died. The settlement was to be free to all "trinitarian Christians", so that even Roman Catholics were sent over and settled there. But although they maintained their Catholicism in great part as we shall see later (Chapter XIX), and still give color to the religious life of the State, they never carried on propaganda outside the State, and never really affected the religious tradition of Dissent, by which they were soon to be overwhelmed. This story is not a pleasant one. The Puritans of Virginia felt aggrieved by the attempted introduction of a stricter Catholic tradition into the State Church, and taking advantage of the very liberal and tolerant terms of Maryland, passed over in large numbers, some say over a thousand, into the neighboring settlement; then they proceeded to snatch the political power from the Roman Catholic population, and in 1692 established the State Church of England, and in 1715 the unfortunate Roman Catholics were disfranchised. This was made possible in part by the conversion to Protestantism of the proprietary house in England.

When in 1664 the English took over New Amsterdam from the Dutch and called New York into being, they also took over the tolerance that had become traditional in Holland. The Dutch Reformed Church was a strongly Calvinistic body, with, however, that touch of Humanism that had colored so much of the religious life of Holland, and had strongly affected the Arminian wing of the National Church. The Established Church of England was left in a somewhat anomalous position in New York, but happily common sense and religious indifference in about equal proportions saved the situation, and the question of religious freedom was never seriously debated. For though in 1691 an attempt was made to disfranchise Roman Catholics, this act was disallowed by the English Government, and the issue seemed settled. Nor would it have been possible to really enforce upon a population already exceedingly mixed any uniformity of religious faith. The Dutch Reformed Church, in its mild tolerance of everything save things socially disreputable, and the Established Church of England in a rather unchurchly garb commanded the situation outwardly, but already

the varied population was making also a variegated sectarianism, a characteristic note of what was becoming a
great urban population. German and Swedish Lutheranism, Irish-Catholicism, Scotch and Scotch-Irish Presbyterianism, Congregationalism from the North as well as Baptists and Quakers lived together and any measure looking
to the exclusive domination of any one body would have
united them all in a struggle for the freedom each needed.

The actual number of those who controlled the civilization of the colonies was relatively small; little groups of
non-Anglo-Saxon peoples neutralized each other; scattered population gave a few such centers as Boston, New
York and Philadelphia very undue influence; the educated
leading Anglo-Saxon groups came more and more, as the
eighteenth century ripened, under the influence of the
English rationalists, Hobbes, Locke, Adam Smith, the
Deists and the French Encyclopedists. With such men
religious toleration was a matter of course, and the formal-
ism of the religious life in the leading traditions was a
blessing, in so far as it damped any impulse to force religious convictions upon an unwilling incoming population.

When we put the question—What English religious
tradition largely controlled the thinking of the closing
years of the colonial era?—the answer may best be reached
by some exclusions. It was certainly not the Anglo-Catholic tradition. Even over the nominally established Episcopal Church, this tradition had little or no influence,
and the Episcopal Church did not even nominally minister
to a tenth of the population. Nor was it the tradition that
inspired the Westminster Assembly. This influence was
confined, as we have seen, to the Scotch and Scotch-Irish.
It was, in fact, the dissenting tradition but in the new
garb of material prosperity, with its tolerance of new ways
of life, and its skepticism and individualism working out

their inevitable changes in the outlook upon life and the conduct of the individual and the group. Some Anglo-Saxon prejudices survived the decay of religious faith and divisions of Dissent. The Anglo-Saxon Sabbath is not, as is commonly thought, a Puritan institution, but has its roots in Anglo-Saxon history. Fines for not going to church dot the pages of the accounts of Bishop's Courts and the "Concilia magnæ Britanniæ" from the earliest times. The admonition of the Archbishop of Canterbury in 1359 in regard to keeping the Sabbath Day could have been written by the American Sabbath Alliance.[1] The question of how the "Lord's Day" should be kept depended quite as much upon the economic status of the class involved as upon the particular religious tradition of the class. The gradual toleration in regard to all questions of conduct in colonial times was part and parcel of the growing indifference to the older standards of a life left behind in England. The theater was taboo in the lower strata of dissenting circles, but in New York and in the Southern States, and even in certain classes in Philadelphia, it gained just about the status it had in England. Nothing separates society so sharply into classes as inequality of possession, for the amusements and occupations of the wealthy are generally impossible to the poor, and as the wealth of the land increased, and as black slavery in the South together with the temporary white slavery of indentured servants gave ever greater leisure to a small class, its world changed, and its toleration of what had been once condemned increased.

Tolerance of religious opinion was also much easier to gain in the colonial world, because Dissent has always emphasized conduct rather than opinion, and has always rather taken orthodox theological opinion somewhat for

[1] Wilkins. "Concilia magnæ Britanniæ." Tome III, 43.

granted. It was easier for Harvard College to take up Unitarianism than it would have been to introduce at that date sports on Sunday. The watch of the small autonomous dissenting church was rather over the conduct of the member than even over strict orthodoxy.

In trying to estimate aright the progress of toleration in matters of religion in the colonial era, it is hard to avoid extremes of overstatement and understatement. Not even Rhode Island held fast to complete religious toleration, but excluded Roman Catholics from the lists of freemen in an enactment of 1663, and in 1665 even passed a law authorizing the seizure of the estates of Quakers who refused to bear arms in defense of the colony, though one never hears that the law was actually put into effect.[1] It is vain to claim that in theory the dissenters were much better in this regard than either the Puritans or the Anglo-Catholics; they were only weaker, and had no central authority to enforce restrictions on liberty. Moreover, persecution is nearly always more or less directly connected with questions of vested interests and property rights. A priestly ministry, whether Anglo-Catholic, Presbyterian or Puritan, feels bound to protect the claims of an office, and sees clearly that the dignity and worthfulness of that office are assailed by heresy and unbelief. The dissenter at this time had neither much property to protect nor a professional and priestly ministry to guard the churchly dignity.

All toleration in matters of belief and conduct must be a matter rather of experience and utility than of abstract reasoning, for no State will ever hesitate in time of great danger to pass any restrictive laws that it deems needful for existence. The excuse always made in colonial times for restrictions upon or exclusion of Roman Catholics was

[1] Hinton. "History", Vol. I, 146.

that they were subjects of a foreign prince (the pope) and could not with good conscience take an oath of allegiance to another power. But as a matter of fact, the inclusion or exclusion of certain classes of citizens in the list of the enfranchised has often had rather an economic than any theoretical ground. Cromwell gave the Jews a legal standing in England, because probably England keenly needed the commercial support and experience of the great Jewish merchants. But he did it as a matter of personal connivance, and the petition of the Jews for open right was refused.[1]

All the colonies needed population and could ill afford to drive away those who were raising the prices of real estate. Nor is it possible to draw a sharp line between the religious opinions that are dangerous to spiritual and material interests and those that are not. All the New England colonies passed savage laws against witchcraft and witches. But they were only really enforced in a spasmodic panic, and even when still remaining on the law books were a dead letter after the excitement had passed away.

What really most effectively advanced religious freedom was the growing religious indifference, of which complaints are early heard in all quarters. The clergy are always dissatisfied with the lack of zeal on the part of their flocks and their complaints must be a little discounted. They are apt to think a past age was more religious and the present less religious than the actual facts would warrant. But Bradford and Winthrop both saw very early a waning interest in the things they cared for. Religious zeal does not always pass from the parents to the children; a new generation arose that knew neither the hates

[1] *Cf.* Carlyle's caustic treatment of the incident "Cromwell's Letters and Speeches." Vol. III, pp. 135–136.

persecution had engendered nor the zeal it in turn inspired; a very miscellaneous population was coming from
the Old World, for England was beginning to follow Hakluyt's advice and send the debtor and criminal classes
away to seek their fortunes in America. Even in New England indentured servants, who were little more than white
slaves, were being slowly introduced, though they never
played the same part as in Virginia and the South. No
doubt the fishing population that came each summer
season to the Banks of Newfoundland and the coast of
Maine left many representatives in New England, and
this population has never been famous for its piety.

The government of the colonies was, as has been remarked, in the hands of a very few, and these men were
more or less dependent for their intellectual life upon
England, and there theoretic toleration was making headway. The dissenter class was rising in importance as
England became a trading and commercial country. The
Anglo-Catholic tradition was linked with landowning,
and the dissenting interest with the town and trade.
Jeremy Taylor was writing his "Liberty of Prophesying"
(1646). The Act of Toleration was passed in 1689. The
Tory reaction under Queen Anne never seems to have
greatly affected the colonial life, mainly because it was
so strictly confined to a class influenced by the revived
Anglo-Catholic religious tradition, which, as we have
seen, never had much influence upon even Virginia and
the Southern settlements. Hence the intellectual world
of the aristocratic leadership now growing up in all three
main groups of colonies was that of the rationalism slowly
finding expression both on the Continent and in England.

The writings of Pope (1688–1744), of Addison (1672–
1719) and Steele (1672–1729) and also of Swift (1667–

1745) find an echo in the work of the later colonial writers, and there is up to about 1740 a great abatement of the outpour of theological literature, although in New England there never was any complete cessation. Nor is it accurate to say with Mr. Doyle [1] that the Congregational churches were finely organized. In point of fact, organization was one of the weaknesses of that body as the various attempts at synodical development show. The individual churches were afraid of central authority, and of creedal infringement upon the liberty of the several separate bodies. Where Presbyterianism and Episcopacy had any following at all, as in Connecticut, they more than held their own, because although very much less numerous, they were far better organized, and in New York the Congregational churches were swallowed up by the better equipped Presbyterians. In spite of this, however, the dissenters carried their traditions into every other religious body with which these singularly persistent types had to do. The Congregational churches ruled New England, and gradually worked their way westward. The Baptists and Quakers were predominant in Rhode Island. The Quakers controlled Pennsylvania to a good degree. Even in New York, under the name of Episcopacy and Dutch Calvinism, a dissenting tradition underlay, as we shall see later, the real religious life of the community. Nor was it really otherwise in Virginia, for as already pointed out a really live and self-conscious Anglo-Catholic could not have lived in the atmosphere of bitter hostility to the Catholic tradition which even otherwise seemingly indifferent men and women cherished. For the old English stock, which in Maryland and Virginia had been less mingled with other blood than in Pennsylvania and New York or New Jersey, was from the same general social

[1] The Cambridge Modern History, p. 56.

strata as the New England population and hated High-Churchism.

Extravagant claims are often made for the contribution to tolerance and free institutions by the Scotch and Scotch-Irish, who brought an intensely Calvinistic religious tradition to the New World. This population was widely scattered, but found its way, as we have noticed, largely through Pennsylvania down into Virginia and Maryland, and later it wandered farther to North Carolina and still later to Tennessee. It was an unruly and stubborn stock, but hardy, intelligent, thrifty and fanatical in its hatred of Episcopacy.

In the first place, the proportion of the population that had this blood in its veins has been often greatly overestimated. A well-known Southern clergyman in an address before the Scotch-Irish Congress in 1891 made the claim that at the time of the Revolution it constituted a third of the nation. That is evidently absurd. The tide of immigration only set in about 1725, and at that time the Anglo-Saxon character of the colonies was overwhelming, and as the English immigration never really stopped, and the German immigration was also in full swing, it is hard to believe that the relatively small populations of Scotland and the North of Ireland furnished any such numbers as would be necessary to bring up their numbers to such a proportion. All is guesswork, but the estimate of Judge Temple at the same Congress of about five hundred thousand is more sober. But even this was hardly probable in 1776, and these were scattered fairly widely but were in education and intelligence on a high level; although in course of time some degenerated into the much neglected class of so-called Mountain Whites, on the whole they took a very important place, as we shall see later, in the political development of the South and even of the whole nation. Professor Beard estimates them at one-sixth of the population.[1]

But their religious tradition had nothing to do with tolerance or even with free institutions in the abstract. They were for the most part genuine Calvinists, and Calvinism cannot logically be tolerant, any more than can Roman Catholicism. They only demanded the liberty they themselves needed, and as they were a hopeless minority and could not hope to establish the Calvinistic theocracy, they were bitterly opposed to any established church system. Moreover, the shameful and shortsighted treatment they had received, first in Scotland and then in the North of Ireland at the hands of an oppressing Episcopacy with the State behind it, made them as before emphasized bitter and uncompromising in their fight against everything that seemed to them to savor of the Catholic Church. Then too, as experience has shown, the hard struggle of a new settlement to gain foothold in the new land, and to lay the foundations for material prosperity, acts generally disastrously at first on the cultivation of the spiritual values, and even while attempting, not always successfully, to meet the needs of education by the founding of schools and colleges, there was an evident decline of the religious life of the incoming tide. True it is that this people had to ask for toleration at first, for they were still nominally under the State Establishment of England, but very soon they were strong enough to carry things with a high hand, for they settled in towns and on the frontier, and were not easily coerced. Their activity later shows that had England really seriously attempted to subject the colonial churches to an American hierarchy, this population would have been as intolerant of the Episcopacy

[1] Charles A. Beard and Mary Beard. "The Rise of American Civilization." Vol. I, pp. 83 *ff*.

as the Episcopacy was of them. Moreover, in Pennsylvania they had come into contact with a genuine tolerance, and as they moved out to the South and Southwest they had to carry with them some traces of this spirit.

Later they settled very largely in East Tennessee, and it cannot be seriously maintained that that State has been noted for its attitude of toleration in matters of opinion either political or religious. Calvinism has not only no abstract objection to State support for a "true church", but in point of fact demands it whenever it is strong enough to enforce its own claims to be the one true Church. The Establishment in Scotland and even the declarations of the so-called " Free Churches " that gave up the Establishment for conscience' sake and the attitude of the Presbyterian Church to the "Queen's gift" or "*Regium donum*", which was a sum of money given every Presbyterian clergyman in Ireland, are abundant evidences of this general approval of State support of the true Church. There were many of this stock who later made a brave fight for a neutral attitude on the part of the State toward all forms of religion, and for effective separation of Church and State, but they were mostly, like Jefferson, deistic rationalists, who had forsaken all pretence of maintaining the old Calvinistic tradition. Nor can it be maintained that the Calvinists, from their point of view, were wholly wrong in wanting State support, for where it has been withheld they have often, for reasons we will discuss later, fallen into all manner of heresies, as in England, where their churches almost without exception became Unitarian; or in Geneva, where rationalism swept the field as soon as the hold of Calvinism upon the State was broken. The fact being that where the real Calvinistic tradition can maintain its strict central organization it is a fighting force superior to greatly more numerous rivals, but when it cannot thus maintain its discipline, it falls apart as easily as does its nearest rival, the dissenting type of Protestantism.

The first general synod of the Presbyterian Church, which represented this Scotch and Scotch-Irish population, met in 1717 and was at first hardly representative of the whole body. In the North the tradition was watered down and greatly modified by contact with Congregational and Baptist bodies, and still more by increasing religious indifference. Thus it was often to be found on the side of a toleration that was not based upon any principle, but had all manner of motives—economic, political, and social—behind it. Even in Pennsylvania the Scotch-Irish were intolerant of the Quakers who refused to bear arms in the constant raids of the frontier settlements upon the unfortunate Indians. Sturdy and independent as this particular stock was, its many virtues did not lie on the side of Christian gentleness or of tender and compassionate toleration of other peoples' errors. It was fierce in fight, unbending in debate, stubborn in defeat and desperately tenacious of personal opinion. This was not the soil in which the weaker virtues of forbearance and toleration are most likely to grow.

Looking over the history of the advance of religious toleration and freedom, one must come to the conclusion that the growing mass of religious indifference, the divisions among the various types of religious opinion and feeling as well as the equalization of economic groups have had more to do with the progress of religious freedom than any theory of religious forbearance, and that even the writings of men like Roger Williams, George Fox, William Penn, John Locke and others, with their somewhat limited views as to the possible bounds of toleration of opinion, had relatively little influence; just as the skepticism of Benjamin Franklin, Thomas Jefferson and Thomas Paine was rather symptomatic of the general attitude of the cultivated classes than the actual cause of the spread of doubt. Simply as a matter of experiment men came to the conclusion that religious toleration was possible and profitable, as the wise men of Amsterdam wrote to Peter Stuyvesant. Nor were the English colonies one whit in advance of the general spread of tolerant opinion in Europe; indeed in some respects they were behind it. For in Europe also exhaustion and religious indifference were playing just the same parts. It was not Calvinism but religious latitudinarianism, the child of Humanism and Arminianism that gave Holland its honorable place as the home of toleration.

Indeed until men surrender all faith in religious infallibilities, whether of pope or Church or Bible, it is hard to defend any toleration of error that may involve the eternal loss of millions of souls, if the power is at hand to suppress it; and the example of Spain and Italy shows that vigorous and determined persecution can establish the practically complete outward uniformity of religious habit. It was waning faith in an ethics based upon the hope of heaven and the fear of hell rather than any change of theological opinion that led in both Europe and America to greater religious toleration. Moreover, it was an educated rationalistic aristocracy that was in charge of the political and intellectual life of the American colonies certainly from the third or fourth generation of settlers on, and the very last thing their economic and political interests demanded was an exclusive policy of any kind. Thus there arose a philosophy of life that made a virtue of a toleration, partial and often very illogical, but sufficient for the needs of that extending international population that was yet to come.

CHAPTER XII

It is common in religious rhetorical treatment of history
to speak of the decline of religion in New England from
about the beginning of the eighteenth century. Nor are
signs lacking that the fervor that brought the Pilgrims
to the shores of New England had by this time in many
quarters abated. On the other hand, it is well to remember
that this religious enthusiasm was never as universal as
some would have us believe; there was always a large
number who either had no interest at all in religious
questions, or were relatively indifferent to them. One
of the Pilgrim Fathers had to be hung for murder ten years
after landing, and is described as of "one of the profanest
families amoungst them" by Bradford himself; nor was
the Massachusetts settlement made up of Puritans alone.
The hard life, the difficulty of providing for many children,
the unwonted severity of the climate made an atmosphere
for the newcomers highly unfavorable to any higher
aspirations than food and shelter. One cannot take very
seriously the laws compelling all to go to church, in
communities so scattered as were the settlements of New
England, after the first danger from Indians had disappeared. The religious exhaustion of Europe and especially of England after the desperate struggles of the
Thirty Years' War and the Independent Commonwealth
left men's minds also freer than they had been for some
time.

However, the theoretical faith of the New England population remained substantially the same as that of the class in England from which it was drawn. All professed to accept the Bible as infallible on all possible questions, even of science, history and government. Heaven and hell and a personal devil, as well as rude conceptions of atonement and a judgment yet to come were common property as elements of a conventional outlook upon life. There were numbers of lesser articles of faith to which at least lip service was rendered by practically all. We can really only judge of the faith of the more intelligent, for the humble mass remains as ever relatively inarticulate. We who read and write books easily forget that nine-tenths of all human history is wholly unwritten, and that this unwritten history is forever creating an atmosphere which is handed down from generation to generation, molding often the subconscious and unconscious life of thousands, who deem themselves guided by reason. It is this atmosphere, which the present writer is very sure goes back to the early English reformation in the fifteenth century rather than to the Continental movement, that is reflected in the writings of the greatest mind of New England's early history, Jonathan Edwards. Not that he was himself conscious of the origin of his inspirations; on the contrary we know that he was not. In his sketch of the progress of Redemption he makes no mention of either John Wyclif or the Lollards. He apparently knows nothing of the critical English scholasticism, which formed the groundwork of Wyclif's thought. But in like manner he seems to have made but little use of either the works of Luther or of Calvin. Locke and Berkeley affect his thought, and he was familiar with the main controversialists in the struggle between the Calvinists and the Arminians, but he distinctly disclaims dependence upon Calvin and says: "yet I should not take it at all amiss, to be called a Calvinist for distinction's sake; though I utterly disclaim a dependence on Calvin, or believing the doctrines which I hold, because he believed and taught them; and cannot justly be charged with believing in everything just as he taught." [1]

In truth Jonathan Edwards moved in quite another world of thought from that of Calvin. He is not, like John Calvin, interested mainly in a Church Universal conquering the world, but in a scheme of redemption for the individual saint, with its fruits of individual righteousness. The Church is a body of saints, who have made and are making their calling and election sure by religious experiences resulting in Christian conduct. His most interesting work is on "The Religious Affections." His doctrine of election is not drawn up to insure faith in the ultimate victory of the Church, but to insure to the individual soul salvation resulting in ethical redemption. The historic Church of the first three centuries hardly interests him at all; his whole system is a compound of English critical rationalism and English Bibliolatry. He can only be really understood in connection with his background of congregationalistic Protestantism. His main interest is also ethical in just the same sense as was Wyclif's. This comes out with him as it came out with Wyclif in the struggle to understand the meaning of the sacrament. And just as Wyclif was led to the rejection of the prevalent doctrine of the sacrament by his denial of its magic working, and to placing the sermon as the agency of conversion in its place; so also Jonathan Edwards staked his life's work on the proposition that the sacrament was not an agency of conversion,

[1] Jonathan Edwards. "Collected Works." Vol. I, p. 3.

but a privilege for the elect. This is not to say that he knew anything about either Wyclif or his teaching, but that he moved in a world that was built up on the traditions of separatistic Dissent; a world of thought entirely different from the Continental Protestant type, and the world of thought that has almost a monopoly of the religious thinking of the Anglo-Saxon elements of the American population to this day. Instinctively the foreign elements which were abundantly brought into contact with this dissenting mind were rejected; and almost as instinctively other elements were absorbed and remolded, as for instance in the thought of Thomas Hooker. The fact that the stern predestination of Jonathan Edwards was called Calvinism, with which it had little to do, has led even the theological historians astray.

It lies in the very nature of the dissenting world of thought and feeling that it cannot depend on organization or cult to tide it over periods of relative religious indifference. The Catholic tradition has its historic Church, its priestly ministry, whose function is independent of personal character and faith, its magic sacraments with their grace-imparting efficacy: the radical English dissenting tradition has only individual fervor and the fanatical faith resulting from long minority. Calvinistic Puritanism has its discipline, its historic creeds, its professional ministry all apart from any individual church, its central organization, its presbyterial oversight of the individual. Over against this Dissent has set the revival. It has no æsthetic traditions to equal those of either Roman or Anglican Catholicism, but it makes a powerful appeal to the individual conscience, and in its bringing the individual soul straight into the presence of a righteous God and leaving it there, without mediation of either

Church or priest, it is more Protestant than either Lutheranism or Calvinism.

Hence it was in the nature of the case that American Protestantism should sooner or later enter upon a struggle for existence in the presence of the growing religious indifference, and the moral disasters due to the long struggle with France and the Indians, as well as the difficulties of frontier life and poverty. It was in Northampton in the year 1732–1733 and under the powerful preaching of God's wrath by Jonathan Edwards that a characteristic "revival" set in, with all the curious mental phenomena that have marked in various degrees all similar ebullitions in the religious history of America. Happily Jonathan Edwards himself has set down with painstaking care and evident exactness the early history of a movement which no American historian has properly estimated or fully understood, but which has had simply inestimable influence upon the culture of at least a good third of the population of the United States, and has indirectly influenced even more; which moreover has reacted upon Dissent in England and given it weapons for the struggle with Catholic cult and Puritan discipline.

The revival spread over all New England in various degrees of power, and when the first excitement was over there were memories and inspirations left that were never forgotten. Again in 1742–1743 a similar wave of renewed zeal for a personal religious experience swept the country, and there joined in it two new apostles of Dissent, Wesley and Whitefield, who came not only from England but out of the bosom of the most pronounced Anglo-Catholic tradition. For the father of John Wesley was the steadfast opponent of all nonconformity, and is still known to historians of English culture as the author of bitter pamphlets against the nonconformist schools, which were by reason of their superiority making sad inroads upon the Catholic monopoly of education.[1] Neither John Wesley nor his brother Charles ever left the membership of the Established Church of England, but both connived at separation, although Charles objected to the ordination of bishops of separation by his brother John. Likewise Mr. George Whitefield never really left the communion of the Establishment. He was suspended by the commissary in Georgia for failing to obey a summons, and his appeal in England was never seemingly either allowed or rejected; he functioned as chaplain and never renounced in any way his membership in the Established Church, although he attacked much in the lives of his fellow clergy, and ignored quietly denominational lines. He was buried by his own request before the pulpit of a Presbyterian church in Newburyport, Mass., where he died.[2] At the same time none of the leaders of the movement were really representative of the Anglo-Catholic tradition in its purity. The Wesleys were originally a dissenting family, and the father of John Wesley had been designed for the nonconformist ministry. Whitefield also rose out of those walks of life where Dissent was the religious atmosphere, so far as there was any religious atmosphere. Moreover, from 1688 on, many who still cherished the dissenting type of piety were represented in the Established Church and became what were known as the Evangelical wing of the Establishment. At a much later date (1808) the Reverend Sydney Smith in the " Edinburgh Review " classes them with the Methodists in his blunt way. " We shall use the general term of Methodism to designate these three classes of fanatics" namely "Arminian and Calvinistic methodists, and the

---

[1] "A Letter from a country Divine to his Friend in London." 3d Ed. London, 1706.
[2] L. Tyerman. "Life of George Whitefield." 2 Vols., 1876–1877.

evangelical (italics his) clergymen of the church of England, . . . not troubling ourselves to point out the finer shades, and nicer discriminations of lunacy, but treating them all as in one general conspiracy against common sense, and rational orthodox Christianity."

The revival was surely attended by curious and often depressing symptoms, so that Jonathan Edwards himself had to protest against the demand for physical contortions and hysteria as evidence of the movings of the Holy Spirit. The powerful preaching of men like Wesley and Whitefield stirred up all classes. That Whitefield was a powerful preacher is abundantly attested, but the witness of Benjamin Franklin alone is sufficient. He went to hear him, determined in no way to be moved by him because Whitefield refused to follow some advice he had given him, but under the spell of the preacher he first decided to give all the copper he had in his pocket, then all the silver, and before Whitefield had finished he had poured out all the coin he had with him into the collection.[1] Incidentally he measured off the space in Philadelphia where the crowd stood, to see how many Whitefield had attracted and how many could actually hear his voice. Whitefield made seven journeys to America, and stayed as long as two years in one mission; the last journey was made in bad health, and he died in New England in 1770. It is an illustration of the loose way in which the term "Calvinism" is used as synonymous with predestinarianism that Whitefield is always called a Calvinist, although he himself writes to John Wesley: "I cannot bear the thought of opposing you: but how can I avoid it if you go about, as your brother Charles once said, to drive John Calvin out of Bristol? Alas, I have never read anything that Calvin wrote: my doctrine I had from Christ and His apostles;

[1] "Autobiography." Collected Works. Fed. Ed. John Bigelow. Vol. I, pp. 220–224.

I was taught them of God; and as God was pleased to send me out first, and to enlighten me first, so, I think he still continues to do it." [1]

Neither the Wesleys nor Whitefield brought anything of the æsthetic culture of the Catholic tradition as preserved in the Anglican Church with them to America. Nor do we find in the very disappointing writings of Whitefield the least appreciation of features of the Anglo-Catholic cult which to-day make it an influence far outside the lines of its actual membership. Their gospel was the intensely individualistic proclamation of a way of escape for the soul from eternal damnation. The test of conversion was an emotional reaction rather than an intellectual acceptance of a creedal statement, and neither man was really interested in theology as such, or really competent to deal with its questions. The revival affected all divisions of Protestantism in the colonies, and did not stop before the doors of the Established Church, for in point of fact the overwhelming mass of the population was not only at this time English, but of the one class in England which, so far as any religious tradition had trained it, was under the influence of Dissent.

It was just as the Great Awakening was running its full course that the Scotch and Scotch-Irish immigration set in, but how far this population was affected by the revival it is now hard to say. The later reaction was very mixed. The thoughtful Calvinistic Presbyterian was attracted to the revival preaching by its real zeal for religion; by its generally almost stern predestinarianism, for Wesley's Arminianism came later; by its faithful adherence to the Bible as the sole authority; by its almost fierce emphasis upon a heaven-hell morality; by its emphasis upon the work of Christ for redemption, and

[1] "A Centenary of Methodism." Dublin, 1839. P. 52.

its general evangelical tone; but on the other hand the more educated Presbyterians soon marked the entire lack of any stress upon sacramental grace; they noted also the lack of all feeling for the organized church and its established ministry; they soon also felt the rebellion of Dissent against the authority of churchly tradition in the established creeds, as well as what seemed to them undue emphasis upon the inner light of all men apart from the historic Church. In various ways the dissatisfaction of the churches under the influence of a real Calvinism was beginning to be felt in criticism of the whole movement, when the war clouds began to thicken on the American horizon.

Whitefield did not live to see the Declaration of Independence, but his sympathy had been, it is thought, on the American side of the questions arising. Wesley took a decided stand on the English side, and thus cut himself off from immediate influence on the colonies so far as they were strongly dissenting, for as we shall see in a later chapter strong dissenting opinion went generally with the demand for independence. The political agitation seems to have at once stopped the more active prosecution of the revival activity, although it had also probably reached more than its height before the death of Whitefield. Since Professor Frederick Jackson Turner has so ably turned our attention to the significance of the frontier,[1] it is important to remember the education that the revival preachers, raised up and educated in the movement begun in Northampton, gave the early settlers. The Catholic tradition has always, for rather obvious reasons, been suspicious of all overestimate of a lay element in religion, and in this the Presbyterian

[1] F. J. Turner. "Significance of the Frontier." American Historical Association Report. 1893.

(Puritan) tradition has also shared. The elder was an ordained man, with a life qualification for office, and the layman owed for the most part only obedience. Even Congregationalism had begun to set the stated ministry somewhat apart. One of the weakest things Jonathan Edwards ever wrote was an attempt to divide between the legitimate lay exhortation and the official preaching of an installed ministry. Real historical Dissent knows no such limit to the power of prophecy, and as we shall see later this characteristic of historic English Dissent and American Protestantism has marked every revival of its power from the poor preachers of Wyclif's day on. The revival brought the layman again to the front in the life of the frontier, and gave a training in speaking, leading and influencing men that is hard to compute, but which was undoubtedly very important in an uneducated community much in need of leadership. Of course a paid and professionally trained ministry is instinctively jealous of any encroachments upon its prerogatives and authority, but on the poor frontier there was little occasion for any such feeling, and the lay preacher played a very imposing rôle in the development of the spiritual life of the widely flung boundaries of the colonies.

Although Wesley and Whitefield were still members of the Establishment they seemingly made no move to prevent the rise of a profound dissenting spirit very hostile to any hierarchy, and especially antagonistic to the Established Church. Just what effect this attitude would have had upon the fortunes of the nominally established but really rather impotent Episcopal Church had it not been interrupted by war, it is impossible to say. Sooner or later there must have been a clash, but the movement was still in its infancy when war broke out.

It must not be concluded from the glowing statements

of the spread of the Awakening that it really did profoundly affect all classes even though it reached them as we are more than once informed. It is suspicious how little place it has in any literature of this period, or how little we hear of it in educated circles of Boston, New York or Philadelphia, although seemingly it made a more marked impression on the educated there than elsewhere. All the evidence goes to show that the leading educated class was under the influence of the extreme rationalistic thought of that day in England, and the hysteria and physical manifestations characteristic of the movement were not well calculated to attract to the movement men and women of fastidious tastes. Even Jonathan Edwards himself soon suffered from opposition and reaction against the excitement his preaching aroused. Eventually he was even driven from his pulpit, and he himself bears testimony to the fact that influential families closely related to his own were among his opposers. Even had we statistics of conversions and numbers of those joining the churches, they would probably be untrustworthy, for all religious statistics must be examined with a care they seldom receive at the hands of Church courts. But as a matter of fact we have no such numbers to examine. The population of the whole country cannot have been much above three millions. The town of Northampton had, according to Jonathan Edwards, about two hundred families, and the church had six hundred and twenty communicants or almost the entire adult community.[1] The revival was only an extension of the methods familiar to the community. Edwards' predecessor, Doctor Stoddard, had had five similar times of religious excitement, although not quite so pronounced. Nor is it easy to form

[1] Jonathan Edwards. "A Narrative of Conversions." Works. Vol. 8, pp. 346 ff. Ed. London, 1840.

an opinion as to the effects of such movements upon the morals and manners of the population. The facts as to the level of the morality of the people given by Edwards himself are not enlightening. One asks also how far a minister is really able to get behind the veil of evasion and concealment that courtesy, apart from deliberate hypocrisy, draws to save the feelings of a respected professional ministry. The pictures are generally seemingly overdrawn. False standards of morality are in evidence. Ritual regularity often takes the place of social righteousness, and professions of conventional belief are accounted for righteousness.

Nevertheless there is no question as to the widespread influence of the movement. How far the non-Anglican population was affected it is also hard to say. Among the revival preachers who followed in the wake of Edwards, the Tennents, Wesley, Whitefield and others less well known, one finds foreign names, like Freelinghausa, as Edwards spelt the name. Moreover, there was nothing in the theological teaching that would have repelled the sectarian elements of either the Dutch or the German colonists. Such excitement is moreover exceedingly contagious, and even if the habits of mind born of the Continental religious training were not favorable to such emotional outbreaks, it is nevertheless true that this population felt the same spiritual needs that made such excitement welcome.

Apart from money-making the colonial population was relatively without higher diversions. It had no native literature, no art, no good music and but little organized social life such as even very poor European villagers enjoyed. Fighting, politics and religion were the only fully satisfying excitements open to that third of the population to whom even the theater and the dance were under the ban, and these were the forms of excitement that a body of more or less competent leaders were professionally engaged in promoting and directing. Up to the peace with France in 1763 the colonists had been kept fighting more or less continuously with France and her Indian allies; from that date until the war with England politics and religion had the whole field, but as the War for Independence was on the horizon even religion gave way, and the Great Awakening paused for a period.

There can, however, be little doubt that among those to whom the Great Awakening appealed it had a significance little noticed in the writings of the historians. It was an essentially dissenting movement: its message, its individualism, its lay exhorting, its emotionalism, its whole conception of Christianity breathed the air of English Dissent, and thus prepared the minds of those influenced by it to resist the claims and oppose the power of an upper-class England. It was easy for those interested in carrying on a war against England to persuade these lower-class dissenters that the war was not against England, to which on the whole the dissenter was loyal, but against the Royal House of Hanover, about which they knew little or nothing. And among these fervent dissenters the fear of an Anglo-Catholic hierarchy was again awakened and given all the force of a personal menace. The Great Awakening can hardly be classed as a unifying religious movement; indeed, the history of sectarian division and development, as we shall see later, is generally connected with such periods of revived religious interest. At the same time it brought various regions into closer connection with one another. The preachers traveled widely. Edwards was in New Jersey and Pennsylvania. Whitefield swept up from the South to the North several times. The Tennents were well known everywhere, lesser men traveled far and wide with the object of spreading the gospel as they understood it. Something of the old freemasonry of Dissent that had made it so hard to suppress in England was revived, as wandering preachers claimed hospitality for themselves and their message. Villages vied with one another in exhibiting the success of the revival, and exchanged exceptionally successful workers. The general interest in religion brought together for a little while at least all the various dissenting sects; even the Quakers felt the influence and in 1755 came a great Quaker revival, and a certain formulation of their rules in the interests of greater strictness. About this time the Quakers began to retire from open participation in the politics of Pennsylvania, under the general impression that political activity had injured the society, and they lost control of the colony, but increased in numbers and the leaders thought in spirituality.[1]

Nor did the more rationalistic wing of the dissenting type of Protestantism escape the movement, and already the beginnings of an organized Unitarianism may be noticed. Ministers like the Reverend Mr. Chauncy were compelled to ask themselves where they stood, and to take some position for or against the whole movement. Thus matters were when the war began.

[1] For the literature, *cf.* American Church History Series. Vol. XII, p. 235.

CHAPTER XIII

ORGANIZED CHRISTIANITY AND THE AMERICAN REVOLUTION

The old conception of the War for Independence as a great and unanimous rising of an oppressed people against their oppressors has been abandoned, and the danger now is, perhaps, that the real antagonisms between England and her colonies may be too much overlooked. Without question the economic interests of great groups both in New England and Virginia were the main cause of the war, but these groups could not declare war and much less carry it on without an appeal to the passions and prejudices of multitudes, whose economic interest these very crowds themselves often did not understand. Although the dissenting class had been hardly used in England, and was still deprived there of what we now consider very elementary rights, their children were seemingly not unfriendly to England. Nor are the reasons for this hard to find. From the earliest day of English conventicle Protestantism the fear of the lower orders of England was directed against Roman Catholicism, and England stood out for them still as the leading power in the struggle against the tyranny of the pope. Conventicle Protestantism rose in England, as we have pointed out, as a struggle for the national life. The dissenters in England feared Roman Catholicism so much that in the time of the Stuart régime they were not willing to buy toleration for themselves at the price of conceding it to Roman Catholics.

In the colonies therefore, the support of this class was

unwaveringly given to the Mother Country in all the wars England waged with France on North American soil, more particularly as the Jesuit missionaries were the heralds of France's claims to the Mississippi Valley.

The Quakers may be regarded as in many respects the extremest statement of some of Dissent's oldest positions: such as its anti-war passion, its ecclesiastical formlessness, its extreme individualism, its aloofness from the actual world. The American Quakers were therefore so much opposed to war with England that to this day charges of treachery and traitorous conduct are believed against them, although almost certainly false. The Wesleyan following was so much under suspicion that the English ministry lost nearly all its influence, and all save Asbury seem to have returned to England. Next to the Quakers we may put the Congregationalists as the purest expression of old English conventicle Protestantism, but just at this time their organized strength was much impaired by internal disputes which were now absorbing their attention in regard to the divinity of Christ and universal salvation.

In point of fact, in spite of the Great Awakening, whose influence was still being felt in certain strata of American society, the ruling classes of the colonies were seemingly but little interested in any pronounced religious organization. Nor does it seem to have been important to win official recognition from any of the organized body. John Adams, John Hancock, Elbridge Gerry, Benjamin Franklin, James Otis, Thomas Jefferson, Robert Livingston, were all very respectful toward religion, but it is often hard to say just where they stood in the matter of any of the prevailing traditions making claims for allegiance. True, all save Jefferson and Benjamin Franklin, who have left frank statements of their positions, seem to have had some connection with the churches recognized by law in the State in which they lived, but just as in the case of George Washington, such membership implied no sort of living interest in the issues upon which organized religion lays stress, and as far as one can ascertain their opinions were in general founded upon the prevalent type of philosophy, of which John Locke is the classic expression. The influence of the writings of Thomas Paine reveals the growing indifference to what may be called conventional Christianity, in all its types. For though his "Age of Reason" appeared much later, any one must notice in "Common Sense" and the "Crisis" the fundamental philosophy underlying the argument. Paine was the son of a Quaker, and even in his skepticism this fact appears.

The Quakers were always under suspicion during any war, because they refused military service, and in Philadelphia there was always a rather strong body of Tory opinion. But John Adams writes of "whole companies of armed Quakers in that city (Philadelphia), in uniforms, going through the manual." [1] The charge was made that they maintained disloyal relations with the enemy, on the basis of letters captured by General Sullivan in Long Island in August 1777. Seventeen were banished from Philadelphia and their property taken, but the charges are now vigorously denied by Quaker historians.[2] But whether the charge is true or not the fact that at all their meetings the tone was neutral, and that they protested vigorously against a violent end to the quarrel with Great Britain, made them very unpopular in patriot circles. There arose however a small body of so-called Free Quakers, whose meetinghouse in Philadelphia is still shown to

---

[1] John Adams. "Familiar Letters during the Revolution." New York. 1876. P. 60.
[2] *Cf.* American Church History Series. Vol. XII, p. 247 (Footnote).

visitors, or was in 1890. These advocated independence, and a "defensive war."

On the whole, however, it must be said that no especial influence of any organized form of the Dissenting tradition, commonly called the Puritan spirit, whether Congregationalist, Baptist or Quaker, had much to do with either bringing on the war or in directing its course. Individuals acted according to their lights, but there was no central directing force, and no way of knowing just what it would have done had it existed.

It would have been unthinkable at that date in any European country for a constitutional convention such as that of 1777 to meet and occupy itself so little with religious and church issues. The whole subject is just tactfully ignored. Apart from a respectful reference to the "Great Governor of the World" in the closing paragraph, there is no mention in the Articles of Confederation of the place of either religion or the Church in the State, and no position taken in regard to the relation of the State to the Church. Even the opening of the convention with prayer was at first opposed by John Jay, on the ground that Episcopalians, Congregationalists, Baptists, Quakers and Presbyterians were present; and it was Samuel Adams who with the tact of the born politician proposed that an Episcopalian of broad mind, a Reverend Mr. Duché, be asked to pray. The Declaration of Independence appeals to "the Supreme Judge of the World" and closes "in firm reliance on the protection of Divine Providence." There is however in all the main documents of this period no direct reference to any distinctively Christian faith. In looking over the list of those who were in any way prominent in forcing on the war, there are very few who took any active part, as far as can be known, in the work of any of the various denominations that were represented, and save John Witherspoon of Princeton, there was no clergyman among the signers of the Declaration of Independence. John Hancock was the son of a clergyman and had a brother who was a clergyman, but he himself never seems to have been active in any churchly connection. Samuel Adams is described in his biography as a "strict" Calvinist, but just what his biographer means by that term is open to question, as the term is so loosely used. John Adams was of the same general mind and temper as Jefferson and Benjamin Franklin. Roger Sherman was a devout Congregationalist, but otherwise New England was not represented by men who in any way stood for what is wrongly called Puritanism. And to speak of New England at that time as "strictly Puritan" is to miss the real meaning of the facts.

The traditions of the dissenting classes that made New England what it was were unartistic, severe, thrifty to the point of parsimony, and this was characteristic of the population apart from all theology and even all religion. As we have pointed out, Dissent has always its depths of indifference unlighted by any effective cult to hide the bareness of the board, and then again its times of revival and excitement, when religion becomes for a certain proportion of the population the absorbing topic. Whether as the result of the political excitement or, as is more likely, from a complex of causes, New England was in a period of marked religious indifference when the War for Independence came. The series of religious waves that had passed over the provinces since the time of Jonathan Edwards' predecessor, Doctor Stoddard, had reached their climax even before the death of Whitefield in 1770, and it will ever remain an unanswered question how far the educated class had been affected on the whole by the revival. Many had been very much repelled, and the rise of a skeptical and questioning type of Protestantism may be dated from this repulsion. It reached its climax, as we shall have occasion to see, later on, but already it was felt, and was a factor in the extremely negative attitude all the Fathers of the Republic took toward the subject of religion.

To claim therefore, as once it was the fashion to do, that the sturdy "Puritan" love of liberty was the sustaining cause of the war is unhistoric. Even using the word Puritan loosely to cover the dissenting tradition in its various manifestations it is not true that the war can be traced in any sense to their love of independence. The real Puritan had no love of any liberty except what he himself needed in order to force the Kingdom of God upon men, as he was commanded by God to do. It is the strength and glory of this type of Protestantism that it fears not the face of man, and even in a minority is willing at God's command, or what it conceives to be God's command, to force His will upon mankind. The sovereignty of God does not wait upon a majority vote.

But even in Connecticut, where the name Presbyterian still persisted, after all the real significance of the term had been lost in Congregationalism or in Unitarianism, there was no such inspiration to action. With the possible exception of Roger Sherman, the representation sent to the first Congress in 1777 was, from the point of view of religion, colorless. The pronounced individualism of Rhode Island throughout the whole struggle for nationality, from its hesitation in the beginning until its long delay to ratify the second constitution, doubtless had economic motives behind it, but possibly the strongly Baptist and Quaker antecedents, with their suspicion of all centralized power and their dislike of force, may have been factors. Such imponderable values are impossible to es-

tablish statistically and are liable to mislead. At least
one thing is certain: that the central dream of Calvin of a
theocratic State in which the Church could depend upon
the State to enforce the revealed will of God and to gov-
ern in accordance with the precepts of religion, had by
1777 so completely passed from even the minds of the few
actual Puritans that may have still survived that no one
thought it seriously worth while even to broach the subject. The churches of Massachusetts and Connecticut
were still supported by the community, but they were so
riddled with Arianism, Socinianism, Deism, Universalism
and lesser known faiths that neither friend nor foe regarded them as politically important enough either to
fight or befriend. As individuals devout churchmen and
ministers did their political duty and took honorable part
in the political life, but religion in any of its organized
forms played no part that we can definitely describe.

Quite otherwise was it with a religious tradition that
was akin to the actual historic Puritanism, but which has
never been called by that name. This was the High-
Church Presbyterianism of the Scotch and Scotch-Irish
who began, as we have seen, in the time of the Tory reaction to come in large numbers to the colonies, and more
especially to Pennsylvania, and from there to the Southern settlements. These Presbyterians were actual Calvinists, not only in theological opinion, which they held more
intelligently than the dissenting tradition is likely to
hold its theology, for it forms a more important part of
the religious complex; they were also Calvinists in Church
government and in their theory of the relation of the
State to the Church. Those that came from the North of
Ireland had formed their characters in a continual struggle with a small and very haughty landed gentry belonging to the English Establishment on the one side, and with

a mass of very ignorant native Roman Catholics on the other.

The exigencies of their situation had often compelled them to live in peace with the landed gentry of English origin, because the Protestant interest needed the protection of England and its power to maintain itself against the great mass of Roman Catholics, whose fervor and faithfulness to their tradition was only heightened by the brutality and greed of their oppressors. The causes of the bad treatment of this Presbyterian population were almost wholly economic. The landowning gentry were Episcopalian and controlled the sources of all political power. The Presbyterians were small farmers in large numbers, but the growing wealth of Ulster, whence these people came, sprang from an increasing industry, of which the commercial classes in England were jealous, and which they set out to destroy. In this they were partly successful, and a stream of immigration to America set in that has never quite ceased.

This stock was a fighting lowland Scotch race, and on the frontier they rivaled the Germans as protectors of the inland from both the French and the Indian allies of France. A large element of their religious life was hatred of all Episcopacy, whether Anglican or Roman. They were masters of organization, with its self-discipline and its demands upon the individual; while at the same time they were in many ways, like the English dissenters, afraid of both too much power in the hands of the State and of any weakening of individual independence. Like the dissenters they too were repelled by the luxury of an oppressing class, and stood for severe repression of many of the æsthetic tastes that marked the ruling minority, and that were therefore godless and wicked.

When war clouds rolled up, and England was now the

enemy and not France, this people, in spite of all they had suffered at the hands of England, was not bitterly anti-English as some would have us believe. But they were very bitterly anti-Episcopal. The very thought that the Established Church should become a reality in the colonies, and that England might send bishops to play the same part that they had so often played in Ireland was sufficient to make every Scotch-Irishman a furious patriot. They had, moreover, an influence out of all proportion to their numbers, just as the small English Presbyterian Puritan party had had similiar influence in England in 1642, because of their organization and discipline. All the thirteen colonies had been grouped for their Church purposes in a State-wide general synod. Unlike the Quakers, they had no objection to taking part in politics, and as the Quakers gradually retired from the politics of Pennsylvania, the Presbyterians stepped into the vacant place. A Scotch Presbyterian took a leading part in organizing them for the struggle he saw was coming, and John Witherspoon of Princeton College (now University) was, as remarked, the only clergyman to sign the Declaration of Independence. Calvinistic Presbyterianism, when untouched by Dissent, had nothing to urge against an Established Church, but it must be a true Church. Had President John Witherspoon had his way, and had he been able to include the Dutch Reformed and the Congregational churches in a nation-wide organization, as he wished to do, it might have been harder to keep all questions of ecclesiasticism out of politics. But the attempt failed, and there was no central churchly organization powerful enough to make any claims for recognition. The Articles of Federation as drawn up in 1777 are as completely secular as the by-laws of an insurance company.

It has been customary to consider Calvinism as a leading inspiration in the founding of a republic, and there is something to be said for this view. For a representative republic builds a barrier against the influences of the mob, for which Calvin had a great contempt, and Calvin's theocracy had as its written constitution the Old Testament. But as we shall see later there must be some care used in distinguishing between the cause and the effect. A representative republican organization has been the natural form into which all the free cities both of England and of the Continent have fallen. Both Presbyterianism and Dissent have been nurtured in the town and city; and the dissenting class being driven from the land, and Geneva and Edinburgh being the homes of Presbyterianism. The great mass of the English dissenting class that peopled North America came from a non-landowning population, and brought, it is true, a land-hunger with them; at the same time they were not "peasants" in the Continental sense of that term. The mentality of the small Anglo-American farmer is something quite palpably different from the Continental "Bauer." The small trading town and village of English origin were the homes of the dissenting class; and the question arises how far the religious tradition of the class was born of the town and how far the town and its spirit was born of the tradition.

The Scotch-Irish furnished many fighting men to the Revolutionary army, but their chief service was rendered when the war was transferred to the South, and at the battle of King's Mountain they defeated General Ferguson, and in the end led to the retreat of Cornwallis to Yorktown. Without any doubt the Scotch-Irish Presbyterian ministry was almost to a man on the side of the Revolution, and the General Synod that had been meeting since 1717 was in 1776 one of the most thoroughly organized interstate associations the colonies possessed. This synod met in Philadelphia in 1776, and although Presbyterianism was somewhat divided, the patriot party was greatly in the majority. John Witherspoon was a great power on the side of independence, and led the patriot forces. At the same time it is well not to over-estimate the influence that the Church exerted, for like the Congregational churches Presbyterianism was at this time far from the self-conscious, united body it afterwards became. The Great Awakening under Whitefield had strengthened the body numerically, but had introduced ways of thought more consonant with the thinking and outlook on life of Dissent; the result was division and struggle, and the religious life of the Church was still suffering from these divisions.

As we have seen there was really no Anglo-Catholic tradition in the colonies, in spite of the nominal estab-lishment of an Episcopal Church without any *episcopus*. Two thirds of the signers of the Declaration of Independ-ence were nominally Episcopal, but the war was the be-ginning of a complete collapse of the whole Church. The ministry fled for the most part to England. They had all been consecrated there and felt so far as they needed a spiritual home that it was in England. Those of the laity who had taken their religion seriously, and really belonged heart and mind to the Church, were instinctively Tories, and as the Revolution assumed almost the character of a civil war, these Tories were treated as traitors and hated more than the English soldiers.

The disestablishment of the Episcopal Church was inevitable, for the influence of the Scotch-Irish on the one side, and the rationalism of men like Jefferson and Franklin on the other, made it impossible to tax the community for an institution that had ceased to exercise any influence. So all the States where Episcopacy had been recognized passed easily over to complete secularism. Not that men like Jefferson opposed religion or even the Christian religion, but they viewed it from a purely rational point of view. Benjamin Franklin advised Thomas Paine to suppress a book, evidently his "Appeal to Reason", not on the ground of its untruth, but on the following ground: "Think how great a portion of mankind consists of weak and ignorant men and women, and of inexperienced, inconsiderate youth of both sexes, who have need of the motives of religion to restrain them from vice, to support their virtue, and retain them in the practice of it till it becomes *habitual*, which is the great point for its security", and lest he should offend popular sentiment, for "he who spits in the wind spits in his own face." And Thomas Jefferson in his oft-quoted letter to Doctor Benjamin Rush calls himself a Christian: "I am a Christian, in the only sense in which he wished any one to be; sincerely attached to his doctrines, in preference to all others; ascribing to himself every *human* excellence; and believing he never claimed any other." Again in a letter to Timothy Pickering he says about a sermon of Channing's which he had just read: "When we shall have done away with the incomprehensible jargon of the Trinitarian arithmetic, that three are one, and one is three; when we shall have knocked down the artificial scaffolding, reared to mask from view the simple structure of Jesus; when, in short, we shall have unlearned everything which has been taught since his day, and got back to the pure and simple doctrines he inculcated, we shall then be truly and worthily his disciples; and my opinion is that if nothing had ever been added to what flowed purely from his lips, the whole world would at this day have been Christian."

The dissenting tradition readily lends itself to such respectful rationalism, for it has no point of contact with an authoritative, interpreting Church, and stresses the right of the individual to rely upon his own faith in a personal guidance of the Holy Spirit. Benjamin Franklin and Thomas Jefferson knew their Bibles well, and in this respect were not different from the great body of their educated contemporaries, but it would be folly to call them representative "Puritans." Nor had Presbyterianism escaped the inevitable trend of thought. In England the dissenting tradition had carried the whole body over to Unitarianism. In one place Franklin says: "I have, with most of the Dissenters in England, some doubts as to his (Jesus's) divinity." Even the otherwise rather narrow-minded Scotch-Irish were at this time much under the influence of the prevalent rationalism and its general attitude toward the claims of divinity for Christ. Under these circumstances it is vain to claim that any religious tradition, either of the Anglo-Catholic, the Puritan or the dissenting type, exercised any great influence upon the beginning or the conduct of the war.

The romantic rationalism that marks so strongly the writings of Thomas Paine had no doubt a part in the forming of opinion for independence, but it can hardly have been more than a contributing cause. The rhetorical emphasis upon the rights of man and the glories of personal freedom could not be taken too seriously in a community in which chattel slavery was only denounced by a few fanatic Quakers and Baptists. The common man had about as much or as little political power under the colonial government as he obtained under either of the new constitutions. Much has been made of the assumed equality of the alleged spirit of "Puritanism", but Calvinistic Puritanism at its best is, as we have before pointed out, far from favoring equality. Its strong point is the due subordination of the individual to those he has himself set over him. Of real equality, either in the State or in the Church, there is no hint in Calvin, and as rationalism, both in its romantic, unhistoric as well as in its critical phases took root in Calvinistic Presbyterianism, it left this phase of its thinking relatively untouched. Puritanism is aristocratic and imperial in tone and temper; are not the elect of God to rule the world to His glory? The elect are kings and priests of the High God, and the ministry is a high office before which a John Knox taught kings and queens to bow; moreover, men are not born free and equal, but in sin and total depravity. Jefferson did not get his phrases from Puritanism, but from the prevalent unhistoric rationalism that had grown up in dissenting circles in England and the lowlands of Scotland.

In a very marked way all these men, springing as they did from about the same class and world of thought in England, held on to a few of the traditions of Dissent. The Bible is still for all of them authority, Jesus Christ is the noblest manhood, theology is secondary to conduct, the "gospel" is hid by overgrown dogmas and outworn creeds. John Adams put it in his characteristically rough way: "Where do we find a precept in the gospels requiring ecclesiastical synods, conventions, councils, decrees, confessions, oaths, subscriptions, and whole cartloads of trumpery that we find religion encumbered with these days?" Religion was for them a private affair which, as Benjamin Franklin once said, right-thinking men do not care much to discuss. The separation of Church and State is the work of Wyclif and not of Luther or of Calvin: it was the instinctive reaction of an outlook upon life that deeply distrusted the State, from which had come persecutions and oppressions. No foreign Royal House in England could ever have overcome the resistance of the English aristocracy to absolutism, and George III was in no way fitted by gifts or strength of will to make such absolutism possible, but the conquest of the colonies would have greatly strengthened his hands and the old fears of the dissenting tradition were well played upon, when Jefferson, following in the wake of all the war agitators, denounced George III as a tyrant. The Mecklenburg Declaration has often been urged as an evidence of the part taken by the Church in the struggle for independence, but as is now known, the reported declaration of May 20, 1775, was an inaccurate memory of resolutions passed actually on May 31, 1775, which by no means went to the length of demanding independence, but only contained remonstrances and threats, and there is no such dependence on it for the phraseology of Jefferson's paper as was once alleged. It was, however, an evidence of the feeling of that tradition we have already described as the Scotch-Irish Presbyterianism, for the county committee that drew up the actual resolutions, demanding the withdrawal of the English Parliamentary petition to the king, was a thoroughly Scotch-Irish committee.

Indeed, it is noteworthy that Jefferson, in the Declaration recital of the wrongs of the colonies and the tyranny of the king, makes no charge that any religious interest had suffered or was in any way threatened. The question of an establishment with bishops had created uneasiness; even so sober a man as the Reverend Charles Chauncy, writing in 1767, deprecates on many grounds any sending of bishops to America, and Archbishop Thomas Secker himself in a letter espousing the cause of sending bishops, says: "The powerful objection made at home against our proposal, is, that the Dissenters abroad have terrible apprehensions of being injured by it", yet it is hard to show that very great dislike of the project was exhibited by any save the Scotch-Irish. Certainly the rather large literature of discontent dwells very little on any alleged religious complaints, the fact being that the Episcopal Church was seemingly too weak to be feared. In the letter quoted above from Charles Chauncy, he claims that without the support of the Society for the Propagation of the Gospel in England, the Episcopal Church in America would fade away, as only about eight churches along the whole seaboard were self-supporting.

Religion and organized forms of Christianity are not synonymous terms, and there is no way of judging how far the colonists were more or less religious as the war broke out than at any other time. It can only be noted by the historian that at the time of the war organized religion was exceedingly uninfluential, and was far too divided to exercise a decisive influence on either side of the question in controversy. Had any of the religious parties of older date, like the Anglo-Catholics or the dissenting bodies, flung their whole weight into the scale on the side of England as the Scotch-Irish Presbyterians flung themselves unreservedly against England, and had it been a time of churchly enthusiasm, there is no saying what might have been the outcome, for some think that even up to a rather late period of the war two-fifths of the population were still loyal to England and were only forced into opposition by the employment of Indian and German allies, and by the wanton destruction by English troops of even Loyalist property. As it was, neither the dissenting bodies nor the Anglo-Catholic Church nor anything that can properly be called Puritanism played any great part in bringing on the war or forcing it to a final issue.

CHAPTER XIV

THE COLLAPSE OF ORGANIZED PROTESTANTISM IN THE
NEW REPUBLIC

It is impossible now to really more than guess how far the Articles of Confederation were responsible for the confusion that followed after the War for Independence. Indeed, it is not easy to gauge the actual depth of the confusion. All the "Federalist" writers are sincerely convinced that all the evils of the situation sprang from the weakness of the central government, and that a merely slow and careful revision of the Articles would have been impossible. How the inarticulate masses felt, and how far they were actually benefited by the new Constitution of 1789, no one can now say. The vocal party was that of influence and wealth, and it had the last word.

The confusion was great. The war just closed had lasted seven years and had spread gradually from the North over the whole country and had been carried on at times at least with great cruelty and waste. Certainly it was not a time when it might be expected that spiritual values, either literary, artistic or religious, would flourish. All the evils that follow upon all wars were now in evidence. War profiteering is no new phenomenon, and as the unfortunate soldiers were paid in promises of land— land scrip—which they had for the most part to sell, land speculation with all its attendant evils was added to speculation in national paper.

Amid this confusion the voice of organized religion

could hardly be heard. The most complete collapse was that of the Episcopal Church, which was hastily disestablished and seemingly went to pieces. The ordained ministry sailed mostly for England, and the wonder is that any life seemed left. All the dislike and jealousy of rival religious bodies could now be freely poured out upon a Church so intimately connected with the defeated enemy. It was hardly missed out of the culture of the time, for it contributed to it almost nothing that was in any sense peculiar save perhaps that its set prayers maintained the dignity of worship when a revivalist type of religious fervor left much to be desired in this respect. Rationalism and Deism were the common atmosphere of the educated classes in the States where Episcopacy had flourished.

There can be no doubt that, apart altogether from the truth or untruth of any religious system, when such a system is violently uprooted other values, moral and intellectual, will also be imperiled. That the collapse of Episcopacy was without moral losses is hardly thinkable, but so very slight was the religious influence apparently that it is hard to point to any very tangible evidence of such loss. Life went on in Virginia and Maryland as well as in the other Southern States much as it had gone on before the struggle. Nor was Episcopacy the only organized form of Protestantism to suffer. The "Wesleyan Connection" lost nearly all its ministers, and as Wesley was very pronouncedly against the cause of Independence, only the personal influence of Francis Asbury (1745–1816) was left. He bravely remained and in spite of hostility and suspicion carried on the work, which at that time was still nominally within the possible bounds of the English Establishment.

The Quakers also suffered in both property and influ-

ence. The close of the war found them also divided and
weakened and powerless to stem the tide of secularization that followed upon the return to the main business
that had brought all men to America, that of making
money, and to this end the restoring of the injured credit
of the country. The inherent weakness of all conventicle
types of Protestantism soon appeared, and differences
that led to splits in the connection were already on the
horizon, for although many Quakers were rich, and individual meetings had wealth behind them, the autonomous
character of the individual meeting prevented the accumulation of large corporate property, and nothing is so great
a protection of orthodoxy as large corporate wealth and
a paid ministry interested by natural selection and education in guarding against innovations that might weaken
the fundamental sources of the corporate enthusiasm.
Thus the end of the war found the Quakers on the verge
of open ruptures, that promised ill for the future, and
prevented their exercising any large influence upon the
political developments that were now absorbing more and
more the interest of the country. In the same way the
Congregational churches were in no position to resist the
swelling tide of anti-Trinitarian views that gradually
gave rise to an organized Unitarian Church. The revival
methods of Whitefield and his lesser followers were opposed by men whose cultivation and freer views made
much in the revival movement very distasteful. Among
these were the Reverend Charles Chauncy (1705–1787)
who already in 1747 published a protest under the title:
"Seasonable Thoughts on the State of Religion in New
England," against the playing on the fears and superstitions of weak and uneducated men and women. In this
tract he quotes a description of the preaching of a Mr.
Davenport in these words:

At length he turned his discourse to others, and with the utmost strength of his lungs addressed himself to the congregation, under these and such like expressions, viz: "You poor unconverted creatures, in the seats, in the pews, in the galleries, I wonder you don't drop into hell! It would not surprise me, I should not wonder at it, if I should see you drop down now, now, now, this minute, into hell. You Pharisees, hypocrites, now, now, now, you are going right into the bottom of hell. I wonder you don't drop into hell by scores and hundreds, etc." And in this terrible way he ended his sermon. . . . After a short prayer, he called for all the distressed persons (which were twenty) into the foremost seats. Then he came out of the pulpit, and stripped off his upper garments, and got into the seats, and leaped up and down for some time, and clapped his hands, and cried out in those words: "The war goes on, the fight goes on, the devil goes down, the devil goes down" and then betook himself to stamping and screaming most dreadfully.

The result of these revival excesses had been a strong reaction just before the outbreak of the war, and what afterward was organized as the Unitarian Church was scattered all over the scenes of the evangelical awakening. When the war closed the Congregational and Presbyterian bodies were also in the midst of controversies carried on over anti-Trinitarian views, over universal salvation, and free will. No great theological advance was made; indeed the interest was rather ethical and æsthetic than theological, with strong sympathy for more tolerance of differences of opinion. The result was to weaken greatly the influence of the Churches as lacking in unity and in inspiration. The dissenting bodies both in England and the United States, but especially in New England, became prevailingly anti-Trinitarian, with strong leanings to various types of Universalism. The influence of Jonathan Mayhew (1720–1766) was great and the teachers in Harvard College were all more or less Unitarian in sympathy. Quite apart from the truth or untruth of the various positions held, the questions raised weakened the authority of established Christianity, just at a time when all authority was being challenged. As we shall see later there was gathered a rich fruitage from organized Unitarianism, which is still rendering great service to the religious thought of the nation, but the controversies and bitternesses that arose in the process made any serious social or political contribution by organized Christianity at this time almost impossible.

One of the most interesting of the various expressions of the conventicle type of Protestantism has always been the religious form usually known as the Baptist body. It is impossible to establish actually any literary connection between the Lollards and the primitive English Baptists, but the more one studies the early history of the movement, going back as it does to the time of John Smyth (1612) the more must one be persuaded that it has a much more ancient even if unwritten history. The Anabaptists of the Continent are certainly not the original body, nor is Calvin the probable source of their very hard and unflinching type of predestinarianism, which is more probably of the pure English type. True it is that the Arminian Mennonites at times deeply influenced the thinking of a section of the body, especially in America, but the constant reversion to the primitive way of thinking suggests, at least, a much older story.

Adult baptism, far from being sacramentarian in the fundamental thought, is, as we have already pointed out in another connection, a thorough-going protest against any grace-imparting character. Only men and women who are already converted should be baptized, and that purely as a sign of obedience and fellowship. This primitive body survived the War of Independence better than almost any other Protestant sect. Its main home was in the south and southwestern States, as well as in Rhode Island, but it had a scattered following in all the States.

It has had a particularly honorable history in its ministry to the poor and humble, and can be very proud of its record as the earliest and steadiest advocate of complete religious freedom of thought. In its constant tendency to fly apart on questions of doctrine and cult, but especially of cult, it again only emphasizes its primitive conventicle character. Its ministry to the Negro made it a religious force among this population second to none, and it shares with the Quakers the honor of early protest in the name of Christianity and humanity against chattel slavery.

On the other hand, its primitive conventicle character finds expression in its constant aversion to any mingling of religion and the State. No body was more urgent for complete separation of Church and State than the various Baptist communions. Nor was this hard to understand, for they had been persecuted by practically every State Church with which they had had contact. True they had in nearly all the States gradually won their way, and in Rhode Island, thanks to the sympathy of Roger Williams at one period of his stormy religious development, they always had had a refuge. But persecution has been the lot of the Baptists, and this again is not hard to understand, for they were the early enemies of all those priestly claims that soon make a professional ministry a vested interest bound to defend itself. Like the Congregationalists they have always been the firm defenders of Church autonomy. Like the early conventicles they had little or no corporate property, and this gave the individual church a freedom that has of course led to divisions and splits innumerable, but has also made reunion and restored fellowship relatively simple. One of the great difficulties in the way both of church splits and church reunion is the question of the property of the divided or reuniting bodies.

In consequence both of the relatively humble character at this time of the Baptist bodies, and their aversion to politics, it is impossible to trace any influence directly upon the national life in its stormy beginnings from 1783 to 1789. There can be little doubt that the logic of the Congregationalist, Baptist and Quaker positions would lead them to dread centralization of power, and to oppose any movement that seemed to them to even approach monarchy. But in the stormy debates that preceded the second Constitution whatever individuals may have done there is no trace of any corporate action of Baptist bodies.

Professor Charles A. Beard has raised anew in his two interesting and most instructive books the whole question of the origin of our Constitution.[1] Nor can the result of his inquiry surprise the thoughtful student of the motives that led men and women to give up all that seemed to make life attractive to face the dangers and hardships of colonial life. The material welfare of themselves and their children was the all-prevailing and quite legitimate urge that impelled the vast majority to begin a new life in an unknown land. That ideal and religious motives mingled with the desire for material prosperity cannot be denied, but the wonder is, not that the material motives were in the foreground, but that the other motives, so far as they were in conflict with these, survived at all. They did survive, and indirectly influenced without question the thinking of the responsible authors of

[1] Professor Charles A. Beard. "An Economic Interpretation of the Constitution of the United States." New York, 1913; and "Economic Origins of Jeffersonian Democracy." New York. 1915.

both the Articles of Confederation and the Constitution of 1787, but at no period of our history, probably, were organized religion and social idealism so divided and powerless in their approach to life as at the time of the formation of the Federal Government.

The whole atmosphere of the entire literature is secular.[1] When one remembers that the Puritan principle, so far as it was Calvinistic, recognized the Jewish theocracy as a model for all time for all governments, the fact that the Old Testament is never even alluded to as an authority by the principal authors of the Constitution should give some pulpit rhetoric pause. Indeed, Alexander Hamilton almost goes out of his way to ignore the Old Testament in his recital of the various republics and their history in "The Federalist", and in his list of republics Sparta, Athens, Rome and Carthage, as well as Venice and Holland, are all reviewed; but of Judaism there is no mention. In the list of the causes of war between competing States he never even mentions religion as a possible incitement. His argument is that republics are as likely to go to war as monarchies, and that the thirteen States need a strong central government to prevent the several States from falling foul of each other, and that commercial rivalries, personal ambitions, desire for enlarged dominion will all inflame the passions of the several States, unless a strong central force is in a position to maintain the peace. It is not with his argument either in this or the following paper in "The Federalist" [2] that we have especially to do, but with the striking fact that the repub-

---

[1] *Cf.* Max Farrand. "Records of the Federal Convention", the official reprints of Madison's Notes in "Documentary History of the Constitution." 5 Vols. Washington, 1894–1905. "The Federalist", Ed. Paul Leicester Ford. New York, 1898, and many editions. Justin Winsor's "Critical and Narrative History of America." Vol. VII, pp. 215–266, where also additional literature is given.

[2] The sixth and seventh papers by "Publius."

lic's ablest group of statesmen, in defending the proposed constitution in appeals to the widest public, and using skillfully every argument that would make the new document palatable to the greatest number of people, saw fit to ignore the whole subject of religion. It is not that it is attacked or made little of, but the fact that it is entirely ignored, that marks the entire disappearance of the Puritan theocratic idea. For though "The Federalist" was primarily intended to affect New York it was also an appeal to all the States. Where a hundred years before every case, whether civil, political or criminal, was decided by a reference to the Old or New Testament, and that not alone in Massachusetts, New Haven, Connecticut and Plymouth, but in Virginia and the Carolinas; in "The Federalist" the Bible and Christianity, as well as the clergy, are passed over as having no bearing upon the political issues being discussed.

Indeed, it is very striking to observe the authorities that have taken the place of Moses and the prophets. We find oftenest cited Montesquieu, Blackstone, Hume, with frequent indirect use of Locke and Hobbes without use of their names; and especially used is Plutarch. The eighteenth-century conception of Greco-Roman Paganism has completely supplanted Puritanic Judaism. And all this evidently seemed to that generation quite natural. Long before the date of "The Federalist" the pulpit had been complaining of the shifting of the emphasis from the authority of the Bible to human reason, but there was no effective pulpit protest against the complete and obvious secularization of politics now so plainly in evidence.

When we turn to the Constitution itself, the fact stands out too plainly to be ignored. There are just two references to religion in the amended document. In Article VI it is enacted: "The Senators and Representatives before mentioned, and the Members of the several State Legislatures, and all executive and judicial Officers, both of the United States and of the several States, shall be bound by Oath or Affirmation, to support this Constitution; but no religious Test shall ever be required as a Qualification to any Office or public Trust under the United States." The second reference is in the first Amendment, in which it is enacted: "Congress shall make no law respecting an establishment of religion, or prohibiting the free exercise thereof; or abridging the freedom of speech, or the press, or the right of the people peaceably to assemble, and to petition the Government for a redress of grievances."

The purely negative character of this attitude appears on the face of the instrument. A very small body of firm and intelligent Calvinists protested for years against the ignoring of the name of God in the Constitution, and even ordered its members not to vote until their petition for such recognition be granted. But the omission of such a term as "Christianity" is quite as striking. Nor is the reason far to seek. Before the War of Independence, as we have seen, there were really only three types of Protestantism exercising any influence upon men's thought: an Episcopal type, that had had no Anglo-Catholic tradition to give it consistency and power; a Presbyterian-Calvinistic type, confined almost wholly at that time to the Scotch and Scotch-Irish population; and lastly the dissenting type, embracing the Congregationalist, Baptist, Quaker and allied religious bodies. Puritanism had long disappeared and been swallowed up in Congregationalism. Now of these three, the Episcopal type had lost all influence on the course of events by the defeat of England. Although the Scotch and Scotch-Irish had taken an influential part in the War for Independence, they were really only hopeful of seeing that their hated enemy the Episcopal Church was not established, and their leader John Witherspoon had lost in part his eyesight and seems not to have been active in the constitutional struggle. He died in 1792. There was, it seems, no influential leader of Presbyterianism in the Convention. The only remaining religious tradition was the dissenting one, which by history and habit of thought was on the side of the complete separation of Church and State. The anomalous situation in Massachusetts, New Hampshire and Connecticut can hardly be called a State Establishment of Religion, although the separate churches still received State support, a situation soon corrected.

Among the members of the Constitutional Convention there were apparently no radical thinkers in opposition to organized Christianity, although the biographical material in regard to the religious attitude on the part of many is too slight to dogmatize; even men like Jefferson, Patrick Henry and Thomas Paine were not of the number. It was composed almost entirely of more or less successful business men and lawyers, mostly lawyers. The leading ends were economic and political. The age was secular, the Churches were weak, Christianity was divided and distracted; organized religion was in no situation to wage any battle for recognition, even if the inherited spirit of English lower-class Dissent had inclined the leaders of this tradition to seek it. Hence, as it happened, the new republic was born in as secular a spirit as the later French republic. Not that many individuals were not powerfully under the influence of religion, but that no organized religion had any place, even in the thoughts of the founders, and to speak of a "Puritan Republic" is talking wild historic nonsense.

Indirectly, the new republic was closely intertwined with the radical wing of the dissenting tradition. The unhistoric but penetrating rationalism of the eighteenth century in England is the generally unrecognized child of Dissent, for as we have so often pointed out, almost the mark of that spirit is faith in the individual illumination of the earnest student of the Bible. According to the Quaker, the Baptist, the Independent, and indeed all the dissenting sects, the Holy Spirit can be counted upon to guide the earnest seeker into all truth. But just as soon as religious feeling begins to fade, common sense is substituted for divine illumination. Benjamin Franklin and John Locke both still regarded the Bible as an authority, but it was to be read and judged by each individual according to common sense. Thus there has always been a rationalistic wing to conventicle Protestantism, and it was this stream of thought that dominated the leaders in the political world of that day, though they exhibit various stages of reliance upon reason and the authority of the Bible, and a more or less unconscious and unthinking acceptance of traditional modes of religious attitude. The charge of atheism is a good stone to throw at any offending opponent, but in point of fact, from Thomas Paine to Thomas Jefferson and Benjamin Franklin there were for the most part only different shades of theism with a rationalistic background. None of the men were atheists in any true sense of the word, but they were all thoroughly secular and rationalistic in tone and temper.

The temper of the Constitution is the same as seen in the various State constitutions. Virginia, Maryland and the Carolinas at once disestablished the Episcopal Church. Rhode Island and Pennsylvania never had had any State Church. Up to 1819 New Hampshire, like Massachusetts and Connecticut, continued the support of the Congregational churches, but gradually and without any serious debate or struggle this anomaly ceased, in Connecticut in 1818 and in Massachusetts somewhat gradually from 1811, when all churches received some support, to 1833 when the whole connection between the State government and the Church was severed. The ease with which this was done reveals the instinctive attitude of Dissent toward the State. In many of the States there are found, however, remnants of the tendency to insist upon belief in God, or to preserve the Sabbath Day, and in many States laws against blasphemy are still on the statute books. In New York the situation was complicated by the way the Dutch Reformed Church had been treated as almost on the same plane with the English Established Church, but here also, without much friction or debate, what had been rather an endowment than an Establishment came to a close.

Although the secularization of the State was very complete, indirectly we may see the influences of the same type of thinking that marked Dissent from very early days. The fear of the State was born of its long struggle with a persecuting Church, as seen in so much English middle-class thought, as in Bentham, John Stuart Mill and Adam Smith, and is seen also in the discussions of the Convention of 1787, and in "The Federalist." The strong individualism which the town life and the trading spirit developed in dissenting circles marks the early political life of the rising republic. The fact that the small town and the city have from the beginning dominated the life of the republic is no accident, but may well have its explanation in the landlessness of the class that came from England, and which was more fitted for a town and city development than for a country life. The State particularism which so often threatened the Union, was the same spirit that made Dissent ever ready to spring apart, and the constant resort to pacts and agreements as the basis of corporate activity is the habit of mind generated in the days of conventicle covenants and small group agreements, as in the cabin of the *Mayflower* before the landing of the Pilgrims. The preference for written constitutions, code laws and mutual covenants is perhaps a memory of the same documentary covenants by which every little conventicle gathering tried to protect itself and its teaching. Certainly it is very different from England's unwritten common law, and from that "general customary law" which in Germany, even since codes have been introduced, still takes first place in German jurisprudence.

In the inefficiency of State organization, particularly military organization, as contrasted with the exceptional efficiency of private enterprise even in those early days of the republic, may be seen the same lack of confidence in the State, and lack of experience in its methods that marked a class excluded in England from all participation in the government of the State, but powerfully energetic in the field it then made its own and as it rose to wealth, carrying its prejudices and its experience with it. The shrewd dissenting mind had been trained in the school of experience; only in trade, shipping and industry could it assert itself against a class that had a monopoly of the land, the political power and social prestige. The struggle began with Wyclif and is still going on in England, but with the War for Independence this class won for itself a wider field and a vantage ground from which it advanced to further conquests.

CHAPTER XV

The English Episcopal Church in America found itself after the War for Independence in a most dubious position. It was so hated in New England that the question whether a bishop should be allowed in Massachusetts was seriously debated in the Boston newspapers, and that as late as 1785. When one remembers that the Puritan party was a party within the Established Church, and that for a long time separation from the Mother Church was vigorously denied by even leading ministers like John Cotton, the entire disappearance from New England of everything that even superficially resembled Episcopacy can only be explained by the overwhelming numerical superiority of Dissent.

At their ordination all Episcopal ministers were bound to take the oath of supremacy of the English king, so that when a young man named Mason Locke Weems, who won immortality by his "Life of Washington", appeared before the Bishop of London shortly after the peace between England and the United States had been signed, Bishop Lowth seemingly somewhat brusquely refused to ordain any one going back to America. The archbishop upon appeal laid the responsibility upon Parliament, which in due time acted. But in the meantime there was no American bishop, and it was a curious question how America could get one. The Danish Minister kindly offered John Adams to have young Americans duly ordained by Danish bishops, and even offered to have the service in

Latin, that all might understand. But although the English Church has always recognized the ordination of other national Churches, yet the young Episcopalians were anxious to have the full recognition of the English National Church.

Into the vexed question of the relations of Church and State we cannot of course go. The separation can never be quite complete; it is not quite complete even in America, where legislative bodies are opened with prayer; the army and navy have their chaplains; ministers are exempted from certain duties. The several States take cognizance of the ministerial office in various ways, more particularly in the wedding service, and they also free for the most part church buildings from certain types of taxation and give them other recognition. The High Anglo-Catholic theory of the English Church treats it as the national expression of the one great and universal and historic Church, founded by Jesus Christ and committed to the care of bishops and teachers as well as the deacons of the body. It was therefore a serious question for earnest young Episcopalians how they could be true to the new republic on the one hand, and at the same time obtain the legitimate Episcopal succession, which could alone validate the soul-saving sacraments.

Upon the refusal of the English Church through its archbishop to set apart any one as bishop, who was expecting to return to the United States, Samuel Seabury of St. Peter's Church in New York had himself consecrated as bishop by three non-juroring bishops at Aberdeen in Scotland in 1784. There was no doubt as to the legitimate consecration of these bishops, but there still remained the doubt as to the recognition of the parent Church of the body thus established as a national Church and part of the Universal Church of Christ. In 1787 therefore, after various conferences, the Archbishop of Canterbury set the Episcopal seal upon the Reverend William White as Bishop of Pennsylvania and upon the Reverend Samuel Prevost of New York as Bishop of New York, and three years later upon Reverend James Madison as Bishop of Virginia.

There was thus set up a national Episcopalian Church which, so far as the orders of the English Church had validity, was also in possession of valid orders for the United States. In due time (1792) this Episcopal body set apart of its own authority a bishop for Maryland, Bishops White, Prevost, Seabury and Madison all taking part. Thus also were validated certain steps that had been taken before, looking to a reorganization of Episcopacy in America. Those who were interested in maintaining the Episcopal Church felt, no doubt justly, that it had to be rescued from the charge of disloyalty to the new political conditions that had arisen with independence, and from 1789 a constitution was adopted which consciously followed the lines of the new organization of the supreme political State.

Grave concessions had to be made to the prevailing tone of the population. In the first place, the right to alter the Prayer Book had to be asserted, as otherwise prayers for the English king would have been necessary, and the President of the United States would be left unprayed for. The constitution and the canons of the Church are therefore of primary importance and authority in America. Two most important steps were taken which separate the Episcopal Church in America from the Mother Church in England; it called itself the "Protestant" Episcopal Church, while the Anglican Church, with historical justification, has never admitted that it was a protesting Church or had its origin in the Reformation;

and secondly, in response to the overwhelming feeling of the dissenting class, which dominated the country, it gave the laity almost as much power as the priesthood. As we shall see in a later chapter this brought the Church into line with the prevailing feeling of practically all the religious bodies which had their rise in Dissent, but at the same time it widened the breach between the tradition at that time prevailing in England and the new national Church in America.

The supreme authority is vested in the new Church in a convention which meets every three years, and has two houses, one of the bishops, the other of the presbyters and the laymen, there being four presbyters and four laymen from each diocese; and both orders must agree upon any change. The several dioceses vote as units. A presiding bishop was at first chosen according to seniority, but this office is now elective, and the presiding bishop with a council now sits as an executive committee between the sessions of the convention. Thus the reorganization of the Episcopal Church practically set it upon a new foundation. The Prayer Book was altered again in view of the prevailing Protestant opinion, the Athanasian Creed was dropped, the comminatory or cursing office omitted, and even the wording of the Lord's Prayer altered.

The progress was slow, however, and the War of 1812 with England revived some of the old antagonisms, but from about 1835 up to the Civil War in 1861 there was steady advance, and at times even great prosperity. Nor was the reason for this success far to seek. True it is that the Anglican-Catholic tradition was not represented as the High-Church party, either now or at the time of Laud in England, would proclaim it. The whole tone was one of compromise with the spirit of English nonconformity, but at the same time it protested against much that was now dominating the whole of reorganized Protestantism in the United States. It brought again a feeling for order and beauty into the church life; it emphasized again the churchly feeling that the children of professing Christian parents were not all "little serpents damned justly" to eternal hell forever unless they had each and several a special emotional change, which assured them of the divine favor. It taught that in baptism properly administered a saving grace was imparted, and that the child then grew up in care of the historic Church and with Confirmation after due instruction was ready to partake of the saving sacrament with faith in its efficacy when partaken of with due repentance of sin and acceptance of the offered salvation.

The emphasis thus put upon the Church, the sacrament, the priestly mediation of an appointed ministry took the minds of many off the constant preoccupation with the emotional religiosity which had become the mark of the awakened churches of the dissenting type. The services grew increasingly ornate and the church buildings increasingly æsthetically satisfying. As a class of wealthy and cultivated people grew in importance, with relative leisure and intellectual interests other than religion, the Protestant Episcopal Church became increasingly the home of this element of the population, especially in the growing cities. It made no excessive demands for emotional reaction upon its ministry, and sought rather order, reverence and fair liberality in the support of churchly activities; even in regard to conduct, its emphasis was rather upon respectability and the observance of the conventions than upon any inquisitive scrutiny of personal weaknesses; it emphasized the home and the sanctity of the marriage tie, under the strong feeling of the sacramental character of the vows taken before the altar. In this it directly opposed the old dissenting view that the marriage bond was a purely secular affair and that the vows were taken before God alone, who judged the heart, and that there was no sacramental significance in the wedding service.

Not only did the reorganization of the Episcopal Church raise up again an old and important religious tradition, but it reacted powerfully upon all the various denominations, which were also undergoing change and reconstruction. It did this sometimes consciously and sometimes quite unconsciously, particularly as the fundamentally priestly character of its ministry became more and more pronounced.

The contrast with the reorganization of the newly awakened conventicle type of piety was sharp and became more and more clear-cut. This type one may see best illustrated in the wonderful progress and surprising services of the newly organized Methodist churches. Methodism suffered from the defeat of England in the War for Independence almost as severely as did Episcopacy. The ministry, like the ministry of the English State Church, had been almost all drawn from England, and save Francis Asbury almost all returned to England. Asbury remained, but he was suspect and compelled to remain very quiet, once even suffering arrest. Nevertheless, he continued to work and hope, and even through the war he slowly increased the depleted numbers of the Methodist connection, and when the war closed he was at once at work, raising up not only churches but training leaders and workers.

To understand the wonderful success of Methodism, it is necessary to remember just what the character of this newly organized force was. We have seen again and again that the weakness of Dissent was its lack of organi-

zation, and even its suspicion of too great ecclesiastical
strength. John Wesley, however, came out of a home
where the training had been in the close priestly organization of a very High-Church convert from Dissent. The
various Methodist bodies are expressions of a powerful
combination of the habits and ways of religious thought
that are rooted in fourteenth-century English Protestantism and the close churchly organization characteristic
rather of the Catholic tradition than of Dissent. Methodism retained the bishop, but only as an administrative
officer; it retained the sacraments, but simply as beautiful
memorials of Christian dedication and social service; it
retained a certain amount of ritual and churchly order,
but as administrative machinery rather than as reminders
of historic continuity with a priestly past.

On the other hand, it systematized and reduced to
order some of the most striking features of scattered
Dissent in the older days. It took up the revivalistic type
of religiosity developed by the generation of Jonathan
Edwards, but which was older than the Great Awakening
that brought it into such signal prominence. The revival
became in the hands of the Methodist workers almost a
regular substitute for the Christian year. It was expected,
worked for, prayed for, and its machinery and mentality
carefully studied. It more or less deliberately dropped
any emphasis such as old English Dissent had placed
upon the doctrine of predestination, in order to concen-
trate on the appeal to the individual and work in him
the emotional change which was the sign and evidence
of the acceptance by God of the soul's obedience. For
the old, small conventicle, with its warm but rather inquisitive interest in each member's spiritual welfare,
Methodism set the class meeting, which was to be the
training ground for all in the spiritual life, but especially

the opportunity for the older and more experienced members to draw the younger ones into the immediate activities of the Christian Church.

We shall later see how important a part the lay element was to play in the religious life of the United States; this was not neglected by the various Methodist bodies, but was systematized and organized into the powerful force of unequally trained but zealous class leaders, field preachers, itinerant pastors, who at first were moved from place to place lest the lack of training should mar the ministry. Out on the frontier especially did Methodism do its work. Bishop Asbury set the example, and even the missionary activity of Saint Paul hardly stands comparison. Thousands of miles on foot, on horseback, in peril by land and water the devoted missionary wandered, and before he had closed his career, he saw a reorganized type of Protestantism that has never departed far from the original lines of his laying down. Methodism has split into many bodies, true to its dissenting origin, but it has carried into all its branches substantially the same methods of work. Its theology is quite old-fashioned, but this has never been central to the life of Methodism, which subordinates everything to the emotional appeal, and uses the cross, the blood atonement, heaven and hell, free grace, love and service, in all the varied adaptations to various levels of culture which the Christian experience of nineteen centuries has slowly evolved.

The scattered three hundred members without leadership, which Asbury found when he began to try and gather the fragments, has grown to what the last estimate in 1926 puts at 8,798,745 members of all bodies. Nor are these figures, however we may distrust ecclesiastical statistics, likely to mislead us as to the power of the Church. Next to the Roman Catholic communion, and

alongside the Presbyterian Church, it is the best organized
ecclesiastical body in the United States, and like the Roman communion it is not afraid from time to time to take
a stand in political struggles, as the history of party strife
in Illinois has demonstrated. This neither the Episcopal
Church nor the Presbyterian body is likely to do, and for
various reasons, but chiefly because the laity would not
follow clerical lead in either of these communions, while
the clergy and the lay workers in the Methodist Churches
are more nearly related in social outlook both to each
other and to the great body of the membership. Moreover, even the most skeptical as to statistics can see in
the rising buildings and the expanding activities of the
Methodist communion an evidence of its vitality. Stone
and brick are not evidence as to the truth of any religious
claim, but they do furnish a measure of the strength of
the convictions of those professing that faith.

The Congregational Church, that typical dissenting
body in New England, from which had gone forth a theological formulation by Jonathan Edwards well calculated
to furnish a basis for revival religiosity, had not escaped
severe criticism even at the time of Whitefield's most signal success. Especially had the grandfather of one of
Harvard's influential presidents led the attacks upon the
extreme and sometimes vulgar presentation of the emotional appeal. These critics turned to the intelligent
leadership of New England at a time when everywhere in
Europe various shades of Deism, Arianism, Socinianism
were rife in all reading and thinking circles. The Congregational churches were not, strictly speaking, a
Church but a loose federation of autonomous bodies,
and one by one, as the original revival enthusiasm died
down, these churches went over to various shades of
Arianism and reverent questioning of the revival type of

tradition. At last even Harvard accepted an anti-Trinitarian teacher as a member of the theological faculty. Then arose those leaders to whom reference will be made hereafter, such as Channing and Theodore Parker, whose great gifts and vital religion made them a power in all thinking circles, and a reorganization of Congregationalism on some other basis than that of the past became necessary.

Here was a very serious difficulty facing the strong individualism of all the dissenting churches that still refused any firm ecclesiastical superstructure such as that of the strongly sacramental communions like the Episcopal, Presbyterian or Lutheran Churches. And it was at this time that a form of organization presented itself which was in truth old, but the development of which was due to special circumstances in the State Church of England, as well as in the State Churches of Germany. From the time when a society was formed in England in 1698 "for Promoting Christian Knowledge", because the actual State Establishment was either cool or antagonistic to the type of Christian knowledge to be promoted, there arose in both Germany and England societies for doing that which the State Establishment refused to do. So in Germany there arose the Canstein Bible Institute in Halle and the many pietistic enterprises which still exist either in coöperation with or independent of the State Churches. In England we find the "Society for Promoting Christian Knowledge among the Poor" in 1750. Then Sunday schools in 1785 organized as a "Union." After that came the "British and Foreign Bible Society" in 1804, of which we will speak later. Then came a number of missionary societies, like that of the Baptist body in 1792 and the London Missionary Society in 1795. The "Society for Propagation of the Gospel in Foreign Parts" had always been active in the colonies, having been founded in 1701 by a Virginia clergyman in England to maintain the Established Church in America.

The conventicle type of Protestantism, such as the Congregational and Baptist communions, unwilling to give up its individual freedom, began to seek coördination by means of societies supported in common and dependent upon the like-minded majority. It was easier for the Congregational churches which held on to the traditional theology to coöperate with the Presbyterians in the support of independent societies than to surrender their individual liberty, or to coöperate with anti-Trinitarians. These independent churches were in the habit of forming associations in which like-minded churches and ministers could work together for common ends. Thus, for instance, all the work of the anti-Trinitarian churches was done by such independent associations, which had only advisory power. Hence when the zeal for foreign missions was awakened by the petition of some Andover students, under the leadership of Samuel John Mills, to be sent out as missionaries, the General Association of Massachusetts, which had rejected the "liberal" theology, and still stood for the emotional revival type of Protestantism, with the work of Jonathan Edwards and his teachings in the background, formed the "American Board of Commissioners for Foreign Missions" in June, 1810. But there arose now a new element in the situation. This Board of Missions had prospectively to hold property and administer funds. A gift of some thirty thousand dollars compelled it to seek a charter from the State of Massachusetts, and as churches in the United States have only legal existence as corporations, this charter provided for a self-governing body.

In 1812 some eight Presbyterians, who had rather more

sympathy with the revival type of piety than with the stricter and more theological, as well as more churchly Calvinistic type, were invited to join the American Board and did so. Thus arose a new form of organization with large property interests soon exercising a very great influence upon the whole development of these independent churches. So also the Baptists, who were quite as strongly individualistic, but who had also formed loose associations for mutual protection and common work, were soon found forming a similar society, "The American Baptist Missionary Union", in 1814. The reflex influence of these property-holding corporations was very great. In the first place, such boards and societies had to seek support, and found it only from the like-minded, and thus had a very great interest in maintaining an effective like-mindedness. The Unitarian societies hardened into a sect instead of being simply an intellectual tendency. Shades of special orthodoxy became rooted in the life of such associations and boards. The financial aid that such societies gave to individuals and to churches was more and more conditioned upon these being in accord with the views and prejudices of the majority of those supporting the society by gifts and personal support. They began very distinctly to limit the freedom of individual churches and to exercise an unofficial oversight in questions of orthodoxy and conduct. In the second place, there grew up inevitably a body of officers who were elected to take charge of the affairs of the society, and who in theory had simply to carry on the work in hand. These were generally chosen, however, for their supposed power of management and their knowledge of the supporting body, and as was natural such officers were at work all the time and had all the information with regard to the society in question at hand. The associations to which they had to appeal for funds met only from time to time, and had to trust the reports of the executive officers of the reporting boards and societies. In this way arose out of the relatively formless conventicle type of churchly life a very strong denominationalism and a new type of denominational loyalty.

In this way, for instance, the American Board of Foreign Missions has become for all practical purposes a purely Congregational body. When the wing of the Presbyterian Church that had become strongly dissenting in its spirit through contact with the Congregational churches in New York and Connecticut broke away in 1837 and formed the New School, it did its work through the interdenominational "boards", but on the Reunion in 1870 this support was withdrawn, and from that time on the support has had to come almost exclusively from the Congregational churches. In the same way the work of home propaganda has to be carried on by boards and societies that are legally independent, but whose teaching and policy are determined by the financial supporters to whom the society through its officers must appeal. In this way, in spite of all prejudices against ecclesiasticism, the conventicle type has become and is steadily becoming more churchly in outlook and feeling. The property held by the societies and boards nominally independent is looked upon as denominational property, and the interests of this property demand some kind of unity and cohesion for its protection. Tests of orthodoxy are in various ways quietly enforced, and the ruling executive officers are looked to, as the administrators of the funds entrusted to these societies, to see that no too wide divergence from the average opinion endangers the support. In this, of course, the administrators, who must collect the funds, have also a lively interest.

This interesting development again places the accent upon cult, for it is easier to win men to cult than to opinion. In all the churches of former conventicle type the demand is increasingly heard as the churches acquire wealth for "enrichment of the service." The example of and rivalry with more ecclesiastically organized bodies direct this development. All the administrative boards and societies are directly interested in maintaining and increasing the strength of the giving churches, and in making them on the one hand soundly denominational, and on the other attractive to the youth that otherwise might be lost to the denomination. The result of this process has been a reorganization of all Protestantism. This reorganization began shortly after the War of Independence, but is still going on, although the main lines were already laid before the great invasion by other types of religious experience during the eighteenth century, which we will study later on.

Presbyterianism, for instance, also suffered much from the confusions of the War of Independence. The revival type of evangelism that came into vogue about 1735 was based upon the extreme assertion of the supremacy of God's will found in English Dissent, and was taken up by the Calvinistic Presbyterians and wedded rather crudely to their theology. The result was a mingling of two types of religious experience which in reality are somewhat far apart. The congregationalized Presbyterians, and the presbyterianized Congregationalists took some time to find out the difference, and the result was confusion and often unnecessary division. The reorganization took too little cognizance of the essential differences due to history and religious philosophy. And it lay in the nature of English Dissent to ignore historical authority. As soon as reorganization began, it was on lines of practical experience, rather than upon any feeling for the continuity of history.

Up to the middle of the nineteenth century, the population affected by this Protestant reorganization was relatively homogeneous and was overwhelmingly of Anglo-Saxon origin. It is very surprising that in the histories of this period neither the almost complete collapse of Protestantism in its organized forms nor the remarkable recovery and reorganization of its forces seem to have been noticed. The agitations preceding the War of Independence, the inner struggles and sufferings of the war period, are not enough to account for what can hardly be called less than amazing phenomena. Perhaps it was due to the fact that a revival type of religion had become so completely identified with Protestantism that when the social and political circumstances made this type of activity almost impossible, there were no other forms to take its place; added to which was the fact that those churches in which the ritual and cult might have saved the continuity were deprived of their leadership by their loyalty to England. But another explanation is also possible; this period represented a tremendous economic change as well as a political revolution. The dissenting mind had to adjust itself to another range of thought and experience. It is often hard to say whether the dissenting mind is the cause or the effect of particular circumstances or of special kinds of mentality, but at all events the political adjustments that seemed to be made so independently of all religious tradition nevertheless are marked by just those features which we have so often noticed in connection with the long struggle of Dissent for place and power. We see the intense individualism, the fear of central government, the tough passive courage, the trading mind, the relative formlessness, the æsthetic bareness, the provincialism and the ethics of English Dissent surviving both the collapse and the disasters of the war, and reasserting themselves not only in the re-organization of Protestantism but in the political reconstruction of the new republic. To this economic change we must now turn.

CHAPTER XVI

RELIGION AND AMERICAN CAPITALISM

In a very well-known essay by the inspiring German professor, Max Weber of Heidelberg, who has recently passed away, and which may be found in the "Archiv für Sozialwissenschaft", Vols. XX and XXI (1904–1905), there is a treatment of the question of the relation of Protestant ethics to the prevalent spirit of capitalism, that is already finding echoes in the United States and England. This essay, as well as the volume of Mr. Tawney,[1] contains so much that is instructive and suggestive that it is well worth while to examine the main assumptions a little carefully and critically.

In the beginning of his essay Max Weber emphasizes the undoubted fact that the great capitalistic development of the last century and a half has been largely in Protestant countries and in Protestant hands; and that in countries with a mixed population it is the Protestant elements that in general have come into possession of the greater share of the productive machinery and accumulated wealth. He reviews several historic circumstances that have contributed to this result, and although admitting their share regards them as insufficient to explain alone this social phenomenon. Curiously enough, he omits a biological explanation that has surely something to do with the situation. Since the time of Gregory VII (1073) the Roman communion has steadily demanded that the most religious and most eager members

[1] R. H. Tawney. "Religion and the Rise of Capitalism." pp. 212, 316, 317, 319 ff.

of the body should take orders and remain childless all their days. These are the members, for the most part, who have the greatest desire to learn and to forward the work of the community. To the monastery and the Roman Catholic priesthood the world owes great debts; we need only to think of the manuscripts of the Middle Ages and the scientific work of men like Mendel. But just as far as they are devoted members of their Communion they are forbidden to hand down their gifts to mankind in a posterity worthy of them.

What would Protestant culture seem to be like, were the Protestant manse with its sometimes over-abundant child life left out? Even Wyclif noticed the loss to England and longed for the married priesthood, which the later Lollards introduced.[1] Whatever may be the advantages to the organized Roman Catholic Church, that insists upon this measure, to the Roman Catholic community as a fighting unit in the struggle for existence the losses of a childless manse must be enormous. When one sees what the few Protestant manses have given France, out of all proportion to the numbers of Protestants in France, it must surely raise many questions in a thoughtful mind.

No one will be inclined to minimize the differences between the Roman Catholic communion and the Protestant bodies, but the differences are not nearly as much theological as they have commonly been supposed to be. In point of fact, Protestantism has taken over from historic Catholicism the great body of its theology. The

[1] "*O quam sanctum et fertile foret regnum Anglie, si ut olim quelibet parrochialis ecclesia haberet unum sanctum rectorum cum sua familia residentem, quodlibet regni dominium haberet unum justum dominum cum uxore et liberis cum proporcionali familia residentem; tunc enim non sterilescererent in Anglia tot terre arables nec rarescerent ex defectu iconomie tante caristie artificialium peccorum terre nascencium, sed regnum habundaret omni genere huiusmodi bonorum, adessentque servi atque artifices labori debeto, per civiles dominos mancipati.*" De Civili Dominio. Tome II, p. 14.

main differences lie in the domain of cult, outlook upon
life, attitude to authority, estimates of value, rather than
in that of dogma. Theologians are in fact everywhere
inclined to greatly overestimate the place theological
opinion has in separating various religious bodies. These
theological differences are often a pure afterthought
to justify separations that have a quite difference basis.
Thus with Calvinism and Lutheranism as Troeltsch justly
remarks: "It (Calvinism) desired in the beginning as a
daughter of Lutheranism, only to be dogmatic and
religiously a uniting Protestantism taking up into itself
all shades of correct tendencies." [1] What has always
separated Lutheranism and High-Church Calvinism is
the attitude toward the State, and the ultimate ideal of
the religious life.

It is impossible to do justice in a few words to the two
essays of Max Weber, whose range of reading and shrewdness of observation no one would deny. In general he
tries to show that Protestantism was not so much the
doing away with the regulation of life insisted upon by
the Catholic Church of the Middle Ages as the substitu-
tion of a more flexible rule. The contrast is not between
the unworldliness of Catholicism and the worldly wisdom
of the Protestant, but between types of discipline. He
seeks the explanation of the material success of Protestantism on purely religious grounds, although he admits that
other factors have entered into the situation.

For the spirit of Capitalism he takes Benjamin Franklin's "Advice to a Young Tradesman" and "Necessary
Hints to those that would be rich" as a text. He tries to
show that Franklin's ethics are not purely utilitarian,
but have as their groundwork the "Calvinistic morality
of one's calling" (Berufethik) and that in Massachusetts,

[1] Ernst Troeltsch. "Gesammelte Schriften." Bd. I, s. 609; *cf.* also 611.

at least, the "spirit of modern capitalism" preceded the
actual capitalistic development. He maintains that the
desire for gain in Anglo-American capitalism has its roots,
not simply in desire for what money will buy, but as an
end in itself, as a sign of "efficiency in one's calling", and
that this is due to the discipline of Anglo-American
Calvinism. He points out that the very word "calling"
has, to say the least, a religious undertone, as pointing to
God's will in choosing an occupation. He tries in a very
subtle examination of Luther's ethics of one's calling to
demonstrate the unlikeness of Luther's ethics to the spirit
of capitalism.

He then examines what he calls "ascetic" Protestantism and tries to show that the rise of Methodism, for
instance, is a revival of this ascetic ideal in Anglo-American lands, and that the faith that dominated the Netherlands, England, and France in the sixteenth and seven-
teenth centuries was Calvinism, with its intense expression
of this "ascetic" type of Protestantism. He then groups
together as the principal expressions of this type, Calvinism, Pietism as a child of Calvinism (which it isn't),
Methodism, and the sects "growing out of the Anabaptist
movement" (which they didn't). Then he attempts to
prove that the doctrine of predestination determines the
attitude to the "calling."

One can hardly blame Professor Max Weber, who was
not a theologian, for making the mistake so many theologians have made and treating the doctrine of election
as the distinctive mark of Calvinism. Luther, Zwingli and
indeed all the early reformers shared the views of Augustine, and the majority of great Catholic doctors agreed at
this point with Calvin. Calvin himself would have been
justly incensed had any one accused him of adding anything to the teaching of Paul, Augustine or Tertullian on

this doctrine. Moreover, as we have more than once had occasion to remark, Wyclif and the conventicle Protestantism which was a hundred years older than Calvin, and which was well known on the Continent as the heresy of Huss, was in some measure even more sternly deterministic than Calvinism. What Calvin placed in the center of his thinking was not predestination but the theocracy after the manner of the Old Testament, and it was this that gave Calvinism its tremendous fighting edge and its political significance.

Throughout all Calvin's writing there blows the hot, fierce wind of Old Testament desert prophetism, and that which Max Weber calls the ascetic element in Calvinism is nothing more than the simplicity and self-discipline that is characteristic of all primitive religions, and especially true of all desert religions, and more particularly of that primitive desert Judaism from which Calvin drew his inspiration, and taught his followers to draw theirs. Indeed, there is in all true Calvinism a primitive patriarchal element which separates it in many ways from all modern movements, more particularly from capitalism. Far from finding in Calvinism, as Max Weber does, the spirit of capitalism, a glance at the map will show that just as capitalism advanced, Calvinism declined. The country districts of Holland remained true to Calvin long after Amsterdam and the Dutch towns had adopted Arminianism. It is not in Glasgow but in the Highlands of Scotland that one looks for pure Calvinism, and it is almost alone in the mountains of the South that Calvinism in its purity, untouched by "revision" or higher criticism survives in the United States.

The railway development in the United States began about 1830[1] and at this time began also the great de-

---

[1] *Cf.* McMaster. "History of the People of the United States." Vol. V, 138–147.

velopment of the coal and iron industry, which forms to this day the basis of American capitalism; it was just at this time too that, as we have seen, the Unitarian Church completed its victory in New England and swept out rudely the last few remnants of any Puritanic theocratic thought still lingering there. At the same time, as already shown, the Arminian Methodists practically took over the religious education of the lower classes and the organizing of the religious life of the frontier. We have also seen what an astonishing revival the Protestant Episcopal Church experienced, and whatever one may think of the Thirty-nine Articles, surely no one will assert that they are the center of interest in the Episcopalian communion. It was this Church which did and still does command the sympathy of the wealthier classes, who form the mainstay of capitalism. In fact, only the Scotch and Scotch-Irish Presbyterian immigration saved Calvinism from almost entire extinction. These remained true to the faith of the homeland, and even in the uneducated classes still stood for something akin to the ideals of the Calvinistic Theocracy.

Ecclesiastical statistics are exceedingly untrustworthy, but a glance at the numbers of those churches which bear with any semblance of truth the name Calvinistic, shows that they are hardly three millions against almost ten million Methodists, three million Baptists, two and a half million Lutherans, not to speak of the sixteen million Roman Catholics.[1] And the proportions have not much

---

[1] The latest estimates the writer can find are as follows:
"The World Almanac for 1928."

Baptist Convention, Northern...................1,052,105
Baptist Convention, Southern...................2,009,471 (Should be 3,700,000)
Disciples of Christ...........................1,441,462
Congregational............................... 700,000   Non-Calvinistic.
Congregational Church in U. S................... 914,698
Lutherans (all bodies).........................2,546,127
Methodists (eight bodies)......................9,920,565

changed since what we have described as the reorganization of American Protestantism.

Indeed it may truthfully be said that the intellectual life, not only of New England but of the whole northern part of the United States, was from the year 1800 completely under the sway of the Unitarian religious movement in as far as any religious teaching commanded common assent. Even in New York in the so-called orthodox churches, the membership was regarded as

Norwegian Lutherans	289,283	
Protestant Episcopal	1,178,679	
United Presbyterians	130,348	
Presbyterian Church in the U. S.	1,868,055	
Presbyerian Church (South)	462,177	Calvinistic
Reformed Church in America	153,739	
Reformed Church in U. S.	349,771	

"The Christian Herald" census of church membership for 1928, under the guidance of Doctor Carroll, gives these figures as the latest estimate.

Roman Catholic	16,735,691
Methodist Episcopal	4,592,004
Southern Baptist	3,765,001
National Baptist (Negro)	3,253,369
Methodist Episcopal (South)	2,567,962
Presbyterian	1,885,727
Disciples of Christ	1,481,376
Northern Baptist	1,392,820
Protestant Episcopal	1,190,938
Congregationalists	914,698
United Lutheran	890,671
African Methodist Episcopal	781,692
Lutheran (Missouri Synod)	645,345
Latter Day Saints	567,319
African Methodist Episcopal Zion	500,000
United Brethren in Christ	396,946
Jewish Congregations	357,135
Reformed in United States	351,926
Evangelical Synod of No. America	336,118
Colored Methodist Episcopal	333,002
Churches of Christ	317,937
Norwegian Lutheran	294,227
Greek Orthodox	285,000
Lutheran Augustana Synod	224,529
Evangelical Church	217,935

But from the personal experiences of the writer with church statistics, he would be inclined to take at least fifteen to twenty per cent. off. The temptation for the individual church to exaggerate its numbers for the higher courts and assemblies is overwhelming and seldom resisted.

generally in sympathy with the broader views. The Dutch
Reformed Church was cold and formal, and the Protestant
Episcopal Church was still pervaded by deism and
rationalism. Professor Weber sees in Benjamin Franklin
the incarnation of the spirit of New England thrift and
worldly wisdom, and in this he is quite right, but he does
not see that Benjamin Franklin incarnates not the spirit
of the old and aristocratic Boston ruling class—for that
one must look to John Adams—but is the incarnation of
the class that in England produced Defoe and Cobbett,
and that neither John Adams nor Benjamin Franklin had
anything whatsoever in common with John Calvin. It is
probably quite impossible to rightly estimate the educa-
tive value of Benjamin Franklin, John Adams, Thomas
Jefferson, Thomas Paine, Alexander Hamilton and Madison. They laid firmly the foundations for the coming age
of commercial and industrial expansion, but to call these
men pupils of Calvin or to attribute their peculiar virtues
to Calvinistic training is to approach the absurd. John
Adams appealed to the upper class of Federal politicians,
and even when they were apparently defeated, they never
really lost control of certain situations, but behind the
scenes worked their will. John Marshall was their devoted
defender, and wealth, station and intelligence only seemingly withdrew from the political field and worked behind
the scenes where they still are.[1]

Benjamin Franklin did not live to see the effects of his
anthracite stove, but he made the capitalistic development
of Pennsylvania possible. He was quite right in feeling
more at home among the Pennsylvania Quakers than
among the high-born of Boston, for he belonged with the
dissenting butchers and bakers and candlestick-makers
from whom, however, the Boston aristocracy was also in

[1] *Cf.* Woodrow Wilson's "New Freedom."

large part descended. It is also perfectly true that he scented from afar the coming commercial supremacy of the class to which he by inheritance, taste and education belonged; but this class had nothing whatsoever in common with the aristocratic little Puritan clerical minority that so vainly dreamed in 1628 of making an aristocratic theocracy on the shores of New England, and that had long since been quite swallowed up in the great tide of dissenting immigration.

The dissenter class was, as we have so often noted, a landless class in England, where a Normanized aristocracy had made land the measure of value and its possession almost the only approach to political power. Trade, shipping and handicraft in towns and free cities gave the only chance at accumulation of the money and credit that even the landed aristocracy could not despise; out of this atmosphere came nearly all the Anglo-Saxon settlers in the New World, but it would be folly to suppose that this class was all dissenting. All we can say is that so far as it had religious ideals they were prevailingly dissenting. As we have seen, not two-thirds of the Massachusetts colonists cared enough about the churches to join them, although that membership meant the acquirement of franchise and a certain measure of social standing. In the New World land could not become the measure of value, because there was too much of it, and the colonists brought with them money and its ideals. Nor had the Calvinistic pronouncements on the subject of usury any more influence than the Roman Catholic. Roman Catholic Lombardy taught capitalistic methods to Protestant London. The morals of trade and usury are subject to class convictions and not to priestly prohibitions; the morality of Defoe's "Complete Tradesman" and of Franklin's "Advice to a Young Tradesman" is on the level of "The Wisdom of Sirach" and of much of Proverbs; and both have their origin in the stage of culture and not in subtle theological distinctions.

Of course Professor Weber was too wise a man to claim that religion was more than a factor in the rise of capitalism, but he jumbles together in his list of religious factors "as chief supports of the sense of calling in one's occupation within an ascetic Protestantism" such various things as "Calvinism, Pietism, Methodism and the Anabaptist movement." And he leaves out Luther, who taught that the servant girl sweeping out her room was engaged in as holy an office, if she did it well, as the preacher in his pulpit, and that the servant who cooked well for her master and mistress could say that she was cooking for the dear God.[1] Indeed Calvinism gave no more inspiration for the faithful performance of daily duty than do not only all the forms of Protestant piety, but of active Roman Catholic piety in many of its best phases. The struggle between the several advantages of the *Vita activa* or life of religious activity, and that of the *Vita contemplativa* or life of contemplation, is as old as religion; one thinks of Mary and Martha and Jesus' attitude; it is to some degree a question of climate and to some degree a question of class and age. True, official Roman Catholicism flung itself upon the Oriental side and in theory proclaims the life of contemplation as the higher, but not without strong opposition.[2] Modern industrial Germany is no more the product of Lutheranism than is Pittsburg a child of Puritanism.

More to the point is the fact that English Dissent is the religious expression of a class fighting a bitter fight for political power and social recognition, and in this

---

[1] For the references, *cf.* Hall's "History of Ethics within Organized Christianity", pp. 475 *ff.*

[2] *Cf.* Hall's "History of Ethics within Organized Christianity", Ch. IV, sects. 1 and 3 for further discussion.

struggle emerge the virtues that minister to the success of individuals of the class, such as hard work, a primitive type of honesty, shrewdness and temperance, whereas the luxury and leisure of the upper class are regarded as godless and irreligious. Professor Max Weber and Tröltsch, following him, are not happy in their choice of Richard Baxter as a representative of "Puritan" morality, for he was constantly wavering between the two opposing camps of Puritanism on the one hand and its deadly enemy at that time, "Independency", on the other. His very influence was to some degree based upon his blowing neither too hot nor too cold to displease any, and even in Anglo-Catholic circles he was read and enjoyed. In Baxter one finds quite impossible positions: he could defend on the one hand the Westminster Assembly and on the other hand denounce election; he even hoped that autonomous independency might maintain its independency under English bishops!

The struggle of both Puritanism and Dissent alike against the amusements and frivolities of a wealthy upper class has very little in common with the Oriental asceticism taken up into Roman Catholic Christianity, and is surely quite different in its motives and outcome. The so-called Protestant asceticism is purely a matter of obedience to supposed commands of God in the Bible to abstain from sinful occupations; it has no trace of that Oriental urge to free the spirit from all material entanglements, no matter how otherwise legitimate. Moreover, this so-called asceticism is very different according to class and manner of life. The judgments of Milton and Colonel Hutchinson and even William Penn were very different in such matters from those of Bunyan and the poor struggling Baptists. The Puritans sprang from a much more prosperous class on the whole than did the sects, and were therefore freer from many prejudices of the poorer "Independents." This fact Butler brings out in his "Hudibras."

Those who have lost the feeling for the difference between Puritan and dissenter would do well to sharpen again this sense, once so quick, by re-reading with care Butler's "Hudibras." In this exceedingly informing and witty poem Butler carefully distinguishes between the two types of mind. And it is worthy of note that Hudibras himself is a Presbyterian, while Ralpho is of the lower order and is his servant and a dissenter or independent. Thus Hudibras is the theologian, while Ralpho constantly turns to conduct and the practical side of life. He is also thoroughly well acquainted with Lollard doctrine, showing how persistent Wyclif's teaching was. Thus he says:

> For tho' success did not confer
> Just title on the conqueror;
> Tho' dispensations were not strong
> Conclusions, whether right or wrong;
> Altho' out-going did confirm,
> And owning were but a mere term:
> Yet as the wicked have no right
> To the creature, tho' usurped by might,
> The property is in the saint,
> From whom th' injuriously detain't;
> Of him they hold their luxuries,
> Their dogs, their horses, whores and dice,
> Their riots, revels, masks, delights,
> Pimps, buffoons, fiddlers, parasites;
> All which the saints have title to,
> And ought t' enjoy, if th' had their due,
> What we take from them is no more
> Than what was ours by right before.
>   "Hudibras." Part I, Canto II, 1003–1020.

Here we have a gross caricature of Wyclif's doctrine that all dominion or possession was by God's grace, and that the wicked only possessed by usurpation. And lest we be left in any doubt just at whom he is aiming, he makes Ralpho say quite plainly:

> Sure 'tis an orthodox opinion,
> That grace is founded in dominion.
> "Hudibras." Part I, Canto III, 1173–1175.

Poor Ralpho, it is true, gets the cart before the horse, but that is a favorite trick of Butler's. The whole poem is exceedingly instructive, and reveals the fact that Lollard teaching had not died out even in the time of the Stuarts.

In Holland, for instance, which according to Professor Max Weber was pushing to the front as a capitalistic country under the influence of an ascetic Calvinistic Protestantism, the life there reflected very little of what he calls Puritan asceticism. In fact, the more it prospered the more uproarious did its life become. He himself sees the difficulty, but his explanation is more complicated than convincing. He does not take into account the fact that Holland was the battleground of all Europe, and that to the demoralization of war was added the strong reaction from its sufferings in a renewed prosperity. This the poor oppressed Plymouth pilgrims felt very much in Leyden. Indeed, it is hardly too much to say that as Holland became capitalistic, it was Erasmus and Spinoza and not Calvin that dominated such minds as are at all likely to be influenced by higher spiritual considerations.

Is it not easier to explain such differences as exist in the several estimates of the pleasures of life in the Protestant Netherlands and in Lutheran Germany on the one hand, and English Puritanism and Dissent on the other, by the fact that the Reformation in Holland and Germany took hold of all classes; the princely house as well as the lowly cottage of the peasant; whereas in England one economic level adopted a special type of

Protestantism, while the upper and ruling class remained true to a Normanized and nationalized Catholic tradition? Out of the difference rose a long series of judgments of value in relation to æsthetic, intellectual, ethical and spiritual matters, in which each class passed judgment under the sway, we will not say of its economic interests, but of its class prejudices, likes and dislikes, born of the entire environment in which each class lived. Naturally the lines were not always sharply drawn, and especially as from time to time the ranks of the ruling class had to open to take in great numbers from the lower orders, and the Army, the Church and Wealth were always opening up the way to power to especially favored individuals.

Thus the English dissenting class that peopled America came with the impoverished æsthetic ideals that still mark English lower-class life. This does not, however, inhere in Protestantism as some would have us believe, for Continental Protestantism gave under the leadership of Cranach, Bach and many others a new and most interesting art, most distinctly Protestant in its feeling and spirit.

Critics of American life, both in England and Germany, have remarked upon the "acquisitive" character of our ideals, and generally laid the blame or praise upon the broad shoulders of "Calvinistic Puritanism." Here again it is no particular theological system that has anything to do with this characteristic, which undoubtedly exists. This belongs to the mentality of any race or class shut out from political power and social distinction and struggling for its possession, as in the case of the Hebrew people. The poor little conventicle Protestants of early English history gloried in the protection any gifted member brought them, when by thrift or genius such a member had accumulated wealth and power and still remained true to the conventicle. Thus accumulation of wealth became more than an individual greed, but a duty the member owed to his little communion, for it gave power to it and his class. Moreover, accumulation of money was in the beginning the only way for self-expression, for political power based upon the ownership of land was too close a monopoly to be easily obtained, and even the Army and the Church were often in the lands of the ruling class. When the same class had in the New World to reshape as it were its ideals in accordance with the new situation, there arose an aristocracy of wealth as a natural result of the two hundred years of training in conventicle ideals. Thus in Harvard, Yale and Princeton the classes were arranged not in relation to scholarship or the alphabet, but for a long time according to the social standing of the family based upon possessions. For the conventicle was far from any "democratic" ideals, to use a much abused word. It fairly cringed to any member who gained power and distinction and did not then desert it to join with the oppressors. Defoe and Cobbett are crown witnesses to this feature of Dissent, but its literature from Bunyan to Spurgeon abounds in demonstrations of it. And this worship of success had its nobler and ennobling side; for the individual worked not only for himself but for his group and his ideals. It is true that the ruling class could and did all too often buy such successful dissenting members and adopt them into the class; but that is the experience of all civilizations, and indeed the existence of a ruling class will often depend upon its ability to thus renew itself and its willingness to be thus reënforced.

At the same time the humble conventicle praised God for all such success and regarded the protection it brought as a signal sign of His favor. All this has absolutely nothing to do with fine shadings of theological opinion, and more particularly nothing to do with Calvinism as

such. It is unfortunate that a sort of Calvin mythology
has been propagated by the older writers of American
history and furthered by pulpit and after-dinner eloquence. From some of these utterances one might suppose
that the shortest road to wealth and distinction was to
become a Calvinist. But unfortunately the annals of
American success in business will not bear out this assumption. The capitalistic development of America is
linked with the success of individuals, and in the list of
such notable personalities there is no such preponderance
of "Calvinists" as the Calvinistic mythology assumes.
From the earliest capitalist John Jacob Astor, of German
descent, to the late Mr. John Pierpont Morgan, the
Episcopalian, there are found not only seemingly all
religious traditions but all nationalities.[1] In a list of
twenty-one of the richest families in New York City, as
estimated on the basis of income-tax returns at a time
when for a short period the returns were public property,
one-third were not even of Anglo-Saxon origin and only
one family might with certainty be reckoned the "old
Puritan stock" of which one hears so much.[2] In John
Moody's "Truth About the Trusts" there is an analysis
of about eighteen "groups" controlling a large part of
America's capital, and these are grouped about the
holdings of two families, neither of which are of "Puritan
Calvinistic" stock, and in these groups we find all religious
traditions represented and all nationalities, and about in
proportion to the estimates of nationality contained in
the census reports for 1900.[3] Such facts reveal the danger
of too hasty generalizations on the basis of very imperfect
impressions, and also the difficulty of any statistical study

[1] *Cf.* Gustavus Meyer's "The History of Great American Fortunes." 3 Vols. 1910.
[2] "World Almanac." 1925. P. 491.
[3] John Moody. "Truth about the Trusts. A Description and Analysis of the American Trust Movement." 1904.

of such elusive realities as religious leanings. Even Roman Catholicism, which has only recently reached any large numerical place in American life, is well represented in the list of successful accumulators of capital.

In trying to trace any connection between American capitalism and any religious faith, an honest student will be faced with the initial difficulty of determining just what constitutes a "religious faith." At this point Dissent is at a great disadvantage statistically, for the general demand in these circles is that all church membership depend upon a personal confession of faith in something approaching adult years; whereas in the Roman Catholic Communion all who have been baptized are reckoned as members, and in the Anglo-Catholic and Lutheran churches all those who have been confirmed, and confirmation is regarded as almost a matter of course and rather of family and social significance than of profound personal religious experience. The Presbyterian-Puritan tradition has in Scotland, Ireland and America rather illogically rejected confirmation, which the Reformed churches of the Continent have retained; for the Calvinistic conception of the Universal Church with an historic faith and a responsible ministry suggests rather Calvin's attitude than that of John Knox.[1] But the influence of old English dissenting circles was very strongly felt in southern Scotland, where Lollardism had made great headway long before the Scotch Reformation, and probably the hate of everything even verging upon papacy was the cause of the rejection of confirmation, so that membership in the various Presbyterian groups, like membership in dissenting bodies, depends upon a personal and relatively adult confession of faith.

Without underestimating the educational value of any

[1] Calvin's Institutes. Tome IV, Sect. 4-13.

religious tradition, it is very hard to separate it from other educational factors. All persecuted and energetic minorities, suffering under political and social disabilities, are seemingly trained thereby in the art of acquisition of wealth; one thinks of the Armenians, the Jews, the Greeks under Turkish sway, the Huguenots in France. And for this reason it is hard to say how far Quakers were trained by their faith and how far forced by the folly of their critics to cultivate the art of capitalistic accumulation; but it is worthy of note how dissenting minorities have often impressed themselves upon the life of America by their capacity in business and commercial undertakings. But about all one is really justified in concluding is: that the great and most influential proportion of the North American population was of Anglo-Saxon origin, and that the larger proportion of these came from the class that in general supported English Dissent; and that the ways of thought and general characteristics developed in this class by its struggle for power, by its religious tradition, and by its racial traits made for industrial and capitalistic progress, and that the slower processes of land cultivation were less liked and more seldom followed.

CHAPTER XVII

RELIGION AND AMERICA'S AWAKENING INTELLECTUAL LIFE

Without question the reorganization of America's political life, of American Protestantism, as well as the reorganization of her economic activity and the awakening of a new intellectual interest are all connected; but in just what way and how far they are interdependent is a difficult subject of inquiry. It is certain that the closing years of the eighteenth century were marked by an intellectual awakening that forms in American history a period to be compared in importance for the national life to the weighty period of Queen Elizabeth in English history. But as might be expected, the subjects of attention were quite different from those in a more settled culture. Artistic literature that appeals primarily to the tastes and emotions must first find a class with at least some leisure to give to the cultivation of these.

It is quite unfair to make any comparison between the intellectual achievements of some million and a half Anglo-Saxons of the poorer sort, struggling with a new climate and in altogether different circumstances from the old home, and the work of England at the same period in the field of artistic literature. Even the mixed population was in the way. The proportion of French, Dutch, Swedish and other non-Anglo-Saxon settlers was surely somewhat large, and these could not be expected to add much in the way of literature until English had become thoroughly their language. To compare the literary output of the colonies up to the Revolution with that of England is well-nigh childish. That we have so much honest work like the history of Plymouth by Bradford, and of Massachusetts by Winthrop; and that at least one theologian and thinker like Jonathan Edwards stands out as a permanently interesting contributor to the world's thought, is surprising, and is more than most new colonies can show.

Moreover, when a thoughtful writer speaks of a comparison with the literary achievements of England, he should ask *what* England? It is evident on the surface of English literature that several streams of national ambition and feeling run side by side through its pages; that when a comparison is made with the American colonies it should be class with class, stream of thought with stream of thought. One whole class, and that the most influential and powerful, was in England ruling her destinies. To this class artistic literature owed its main support, if not its main contributors. Without this class the English literature of that period would be unthinkable. But this class was wholly unrepresented in the northern American colonies and rather feebly by one or two representatives in the South. The old and æsthetically highly fruitful Anglo-Catholic and Roman Catholic population was barely represented; and what would England be artistically today were they and their work missing from English life? As we have seen, a real Catholic tradition never seems to have influenced colonial life, even at a time when it dominated the Established Church in the homeland. One influential writer on American literature kept constantly calling our attention to English common law as the foundation of our civic thought, when, as a matter of fact, one of the evidences that a different class ruled the colonies from that which ruled England is the rather remarkable circumstance that, like Cromwell's Independents, the colonists demanded written constitutions, and that no doubt from a well-founded fear of unwritten law in the hands of a class other than their own. The basis of American jurisprudence is constitutional and code law, in violent contrast to England's common law.

The intellectual activity that was soon to appear in a literature of taste and leisure awoke seemingly about the time when organized colonial Protestantism was showing signs of weakness and decay, and it has therefore often been hastily assumed that the breaking down of the "Puritan" tradition was the cause of this new activity. Now in the first instance anything that has a right to be called historic Puritanism was dead long before that remarkable awakening; and in the second place the broader religious tradition which has loosely been called "Puritan" did not, as a matter of fact, break down, but only demonstrated its vitality by that reorganization to which we have called attention. As we have shown, we hope, the reorganization of American Protestantism is based upon the essentials of the old dissenting faith.

Yet it was a time of great freeing of the spirit of mankind. The question is: What was the nature of the freedom gained that gave the colonial population such new life? It can hardly have been freedom from the British yoke, for a large part of the population did not feel the British yoke to be galling, and moreover political freedom came as a result rather than as a cause of the new sense of life and responsibility. Surely there is one possible answer to the question that has been thus raised. Every one has realized the political effects of the Anglo-Colonial victory over France, but had this not also important intellectual and spiritual results? The fear of France and still more of France's allied Red Men must have lain like a pall upon the whole long frontier, shutting out the West from the settler's imagination, and forcing home even upon those who were not immediately exposed to the danger the advantage of dependence upon England for protection. Allies in war always praise each other publicly and hate each other privately, and are both thoroughly convinced that they would have won the war alone, anyway. Now the colonies were free and had fought their way to freedom, for the Heights of Abraham had been stormed, and France was no longer a menace.

The first signs of that spiritual freedom were on the side of political speculation, and the common-sense philosophy of Benjamin Franklin. "The Federalist" as a simple literary achievement can be put with the best of the world's writing, and will have an immortal place, even when men may have abandoned the primary assumptions of the document. It would be folly for these pages to try and repeat the story of the political reorganization of the nation's life as told by Von Holtz, John W. Burgess, Charles A. Beard and others; moreover, we have seen how little organized Protestantism had to do with it. But hand in hand with the reorganization of both the political and the religious life of the nation went at last a burst of song, and an appeal to the artistic side of man's nature. This new-born sense of form and the beautiful had nothing to do with "breaking the shackles of a Puritan tradition", for it arose in the Middle States, where a Puritan tradition never had existed. Washington Irving (1783–1859), William Cullen Bryant (1794–1878) and James Fenimore Cooper (1789–1851) in no way embody any distinct type of religious tradition. Bryant, although born in New England, may be claimed by reason of long residence for New York, and alone of all three exhibits perhaps in his morbid attitude to death some traces of the dissenting feeling as seen in Gray's "Elegy in a Country Churchyard." But on the whole we have a quiet, respectful ignoring of all dogmatic Christianity, or an artistic interest in it as a part of the particular life described.

Nor was it strange that New York should see the first fruits of the new intellectual and artistic awakening, for here in a very mixed population was to be found the beginning of a leisure class and all that this implies. But it is an evidence of the overwhelming preponderance of the English lower middle class in the settlement of New York, that in spite of the fact that the English State Church had been the established Church up to the peace of 1783, there is no trace of the Anglo-Catholic tradition in either the form or content of the work of any of these early American singers of a new American song. Indeed, it is remarkable that in the work of Washington Irving, in spite of the fact that he turned with affection and interest to English life, and gave ample evidence of his sympathetic understanding of the sides of it which he saw, his romanticism is rather Continental, German and Spanish, than English.

We have seen that the development in New England is rather to be taken as the, perhaps, somewhat one-sided revolt of dissenting rebellion against all churchly and priestly authority than as a reaction against an alleged Puritan spirit, which was confined to a small governing minority and was soon overcome. This rebellion had at last free course, and with the awakening of the new life it found its expression in a new and profoundly interesting literature. Organized Unitarianism is one of the marked forms of this dissenting tradition found in America. As we have seen, it found many forms of expression and a good deal of variety in its dogmatic assumptions, but it sharply and almost fiercely emphasized at last all that Dissent had stood for in its long struggle with an historic priestly and sacramental Church. Ralph Waldo Emerson (1803–1882) is to the dissenting English tradition much what Emanuel Kant is to the Continental Protestant type of thinking. Nothing could be more characteristic of the old Wyclifian attitude toward the sacrament than Emerson's and for that matter his congregation's. He had simply lost interest in it, as perhaps Wyclif would also have done had he lived long enough, and as the Quakers did later on. Whereas Emerson's congregation would have liked to keep it, leaving every man free to take it in the sense he cared to. This attitude of relative indifference marks more strongly the tone and temper of the dissenting mind than even any open opposition. The sacrament has once and for all been relegated to a secondary place as a pious symbol, which may be kept if not abused. "I have no hostility to this institution; I am only stating my want of sympathy with it," said Emerson, and went on to say: "I am content that it stand to the end of the World, if it please men and please Heaven, and I shall rejoice in all the good it produces." Nor was the congregation far behind him, wanting him to go on and let them interpret for themselves.

But Emerson was a preacher and spent his life in most laborious and self-sacrificing proclamation of the gospel as he understood it. That gospel was the absolute surrender of the human mind to God's impelling power in reason. It was the dissenting proclamation of the priesthood of every man and woman raised to the nth power. In its very formlessness it reflected the rebellion of the early dissenting mind in the presence of classic models and class judgments of correctness. It was the climax of the long battle against the arrogance of those who had thrust a conquered class into another category of being; an assertion of the divinity of all men.

I am owner of the sphere,
Of the seven stars and the solar year,
Of Cæsar's hand, and Plato's brain,
Of Lord Christ's heart, and Shakespeare's strain.[1]

Its extreme individualism is only matched in the message of George Fox and the Quakers; its determinism is as complete as the sternest theologian could wish, only bound up with that impelling conviction that at last all would be well. "A little consideration of what takes place around us every day would show us that a higher law than of our will regulates events; that our painful labors are unnecessary and fruitless; . . . and by contenting ourselves with obedience we become divine."[2] His message is wrapped up in poetry as primitive in its form in many ways as is possible. The rhyme and rhythm are not classic, but smack of that formlessness that has ever again made protest against the rules a higher culture imposed upon English verse, a protest heard from "Piers the Ploughman" to Walt Whitman. Carlyle caught at once the note of Cromwell and the Levellers, and marked in Emerson a kindred spirit to these sturdy rebels.

And Emerson cannot be formulated, classified and set down in a system any more than can Dissent; its flying apart in sects and divisions, contradictions and fierce one-sidednesses is characteristic of his whole way of thinking, and as one ponders his poetry one hears in its echoes the clash of four hundred years of struggle.

The living Heaven thy prayers respect,
House at once and architect,
Quarrying man's rejected hours,
Builds there with eternal towers;
Sole and self-commanded works,
Fears not undermining days,
Grows by decays,

[1] Ralph Waldo Emerson. Essays, First Series. Prelude to "History."
[2] Ralph Waldo Emerson. "Spiritual Laws."

And, by famous might that lurks
In reaction and recoil,
Makes flame to freeze and ice to boil;
Forging, through swart arms of Offence,
The silver seat of Innocence.[1]

He has almost nothing in common with Puritanism
even using that term in its broadest sense; he cares nothing
for historical ecclesiasticism; a formal priesthood would
have driven him to paganism; authority and communal
discipline, such as made Puritanism a power when Dissent divided like water, would have killed Emerson;
discipline must be self-discipline, and authority only the
inner voice speaking in terms of Eternity. Pure doctrine
so dear to the Puritan heart that it meant more than
conduct, had actually no meaning for Emerson. Every
real man was his own living creed, growing if he were a
true man with each day's growth, and conduct is all and
all. "The Faith that stands on authority is not faith,"
and "Your genuine action will explain itself and will
explain your other genuine actions. Your conformity
explains nothing."

Some have tried to explain Emerson as a reaction from
Puritanism, and it is easy to show the contrasts, but he
did not have Puritanism really in mind, in the writer's
judgment, but spoke as a prophet to that coming generation which was to bury the virtues of the struggling past
in the conventionalized future of a conforming group of
ecclesiasticisms already, as we have seen, on the horizon
as an organized Protestantism. Perhaps that he was the
last of the great dissenting prophets will be the judgment
of posterity on him. He stands out in American history as
one of the characteristic voices of America's great period.
Emerson's influence in Europe both directly and indirectly

---

[1] Ralph Waldo Emerson. "Spiritual Laws."

through Nietzsche, whom he profoundly influenced, and whose poetry rings with his phrases, is still very great; and it seems likely that one day the world may again humbly listen to his voice, when reaction sets in against the standardization of life and the suppression of personality. No amount of comfort, no speed in traveling, no wonders of workmanship would have for one moment been a substitute Emerson could have accepted in lieu of that intensely personal life and individual freedom which formed the core of his message to mankind.

In the songs of another simple-hearted minstrel we hear the same accents of Dissent, and the same echoes of that long-forgotten Lollard past, when John Greenleaf Whittier (1807–1892) poured out his soul for the liberty of the slave, and yet had faith to believe that it could come without war and bloodshed which, as a Quaker and true to his conventicle past, he hated with his whole being. In him the faith of Wyclif that all unloving violence was evil and of hell [1] finds constant expression, although he had learned his lesson from other sources. As in Emerson so also in Whittier the inner voice is ever man's faithful guide if he will but listen:

> God's love,—unchanging, pure and true,
> The Paraclete white shining through
> His peace,—the fall of Hermon's dew.

In his passionate simplicity Whittier reflects the best of that passive courage which made Dissent in England unconquerable even when without leadership, and when above all without the communal discipline of ecclesiastical organization it still hid in the hearts of very simple unlettered men and women waiting to break forth in God's good time and claim its own.

---

[1] *Cf.* for Wyclif's teaching at this point Hall's "History of Ethics within Organized Christianity." pp. 378–385.

Whittier is not a great poet with large orchestral effects at his disposal; he is a pastoral songster with the flute in hand, and with simple and yet very sweet melody in his heart. His rhymes are often faulty, and his rhythms sometimes halt, but his faith is high, and hardly any of the New England voices that are from now on to express the inward spirit of the newly awakened intellectual life of the young republic did more to bridge the gap between the intellectual strivings of the radical wing of a reorganized Protestantism and the emotional orthodoxy of the revival type of religious expression.

In the history of Harvard College we may follow from the beginning of New England that change of ideals from a Puritan theocracy to the freedom of a very dissenting individualism. Without question Harvard College was founded by men who were attached to an ecclesiastical ideal and with Puritan hopes, and naming the township in which the college stood Cambridge, expressed the loyalty of, it is said, nearly seventy graduates of Cambridge among the Puritan ministry of Massachusetts. But the early surrender at Salem to the dissenting tradition in the acceptance of the autonomous church made it impossible to erect a State-Church university, and although Harvard remained nominally a State institution until the year 1866, it was really an independent corporation. For very soon in its history sectarian educational ideals clashed with the ecclesiastical interest, and in 1654 President Henry Dunster was removed for repudiating infant baptism. In his place was elected Charles Chauncy, the grandfather of that Charles Chauncy who was the chief opponent of the over-emotional type of piety advocated by Jonathan Edwards and the Revivalists.

The triumph of the dissenting type of individualism was complete when Henry Ware was elected in 1805 to a theological chair and entered upon his work as an avowed anti-Trinitarian. At that time the clergy had great personal power, but the individual clergyman was dependent upon an autonomous congregation, which called him and could dismiss him, only nominally hindered by the "advice" of a church council, whose members were of the church's own selection. It might have been possible in the beginning of the colony for the clergy, who were class-conscious enough, to have built up an ecclesiastical structure, and to have forced a common creed and an independent ministry upon the dissenting majority. Doctor Henry Cooke in Ireland under not very different circumstances stamped out Sectarianism and Arianism in the Province of Ulster and forced subscription and a strong and stern ecclesiasticism upon what was certainly a majority of the population by means of a united and self-conscious minority. But a great body of autonomous congregations with a dependent ministry and without a common creed or compulsory cult cannot establish a strong churchly mastery over an unwilling multitude. Hence, when the intellectual awakening set in, it was only a question between various shades of radical Protestantism. On the more constructive and churchly side were Joseph Buckminster (1751–1812) and William Ellery Channing (1780–1842), while on the more radical wing were the younger men like Theodore Parker (1810–1860) and James Freeman Clarke (1810–1888).

The repudiation of ecclesiastical and priestly ways of thinking was now so complete that men like George Ticknor and Edward Everett turned to Germany and not to England, for there they could find a thoroughly secularized and highly specialized instruction. There arose a school of historians, whose interest in religion was keen, but simply as a factor in culture and often with very vague conceptions of the real historic issues. Everything that smacked at all of an older theology was dubbed with the name "Calvinism", and "Puritan" became a general term of praise or blame for almost anything liked by one or disliked by another. Unitarianism left the laity as free to do their own thinking as did the Episcopal Church before the Revolution, and the work of Longfellow, Lowell, Holmes and other lesser contributors to the *Atlantic Monthly* can hardly be claimed by any distinctly marked religious body of thought, however respectful and really religious the attitude generally was.

It is surely a great mistake to rank Emerson with a group that generally bears the name of the "Transcendentalists", however intimate his personal relations were with many members of the group, and still more mistaken is the attempt to unwind the tangled skein of Neo-Platonism, German Idealism, Dissenting Dogmatism and French Rationalism that composed the rather unwholesome diet upon which these æsthetically starved but actively minded persons fed. Actual historic Puritanism had no objection to high art or Greek literature, but the English lower middle class was bitterly hostile in its religious prejudices to anything that savored of the ecclesiastical culture of its oppressors, and in America, up to the Revolution, had neither time nor opportunity to come in contact with high art wholly disengaged from the associations of ecclesiastical oppression; when at last the way was free to enter upon the enjoyment of the world's best art, the effect upon the open-minded ones was intoxication. One can still see the same effect upon stray individuals in America, who have been brought up in old and narrower surroundings and are suddenly given entrance into worlds of feeling and experience they have never before dreamed of as possible.

In some ways Hawthorne's "Marble Faun" is therefore one of his most interesting novels, not because he was in any way fitted to guide us into Italian life and feeling, but because we see there the unfolding of his own mentality, and read with interest the reaction of a highly sensitive mind introduced for the first time into a world that should have been from the first his own. But the narrow bounds of his outlook upon life are not those of any defined religious dogmatism, either 'Puritan" or Dissent, but simply the limitations of a countryside brought up in the simplicity of dissenting religiosity.

Edgar Allan Poe is a representative in American literature of the great mass of respectful indifference to any pronounced religious faith. This indifference is greater the most conventional Americans are probably inclined to believe, because the superstition of a Puritan background for our whole history has been fostered by so many respectable writers that simple facts as to empty churches, long years of marked religious indifference, whole galleries of public men with no claim of any kind to a religious influence or life, statistics of non-church membership and other signs of indifference, are passed unheeded by. Great bursts of national enthusiasm have been at times attended by greatly revived interest in revealed religion, as in the period that marked also a greatly increased interest in literature just after the adoption of the Constitution; but in trying to connect these epochs in some causal relationship the probable fact emerged that the two movements concerned different classes, and that both had their origin in new-found political, economic or intellectual freedom.

The pulpit has been probably in all Anglo-Saxon countries a greater intellectual stimulus than in Continental lands, and for the simple reason that the lay preacher has brought a larger range of subjects into the pulpit, and compelled the professionally trained preacher to widen his field of interests. In no Continental country has the layman had the same place, as we shall see later, in the religious life of the community. Now when the layman preaches he has no stock of past performances of the same kind which it has been his duty to study. He is generally a novice in theology and must deal with life as he has experienced it, often on a wider and always on a different plane from the professionally trained minister. Usually also the layman must interest and hold his audience by his own ability, whereas many a very mediocre preacher is maintained by the organization. Hence it happens that American general literature has probably been more stimulated by the pulpit than German or French letters have been, although not more than English literature. Emerson, like Coleridge, began life as a preacher, and more than one American preacher has in literature done at least respectable work.

Hence it may be adduced, as an evidence of the relatively secular character of American literature, that except Hawthorne no American writer has lit up a whole religious tradition in fiction, as George Eliot has done in England or Walter Scott in Scotland, not to speak of Goldsmith or Anthony Trollope. We have had much description of the ways of churches and clergymen, and some attempts at inseeing analysis, but no penetrating and illuminating work of first class. This may in part be due to the absence from our life up to a rather recent period of any really respectable representation of the ancient Catholic tradition, taking up, as it does, the æsthetic beauties of all the arts. Whether any one dislikes or rejects the Temple with its sacramental magic in the midst, and its ministering priesthood pointing ever to the past in defense of the mystery, no one can live in the immediate contact with these memories and fail to be in some measure moved and even molded in matters of reverence and taste.

As our political institutions rose at a time when organized Protestantism was shaken to its foundation, so also American literature rose side by side with a reconstructed Protestantism, and though not unaffected by it and its struggles and perils, yet in a very marked independence of it, and sometimes with a downright misunderstanding of its power and meaning, and very often in entire indifference to it.

CHAPTER XVIII

THE LAY ELEMENT IN ANGLO-AMERICAN DISSENT

Properly speaking there is no "Dissent" in America, but in England this type of Protestantism is still struggling against the disapproval of the controlling class, and up to quite recent years English Dissent markedly influenced American religious development; hence for convenience we still use the term. From time to time we have had occasion to notice the place the lay preacher has had in English Dissent, indeed, ever since the time of Wyclif's lay preachers the very existence of the conventicle type of religious tradition depended upon the possibility of the layman carrying on the worship and organization of the several groups. We have seen how Brewster maintained the little Plymouth Colony, and directed the religious life and worship to the satisfaction of all. The Puritan attempt to create by means of a theological school a learned and exclusive ministerial class soon broke down, owing to the needs of poor communities that could not support even in a mean way an educated ministry.

In the Great Awakening of 1732 on the clergy led, but soon the old need for preaching, even if more inspiring than instructed, asserted itself, and there was soon a lay or almost wholly untrained ministry in the field. After the reorganization of Protestantism, as we have seen, on a much slighter theological basis than the Continental type of Protestantism demanded, the place of the layman was most distinctly recognized in the Methodist bodies, but practically all American Protestantism made a place and a large place for him. In England the Methodist preacher might not only be a layman but a laywoman. The Quakers also sought not the instruction of the schools but, as they thought, the leading of the Holy Spirit, and even though they soon had regularly recognized preachers, teachers and leaders, every layman might instruct and teach when the Spirit moved him to do so. It was only a question of the acceptability of the layman's ministry.

The rise of corporate property introduced another element into the situation. It was a part of the strength of the old conventicle that it had no corporate property either to hold the body together or to be protected by evasions and conformity. As, however, even the poorest and most insignificant little sect in America began to share in the rise in the value of houses and land in the new Republic, corporate property demanded watching and care, and this task fell naturally to the business class, that had training in such matters and had largely contributed the property. Large vested interests arose, and these also demanded expert advice, which often only the layman was in a position to give. Two of the most famous cases in American Church history are the defense of the taxpayers of Virginia against the demands of the Episcopal clergy, to which we have once before alluded, and the Dartmouth case, in which Webster laid down important constitutional law in the case of a primarily religious charter. And hardly secondary to these is the well-known decision of Judge Patterson in the case of dividing the property of the Presbyterian Church after the division between the New School and the Old.

After the revivals that followed upon the closing of the War of Independence there arose weekday prayer meetings almost wholly in the hands, at first at least, of laymen; and these together with the class meetings of the various Methodist bodies gave the laity a training in public speech and in the conduct of consulting bodies only secondary, if even that, to the training they received in political life. Any one accustomed to the atmosphere of religious life in either France or Germany cannot but be struck on going to England or America by the lay element in the dissenting circles of all denominations. In England, even in the State Church, there arose a demand for activities that the State was not in a position to carry on, as, for instance, missionary enterprise; and there also the "evangelical" party formed societies that were intended to meet such needs, and again laymen were needed not only as givers of the needed money, but as advisers and protectors of the enterprises.

It is tempting to try and connect such lay activity with the lay movement of the Middle Age fraternities, like the Franciscans, from whom, perhaps, Wyclif did actually gain inspiration, or with the craft guilds under religious leadership, and yet made up of laymen. But a closer inspection of the facts will not bear out the analogy.[1] The motivation was quite different, nor was there any such blotting out of the sharply drawn line between lay and clerical as took place in dissenting Protestantism. Lay activity rose naturally out of Dissent's emphasis upon the priesthood of all believers, and the relegating of the ministry to a purely functional office of the autonomous church. The lay brothers of a Middle Age order hoped to share in the treasures of salvation laid up by the order, while no such thought could occur to an evangelical dissenter. The importance of the lay element increased as the reorganization of Protestantism opened

---

[1] *Cf.* Mueller. "Kirchengeschichte." Bd. I., ss. 471-472, 565 *ff.*, 572 *ff.* Also Adolf von Harnack. "Das Moenchtum, seine Ideale und seine Geschichte."

up new opportunities in which they could serve as well or even better than the instructed clergy.

John Wesley is the father of the Sunday school, for he and his little group began as students to gather the ignorant little boys in the slums of Oxford to teach them their letters so that they might read the Bible and the Church catechism, and in 1737 he had already established Sunday schools on the missionary journey to America. But the movement was organized and made interdenominational by the work of Robert Raikes, the son of a printer, who in 1782 established a Sunday-school union that has never ceased to operate. It was soon a matter of experience that laymen and women could just as well instruct children in the elements of reading the Bible as theologically trained preachers and in some respects even better. At first the reading of the Bible and the catechism was about all that the Sunday school aimed at, but it has gradually extended its scope and in some respects its efficiency. As it made its way everywhere in reorganized Protestantism, it enormously increased the activity of the lay elements of the churches, and the general theory was that every converted boy and girl, no matter how ignorant, could trust God's Spirit to guide them in instructing still more ignorant children. This was the firm and humble faith of all conventicle piety, in which the infallible Bible made all men and women equal so long as they had the Holy Spirit to lead them into all truth. The methods of modern pedagogy were then unknown. It stands to reason that with the exaltation of such lay teaching the crude and undisciplined theology that marks even educated Protestantism in America and to a less degree that of Great Britain became thoroughly entrenched. The Sunday school could go with slight expense everywhere, and was the pioneer of the church. It could work with the united ignorance of many different denominations, and it had its crude songs, its still cruder theology and its sincere devotion as a priceless gift to the great frontier as well as to the growing heathenism of the increasingly cosmopolitan city. It did not excite the jealousy of the established clergy, for it readily became attached to the organized church and increased its membership. Not even the Catholic and Continental types of Protestantism in America, in which confirmation classes might seem to make the Sunday school superfluous, could resist the innovation, and somewhat grudgingly even these yielded to the pressure of the lay element inevitably brought in by it, even though foreign to their spirit.

Out of the revival of interest in religion arose all manner of societies, but particularly Bible societies. It was natural of Protestantism to set the Bible up instead of the Church or the pope as the final authority. Already in Germany even before Luther the Bible had been circulated, but Luther's translation gave to Protestantism its arsenal of weapons. Nevertheless the Continental type of Protestantism never thought of the Bible alone without the old historic creeds as a means to its interpretation, until the great reaction against the relative deadness of Lutheran ecclesiasticism gave rise to that Pietism, which has always had a close connection with the evangelical thought of Holland, Switzerland and Great Britain. The Canstein Bible Institute in Halle to which we have once before alluded is still shown to visitors at work as in older days in the distribution of the Bible in many languages. This agency was the work of Baron von Canstein, (1667–1719) who together with Spener and Francke, the founders of German Pietism, was bent upon distributing the Bible in all languages among all people. In England this same motive was very strong. As over against the outward authority of the pope the temptation to put the outward authority of the letter of Scripture was irresistible. Several societies undertook the distribution of the Bible or parts of it, in many tongues, but in 1804 was founded the society which furnished the dissenting type of Protestantism with its model for all lands. The British and Foreign Bible Society was not nominally a dissenting organization, but arose out of the Evangelical Revival in England, that had awakened to new life the Protestant elements in the Established Church. These evangelical clergymen were alike disliked by the conventionally respectable Tories and the politically minded Whigs like Sydney Smith, who grouped them all together with the Methodists as "fanatics" and enemies of the orthodox faith. The Tory so-called "High and Drys" would have had little power to save the Establishment, but the Evangelical party soon aroused to new life the active opposition of the old Anglo-Catholic party, an opposition that sprang to the front as the "Tractarians" and in spite of the defection of some of their ablest leaders, who went over to Rome, soon captured the Church for the historic position, which has been the real religious tradition of the Establishment since very early days.

The evangelical party had at that time the almost undivided support of the revived Episcopal Church in the United States, whose membership was composed in the main of exactly the same class that fought Rome all down the ages. These gloried in the name "Protestant" and hailed the British and Foreign Bible Society as a kindred organization to the many that were springing up in the United States everywhere, and as destined to carry evangelical principles to all the earth. In the British and Foreign Bible Society the lay element had the upper hand, and Dissent was equally represented with the State Church. Had High-Church Anglicanism been at that time really awake this could not have happened in England, though it might have happened in America. Naturally as soon as Anglo-Catholicism became alive to what was happening it took alarm. The Anglo-Catholics objected strongly to sending out the Bible without authoritative notes, and to the fact that the Society accepted the coöperation of anti-Trinitarians. But as yet the Anglo-Catholic High-Church revival had no place in the United States, and as we have seen the Protestant Episcopal Church had made room for that most distinguishing mark of all conventicle Protestantism, namely the layman. The lay element in American Christianity has been greatly emphasized by the spread of foreign missions. The Roman Catholic missions from earliest times were a part of the imperial claim of a priestly Church to rule the world in God's name. They were carried on, for the most part, by men and women who had been set apart by solemn vows to carry the saving grace of baptism to the unconverted and to bring them under subjection to the sovereign pope at Rome. The mainspring of their activity was the establishment of a sacramental church in which all men could find safety. The missionary activity of the great dissenting revival movement had as its inspiration the saving of individual souls. That saved souls would come together in churches was, of course, presupposed, but the saving of the individual soul was the main issue. From the first the lay teacher and preacher have been active, but now medical missions, schools and colleges employ so many lay workers that the whole tone of the enterprise has undergone a distinct change. Not that the old orthodoxy has been formally repudiated; it has simply ceased to be more than a transcendental background with which the ordinary lay worker has little to do. The Heaven and Hell of Dante and Jonathan Edwards have not been actually denied, but the average lay worker on the mission field in the writer's fairly wide experience does not really believe that untold millions of unconverted Chinese and Indian Hindoos are doomed to everlasting fiendish torments because they have not been baptized. And he certainly does not, like Carey on his way to India, write: "Found much pleasure in reading Edwards' 'Sermon on the Justice of God in the Damnation of Sinners.'"[1] Professional theologians still mumble the formulæ, or fence and guard the plain statements that buttress vested interests, but the actual driving force is a gospel designed to produce an emotional experience sufficiently powerful to give the life direction toward righteousness; and what that gospel is depends much upon the level of culture of both the preacher and his audience.

Thus it happens that in critical situations the lay elements in the various forms of American Protestantism exercise an overwhelming influence, both in regard to the inner organization, and also in regard to the form of the gospel proclaimed. Professional scientific theology has but little place in their interest, but familiar phrases must be used, and intellectual innovations are regarded with suspicion. Theodore Parker was long regarded with deep suspicion by cautious Unitarianism in Boston, and creedal changes excite seemingly quite as much opposition among the laity as among the trained clergy.

Another institution sprang directly out of dissenting circles in the North of England and the South of Scotland, where industry and business were calling young men away from their country homes to the city with its temptations.

---

[1] Baptist Missionary Society. Vol. I, p. 165. Quoted by Sydney Smith, in *Edinburgh Review*, 1808. "Indian Missions."

It consisted originally of circles for prayer and centers for Christian young men to gather together, and this idea a merchant of London, a Mr. (afterwards Sir) George Williams (1821–1905) organized in 1844 into a great layman's movement as the Young Men's Christian Association, which today encircles the world. It has reached its highest development in America, but is represented everywhere. In 1925 the active control in the United States and also in Canada passed over to a national body, but up to that year an international committee had managed its affairs. It has always been a strongly and almost jealously lay body. Of the governing board of the National Council two-thirds of the membership must by statute be laymen, and the real direction of affairs has always been in the hands of laymen, and it bears the marks of this characteristic development. Springing directly out of the evangelical revival, it cherishes almost fiercely all the catchwords of that great movement, without having any really definite theological basis, but relying upon the emotional appeal, and the power of the great and often tender associations embodied in the evangelical movement.

The influence of the Y. M. C. A., as it is generally known, upon the religiosity of America is very great, for although it hardly reaches directly the manual laboring class, it indirectly attracts or repels great masses of young people and molds their thought, for to many it has become the only symbol of Christianity with which they are really at all familiar. The lay secretary of the Y. M. C. A. is almost as familiar a type as the monk of the Middle Ages, and like the monk he has become the poor and badly paid idealist, who guards great vested interests. There were in 1927 some one thousand five hundred recognized associations in the United States and there must therefore be over two thousand secretaries engaged in the oversight alone, as well as a great body of teachers and various employees. The requirement of membership in an "evangelical" church is so vague, and the lack of any adequate machinery to test men for orthodoxy is so complete, that the Association will, no doubt, always dimly reflect simply the average religious opinion of the class that mainly supports it. In like manner the Young Women's Christian Association is a lay movement, and will, like the Y. M. C. A., mirror the opinions and faiths of the supporting class.

There is, of course, a good deal of quiet distrust of the whole lay movement on the part of the professional ministry, partly sincerely honest uneasiness in regard to the intellectual trend away from exact theological standards, and partly more or less unconscious jealousy of the rivalry with the Church. To many young people the Y. M. C. A. hall is all that resembles a church which is really frequented, and the High Churchman sees here no sacrament, no established priesthood and no adequate creed. The connection with the various churches is, of course, important for the association, since the funds come eventually out of the pockets of the membership of these bodies. At the same time there is no way for these to affect in any way directly the policies of the Association, and there is bound to grow up an unchurchly type of religious tradition over which the various churches will have no control.

In a less degree is the much more recent "Young People's Christian Endeavor" movement a promoter of lay religion. It is more closely united with the Church, and is more dependent upon the good offices and services of the paid ministry, the particular meeting bears the denominational marks more distinctly, and yet it also makes for an undogmatic and often very sentimental type of piety. Its effects as an intellectual trainer of youth have yet to be duly estimated, for the movement is too young to have brought forth all its fruit.

But already we may see on the horizon a very distinct type of undogmatic religiosity rising up. Having its roots deep down in English dissenting history, it is utterly unhistoric in its interest, undogmatic in its spirit, with a certain formlessness and adaptability that enable it to take up superficially into itself elements sometimes seemingly strange. The rude Methodist conventicle trying to clothe itself in the stately temple forms of the Middle-Age sacramentarian and priestly cathedral suggests irreverent reflections. Where the sermon still stands where Wyclif put it, no church form could be worse adapted to the needs of a worshiping dissenting body than the Germanic-Norman Gothic in which the pulpit is an afterthought and is attached to any pillar. Then, when that Gothic is reproduced with steel girders and cement and the whole is lit by electricity and steam-heated, the travesty becomes positively painful.

Naturally the social system in which any religion lives controls the forms of that religion. The power of the purse will, of course, be felt a little more directly where the lay element predominates, but the power of the purse is no worse than the political power to which every priestly religion seems sooner or later to surrender. Whether such a lay religion will produce a simpler and more rational theology than has grown up with the ages is a matter of pure speculation, but as yet there are no signs of such a process. Slight as is the real interest in the questions that theology raises, all that has been done hitherto is mainly to repeat or to deny the older statements.

Like the boards and committees which, we have seen,

played such a part in the reorganization of Protestant-ism, all these various lay movements have generally em-phasized in a wholesome way the interdenominational character of religious activity, but they have never really affected any definite unity, because the vested property interests, which for the most part keep the several or-ganizations apart, have remained untouched and un-discussed. And as these interests become more and more important, at least relatively, there is seen a tendency to withdraw from such undenominational efforts, and to erect more strictly denominational substitutes. Church houses take the place of the Association Hall, and supply under denominational supervision the same kind of instruction and amusements. Denominational missionary societies take up the work that the older interdenominational societies once did. Every such extension of denomina-tional work raises up a large class of secretaries, and other paid functionaries as well as a whole army of unpaid officers, who are all interested in the support of the machinery and honestly believe that any changes in the management would be harmful if not disastrous to the interests they have at heart.

The historic tendency of Dissent to fly apart is, it is true, somewhat counteracted by the vested interests that suffer under every division, but these also tend to per-petuate any division that has once taken place. More-over, as the Roman Catholic imperialism saved itself more than once from the peril of division by adopting an order or founding a brotherhood to accomplish some needed reform, so also the energies of dissenting bodies have often been given to various reform movements like Temperance, White Cross societies and similar move-ments, and restless spirits have been fully occupied with-out the necessity of founding a new denomination.

Not that new denominations do not arise, but an examination will generally reveal the fact that they are not, as once was the case, a result of strife over questions of cult and dogma, but are the outcome of the energy of individuals, often laymen, discontented with the failure here or there to maintain old standards or to welcome some seemingly needed social reform. Thus Mormonism, for instance, is, as we shall see later on, to be connected directly with the dissenting movement, but has its roots in a primitive communistic ideal, and may trace its relative success rather to its coöperative life, and shrewd leadership than to any religious innovation.[1] The use and misuse of the Old Testament can hardly be relied upon to link it up with English conventicle Protestantism. It was primarily a protest against the excessive individualism of frontier life, and is to be rather likened to such religious-economic experiments as came out of Germany and France, and especially Württemberg in Germany in the eighteenth century. These various experiments attracted indeed many Anglo-Americans of the class that has furnished the great majority of the dissenting sects, but the inspiration was almost always foreign. The part that communism plays in most of them might suggest early Lollardism, but in fact there is probably no such connection. The communistic and revolutionary elements in Lollardism have been evidently greatly overestimated; very seldom do we read of any such charge as being revolutionary being made in the great number of trials of Lollards of which we have any record.[2]

[1] *Cf.* Eduard Meyer. "Ursprung und Geschichte der Mormonen," Halle. 1912. This exceedingly interesting comparison of the rise of Mormonism to that of Islam and early Christianity, passes the economic meaning over rather lightly, but is the best study the writer has come across of the subject.

[2] If any one will go through the list of the well-known religious-communistic enterprises, he will almost invariably find Continental influences at work in the primary inspirations. The Shakers are the nearest approach to any dissenting sect of pro-

Contrary to the received opinion historic Calvinism has very little place for the layman. The laity indeed elect those who are then set apart by ordination as elders, and these with the minister, who is installed by the Presbytery, then rule the individual church under the Presbytery, which is wholly made up of ordained elders, ruling and teaching. To the ruling body the congregation promises obedience in the Lord, and ordination is for life, save in case of discipline by the Presbytery. But in the United

nounced communistic character, but their inspiration came from the "French Prophets", and although the dissenting class furnished the majority of the adherents, their general tone is primitive apocalyptic Prophetism. The oldest one of such communistic experiments is the Ephrata Community, founded by Conrad Beisel in 1732, unless the Labadist Community of mystics is included, which, however, had a very short life. Both were of German origin. Württemberg gave also "The Harmonists" and the "Separatists of Zoar" to the world. The American "Phalanxes" and "Brook Farm" owe their inspiration to the French influence of Fourier; while the communistic experiments of Robert Owen had an anti-dogmatic basis, also in the end Continental in its original inspiration. The most successful of all these enterprises is the Amana Community, and it is German through and through, still using the German language. The "Jansonists" are Swedish and Lutheran, as are also the "Bethel-Aurora Communities"; whereas the "Icarians" are French. (See the articles dealing with the several communities in W. D. P. Bliss' "Encyclopedia of Social Reform", New Edition. Also Noyes' "History of American Socialisms", William A. Hinds' "American Communities" and G. J. Holyoake's " "The History of Co-operation", Vol. II, pp. 453–465.)

The trend of English Dissent has not been toward Socialism but toward individualism, and self-expression, and although there has always been a certain primitive strain traceable in the development of English Dissent, due to the supreme place of the New Testament in its thinking, yet the conventicle type of religion has remained almost unduly negligent in regard to economic questions as well as political ones. The early communism in land in Plymouth and some of the early American settlements had no economic or religious theory behind it, so far as one can see, but was purely the result of the convenience of the moment, and passed quietly away as soon as the community was better organized and did not have to live from a common store.

Primitive religious communism does now and then, like the hope of the second coming of Christ, attract a few minds, and the apocalyptic elements in the New Testament are too obvious to entirely escape attention, but on the whole when these receive undue attention it is fairly safe to assume that some outside influence has been at work. These apocalyptic hopes, like communism, play a rather common part in the small Continental groups, in strong contrast to the very matter-of-fact mentality of the churches descended from English Dissent. Nor should anyone be led astray by the fact that reaction against the formality and spiritual deadness of a State Lutheran Church at times has produced in some of these Continental communities a very similar state of mind to that found in English dissenting bodies, as for instance in the case of the Swedish Jansonists, without at all proving dependence upon one another; indeed a closer examination will usually show that the similarities are superficial.

States the influence of the dissenting mind has been so great that historic Calvinism has had to give way and make a large place for the layman in Presbyterian churches. The American State takes no cognizance of a church save as an incorporated body under State law. The Dutch Reformed churches, in true Calvinistic spirit, make their elders the trustees required by law to guard the property. But the American Presbyterian churches generally elect unordained trustees, who are not required to sign any confession of faith as the elders have to do at their ordination, and these may be Universalists, Unitarians or even Agnostics so far as any rule goes. The trustees are chosen rather for their business experience than for their orthodoxy, and American Presbyterian churches may be often rudely divided into "trustee churches" and "elder churches" according to whether business or orthodoxy controls the life. Thus the layman has come to play as great a part in American Presbyterianism as in any of the churches more nearly descended from English Dissent.

Nor has even High-Church Lutheranism been able to wholly resist the increasing demands of the laity for recognition and power. The influence is often, perhaps, subtly exercised, but without question in the United States the layman has a place in the church life of Lutheranism ever more akin to the place he holds in Anglo-American churches.

CHAPTER XIX

From earliest times Roman Catholicism pressed heavily upon the English colonies; in the South it was mainly the Spanish form of the Catholic faith, and in the North it was the French type.

The War of Independence brought with it a reorganization of the Roman Catholic Church as well as of the Protestant communions, for up to that time the somewhat scattered members of the Roman communion were under the jurisdiction of the Vicars Apostolate in London. The number of these adherents is uncertain and the estimates vary from twenty thousand to thirty thousand of which the larger part was found in Pennsylvania and in Maryland. It is not true to say with Bancroft that Maryland was founded upon religious freedom, for only Trinitarian Christians were ever legally permitted, and in 1692 the shameful penal laws against Catholics, which disgraced the legislation of England, were enacted for Maryland. Moreover, twice the Roman Catholics were ruthlessly plundered, and although they were thought to have constituted in 1645 about three-fourths of the population, which was at that time about four or five thousand, they were always more or less subject to suspicion and opposition.

In 1632 George Calvert, the first Lord Baltimore and in 1623 a convert to Roman Catholicism, received from Charles I a grant of land immediately to the north of Virginia as noted in another connection. In the year of the grant he died, but the grant was confirmed to his son, Cecilius, who with his brother Leonard desired without question to found a sort of refuge for their persecuted countrymen. The Calverts were too wise to wish to confine the immigration to Roman Catholics. The second Lord Baltimore sent out his brother Leonard with two or three priests to take charge of the settlement, and only the upper ruling "gentlemen" who accompanied the three or four hundred lesser folk seem to have been Catholics. The Roman Catholic historians claim and, it seems to the writer, with good grounds for the assertion, that the greater number of those in Maryland who were at the Revolution Roman Catholics, were in fact converts to Rome, made by the labors of very faithful Jesuit priests, who defied all persecution and continued their work often amid great difficulties.

It was therefore rather natural that the Roman Catholics were on the whole earnest supporters of the cause of Independence. One of the signers of the Declaration of Independence was the famous Roman Catholic, Charles Carroll of Carrollton, who together with George Washington was constantly named as the wealthiest man in America, and whose well-known letters as commissioner to Canada to try and secure that country's adhesion to the cause of the revolting colonies are an important source of historical information.[1] His cousin the no less equally able and famous Reverend John Carroll, a Catholic priest, accompanied the expedition and thus came in contact with Benjamin Franklin and won his confidence and respect.

When we remember the relatively small number of Roman Catholics in the thirteen United States in 1787 it is not a little remarkable that two Roman Catholics

---

[1] *Cf.* Mary Mason Rowland. "Life and Letters," 2 Vols. New York, 1898.

were among the authors of the Constitution, Daniel Carroll of Maryland and Thomas Fitzsimmons of Pennsylvania, both men of great wealth and influence, not only in their several communities, but in the country at large. The history of Catholicism in the United States is bound up in its beginnings with the life and service of the Reverend John Carroll, whose Irish ancestry gave tone and color to the whole development of the Roman Church in America.

Important as are the contributions of individual members of the Church to the life of the United States, it is yet worthy of note how small the part is that the Roman Catholic Church has taken in the formation of the general culture. The old classic tradition of Rome has maintained itself as a theological factor without serious heresy or much deviation from the Continental type, but Roman Catholic art, Roman Catholic mysticism and literature as well as Roman Catholic music have not until quite recently been even very distinctly recognizable as the important contribution they might have been to the enrichment of the early life of the United States. An impartial survey of the history of the reorganized Church will in part explain this fact.

At the suggestion of Benjamin Franklin the reorganization of the Church was taken out of the hands of the London Vicars Apostolate and placed in 1783-1784 in the hands of John Carroll as Prefect Apostolate and Superior of Missions. Later, in 1788, Baltimore was made a See of Rome immediately under the Congregation of Missions of the Propaganda. The ability and industry of Bishop Carroll, as he now became, were beyond all praise, but the difficulties in his way were enormous. In 1808 Carroll became archbishop with suffragans in New York, Philadelphia, Boston and Bardstown (Kentucky). The influence of a very pronounced type of Protestantism made his administration difficult, for the layman has played a part in the development of American Catholicism somewhat similiar to that taken by the business man in the reorganization of the Protestant Episcopal Church, and with a result not wholly dissimilar. Supported by influential laymen, wayward priests have given the bishops much trouble in maintaining that centralized administrative authority which is the soul of the Catholic tradition, whether in its Roman or Anglican aspects.

In addition to the administrative difficulties there came the fact that the increase of the Church was largely by conversion from Protestantism or by immigration, and that in both cases the cultural unity was lacking. The hierarchy was prevailingly Irish in its ancestry, and long years of brutal suppression by a stupid English minority had well-nigh destroyed the rich artistic inheritance of the Irish Catholic Church, and reduced its membership to a poverty that precluded the cultivation of art save in its most simple forms. The passionate devotion of the Irish to their land and their religion could not supply the place of an almost demolished culture, and in the New World their contribution was therefore in other fields.

Somewhat the same may be said of the Polish immigration, which came rather later, but which brought with it the same artistic and temperamental bent characteristic of the Irish from the South of Ireland. Now capacity may be passed on by inheritance, but even the most fanatical advocate of race importance will hardly contend that old and formulated traditions are thus passed on. The oppressed and poverty-stricken peasants who constituted the great mass of those coming to the United States were not well calculated to be the bearers of the very elaborate and well-developed Roman Catholic culture.

The early Roman Catholic church buildings were as bare and uninviting as the most severe dissenter could desire. The paintings of the saints and the decorations of the altars revealed the extremely limited resources of the struggling Catholic population. The services were "of the plainest and in most cases no music", reports a Roman Catholic historian. The suppression of the Jesuit Order by Pope Clement in July, 1773, acted badly upon American Catholicism, as it lowered the general level of preaching, upon which the Catholic missions in America have always had so much to rely. We pass no judgment upon the famous Bull *Dominus ac Redemptor*, but its effects in America were hardly to promote the art of pulpit appeal, which the Jesuits had done so much to advance.

The chief difficulty with which the Roman Catholic hierarchy had to contend was the question of nationality. Wave after wave of European Roman Catholic immigration passed over the reorganized Church. Germans and Irish, Poles and Bohemians, Italians and French-Canadians were only the more noted of the various nationalities. With the best will in the world it was impossible to absorb without friction all these elements into the body of the Church. And the effect upon the Church as a messenger of its own culture was well-nigh disastrous.

The strength of the Catholic tradition in all the ages has been its capacity to adapt its central teaching to the local and artistic wants of those to whom it appealed. The central place in all Roman Catholic art must be given to its sacramental life. On the altar God is, for the Catholic, actually present, and for His adoration exist music, painting, sculpture and architecture. These must be the highest and best the community can produce; moreover, to be really good art they must have their source in a living faith in the reality of the divine presence

they join in adoring. Thus it happens that in all Roman
Catholic art there has been the very greatest national
divergence bound up with the most marked underlying
unity. Where, however, there is no native art, all that
can be done is to transplant various national types, and
this involves in the first instance wild confusion and
superficial contradiction. No doubt if the Catholic tradition retains its power over the actual lives of men in
America, there will rise again out of this central sacramental faith a living native art expression, but at the time of
the reorganization of the Church, Archbishop Carroll and
his successors had neither the time nor the means to
realize the full cultural power of the sacramental faith.

The Roman Catholic hierarchy in America has been
substantially Irish. This came about not only because of
the heritage of the Carrolls and the numerical superiority
of the Irish nationality, but also for several other reasons.
One of these was the experience the Irish had in resisting
the Protestant influences bent upon their destruction.
The education of the Irish priesthood has been unique
and given that priesthood an international experience
second to none, for France, Italy and Germany have all
been carefully drawn upon to furnish the most able Irish
priests with the best education these lands could give.
It cannot be claimed that the Irish-Catholic priesthood has
always dealt tactfully with other nationalities, but it may
be safely affirmed that probably no other nationality
would have done nearly as well, for German Catholicism
or Italian Catholicism, for instance, are far more deeply
rooted in their several national lives than is the Irish
priesthood in Irish life, and that because of its wide
international education. Reverend John Carroll, for instance, was forty years on the Continent as student and
teacher before he returned to Maryland.

Nevertheless the result has often been that the Irish hierarchy has overshadowed the cultural contributions of other lands, and in the general restlessness among other Catholic nationalities there has been much loss to the Church, at least in numbers. For although the Roman Catholic Church in the United States has grown with great rapidity, it has hardly retained all the incoming tides and their natural increase. At the same time the losses have often been really very nominal, for numberless men and women who have in the Old World been reckoned as belonging to some State-supported communion, either Protestant or Catholic, but who in fact had no real interest in the things these Churches stood for, simply dropped their connection in the new surroundings. They were no strength to the communions to which they belonged on paper, and they would only be weakness to any they merely joined from habit in the New World. More than half the American population has no sort of living interest in anything that can properly be called religion, and it makes very little difference by what name it goes.

As over against dissenting types of Protestantism Roman Catholicism demands a close and centralized organization. Some one nationality had to take such a place in American life as the Italian hierarchy takes in the life of Europe. No other nationality was as well fitted to take this place as the Irish; the fact that they spoke and wrote an exceedingly virile English alone gave them a great advantage over Germans, Poles, French, and other nationalities. Moreover, the Irishman loves his land, but at the time of the greatest immigration he had no country; he was a hated rebel in his own island. Hence he readily became "Americanized" and plunged into the life of his new country with enthusiasm and success. It would be ill-fitting to belittle the services of the Irishman as an

American patriot; for these have been not contemptible; at the same time he brought few formulated cultural achievements with him from his desolated home; the English Pale, Cromwell's Ironsides and selfish and short-sighted English landlordism had done their work too well; but he brought that feudal organization and feudal loyalty which the Catholic Church had preserved to him, and in the individualistic anarchy that so often character-ized the growth of American cities he had his chance and took it, and soon ruled the city centers of the eastern coast by virtue of his feudal cohesion.

Many a good Catholic would be the first to lament the entrance of the Roman Catholic Church even indirectly into American politics, but the heritage of hate brought from England by the dissenting class had raised up a growing and fanatical opposition to the evident increase of the Roman communion. The so-called "Know Nothing Party" was one of the first violent and organized attempts to put down Roman Catholicism by force. It grew grad-ually out of an "order" whose aims were to limit power to native-born Americans and to check the advance of Roman Catholicism. It entered the national political life in 1854 as the "American Party" and won at once several States, and put a candidate into the field for the presidency in 1856. This gave the leaders of Catholicism in the cities a good excuse, if they needed one, for entering into local politics as a mere matter of self-protection.

In 1844 churches were burnt by anti-Catholic mobs, and houses were destroyed in Philadelphia mainly oc-cupied by newly arrived Irish. And ten years before, a Roman Catholic convent in Boston was burnt down under very disgraceful circumstances. The rioting was not wholly religious in origin, for the cry that cheap labor was threatening the working class was also raised, but it was at this time that the immigration to the United States began to be almost wholly from Roman Catholic countries or from those sections of Protestant countries in which Roman Catholicism was dominant.

In a land so completely under the control of what had been Dissent in England, and in which a dissenting tradition had so thoroughly mastered the thought and feelings of even many in no way very religious, it was inevitable that there should be much friction between the incoming Roman Catholic masses and the native population. The wonder rather is that there was relatively so little. The older American Roman Catholic families in Maryland, Virginia and Pennsylvania felt themselves almost as strange in this new Catholic world as did American Protestants. They resented the social implications that the relative poverty of the incoming population necessarily involved, and shut themselves off in some measure from the new Irish hierarchy. The layman type of religious activity could not fail to influence even Catholicism. It won over Anglo-Catholicism in America, and the Roman Catholic hierarchy in the United States had many a bitter struggle with laymen in regard to the power over the property they were set in charge of by the law. For, as in the case of all churches, the Roman Catholic churches could only be recognized by the law in so far as they were incorporated bodies, and the trustees for these corporations were laymen, who, it was charged by the bishops, exceeded their powers and tried to dismiss or instate in ecclesiastical positions persons the bishop disapproved of, or was friendly to. In a series of court decisions the legal status of Roman Catholic property has been now fairly well defined, but the hierarchy still has difficulty in controlling willful priests who have strong political or financial backing, and to whom the laymen of the parish are friendly.

Occasionally small splits have taken place, like the rebellion of the "Free Polish Catholic Church" of Chicago. But as the Roman Catholic Church has gathered weight, and even begun to carry its conquests into the ranks of the ruling class, and compel political respect, these small divisions become more and more difficult and unlikely.

The Civil War of 1861 did not divide the Roman communion, but it greatly weakened the older and wealthier Roman Catholic class in the South, and thus in part removed one of the barriers to a greater social unity. Roman Catholics by all accounts did their full duty on both sides as soldiers and patriots, and on the close of the war the great tide of an immigration that had had no place in the conflict, and had no prejudices one way or other made the actual spiritual unity of the Church easier.

The world into which Roman Catholicism thus came was a wide one and relatively unorganized, so that it ran along with the dissenting tradition with less friction and with less influence upon its hostile environment than might have been expected. The older Roman Catholic families of the South had consciously kept from propaganda and viewed the eager work of some new-comers with some suspicion and dislike. Almost the only influence they had, so far as religious life went, was exercised through the exceedingly good if somewhat old-fashioned schools for girls, which were very popular both with the wealthy Protestant families and their own class. Thomas Jefferson, for instance, sent both his daughters to such a nun's school. The education was by all accounts limited in its range; French, music, drawing, needlework and exceedingly good manners were the chief acquirements; nor did the sisters seemingly make undue efforts to "convert" their young Protestant pupils, but the quiet and gentle refinement of the life did in fact often make an impression that perhaps more deliberate effort would have failed to do. At least Jefferson had at last to take his daughter away lest she should give herself to the life that had made such an impression upon her. That was, it is true, in Paris, but these schools were nearly all from France and all breathed the same atmosphere.

Later on in its history the effects of Protestant thought, both German and American, were felt in what came to be called "Americanism", of which Father Hecker was regarded as typical. The American Protestant reader of Leo XIII's Bull *Testem Benevolentiæ*, or rather letter to Cardinal Gibbons, for such the Bull really is, will often hardly quite comprehend what the issue was. In point of fact the ultimate question was whether an American-Catholicism could be called into being similar to the Anglo-Catholicism of Great Britain, in which room for national thought and feeling as over against Roman might have place to develop. This question Leo XIII answers in the negative, and for the time being the answer is final. There may arise an American Wyclif or Luther to challenge this answer, but so far none such has appeared. Moreover Rome came to have such confidence in the loyalty of the hierarchy that the American Church in 1908 was separated from the Congregation of the Propaganda and the ministry is no longer considered as working *in partibus infidelium*.

Curiously enough, the Italian immigration was at first very much neglected by the Irish hierarchy, and the wandering character of much of the Italian population made the proper care of them very difficult, but now the machinery of the Church is so large and embraces so many nationalities that, no doubt, the hierarchy will become less exclusively Irish and be in part at least unified by American training and education. From the earliest

days the Church in America has been faced with the task
of dealing with very diverse elements, from the time when
some nine hundred poor Roman Catholic Acadians, whose
fate Longfellow has so plaintively sung, entered Maryland
and had to be taken care of there, to the present day,
when from all parts of the world members of the communion seek refuge in the New World.

The full effects of Roman Catholicism upon the religious
life of America cannot be realized until it has ceased more
than it has yet done to be the Church of the newly arrived foreigner, and has successfully challenged the
dissenting type of Protestantism for possession of the
ruling class, not only in city politics but in the control of
the thinking and feeling of the great mass of the American
people. For this purpose it must have at its disposal
something of the dignity and beauty that has made its
ministry in Europe one of the elements of culture that
cannot be forgotten, and already such a beginning has
been made. From the earliest times the hierarchy has
recognized its great advantage in the matter of a worship
that makes a sensuous appeal, and has wisely tried to
build cathedrals and churches that would make such an
appeal more possible, but poverty and the cramped
circumstances of colonial life have greatly limited its
scope. The Roman Catholic Church is not "democratic",
but patriarchial, and that on principle; it is founded not
on the authority of the people, but on the authority of the
past, and that authority is incarnated in ordained persons with a head who, from the Catholic point of view,
is endowed with infallible authority when speaking from
his official seat on doctrine, and with plenary administrative authority, given him as God's representative on earth.

As over against the Protestant bodies ranging from the
extreme individualism of the Quaker to the churchly but

divided Continental type, the Roman communion has the great power of centralized authority; in many of its aspects it is better fitted than are its rivals to deal with the rapidly centralizing capitalistic State, and this pressure may have something to do with the increasing demand of thoughtful Protestants for greater unity and for some sort of federal bond. It remains, however, to be seen whether the sturdy independence of the old conventicle Protestantism will so far give up its heritage as to really make such unity effective.

As the Southern States recover economically from the war, the old and influential Roman Catholic families are certain to gain in power and social standing and will no longer hold aloof from the increasingly effective organization of the Roman hierarchy, and no Ku Klux Klan or nativistic party will be able to resist the recognition of the Roman communion as of equal standing with all other ecclesiastical bodies. The High-Church wing of the Episcopal Church will continue to give many members back to the Roman communion, for it is hard to see why such should remain Anglo-Catholic in America, when the older communion is open to them. What changes the various types of religious expression will undergo in the struggle for place and expansion no one can tell. But already the influences of the several types upon each other are quite noticeable and will continue, no doubt, to increase.

Note on Ecclesiastical Statistics

The difficulties in the way of securing any really trust-worthy statistics of church membership are very great, and partly because the definition of membership varies so much. The individualistic dissenting type of Protestantism demands for church membership a special emotional experience on the basis of which the individual "joins the church" of his or her choice. The Continental type of Protestantism counts all as church members who have been baptized and confirmed, and who take no steps to disavow membership. The Roman Catholic communion demands that members avail themselves of the four chief sacraments, and after baptism, confirmation and confession, that the member at least once a year go to confession and partake of the Eucharist. The Established Church of England counts all members who demand the privileges of its membership, whereas the Protestant Episcopal Church of the United States, like churches of the Continental type, calls all members who have been baptized and confirmed, but unlike these has special church rolls of individual membership in separate parishes. In Presbyterian churches there exists the distinction between a member of the congregation and a member of the church. Any pewholder or subscriber to the support of the church is a member of the congregation, but only those who have made a profession of faith are enrolled as full members.

In trying therefore to estimate the strength of the several types of ecclesiasticism in the United States these differences must be borne in mind. But even then there still remain great difficulties born of the way church statistics are collected. Apart from more or less deliberate swelling of the numbers returned to church courts, there is an almost unbelievable carelessness on the part of those responsible for the lists in the several membership bodies; and even a conscientious "scribe" has often no authority to drop names which he knows should be omitted. Many Protestant bodies have lists on which a third of the names represent nothing.

So in dealing with the estimates of the membership in the Roman Catholic Church in America it is often hard to say just what the reports of the membership signify, whether vague sympathy with the historic Roman tradition or active technical membership by fulfillment of the canonical requirements. The accommodations in the church buildings of Protestants and Roman Catholics give also very little basis for a comparison of relative strength, because the Roman Catholic buildings are used much more intensively than are the Protestant ones.

The estimate of the official census cannot go behind the various official returns, and we are not always told upon what basis these estimates rest. Nevertheless we can get a fair picture of the progress of the various types of religious faith by noting the given numbers and the increasing church accommodation as well as the numbers of the priests and ministers engaged. It will be only relatively accurate however.

The Reverend John Carroll, afterwards archbishop, estimated the number of Roman Catholics in Maryland in 1785 as 15,800, those in Pennsylvania as 700; in Virginia 200; in New York 1500; [1] so that the total would be about 18,200; but the estimate for Pennsylvania is certainly too low, for many German Catholics were already there, and an inquiry by Lord Loudon in 1757 gives the Catholic population of Pennsylvania as 1375; [2] there were also German Catholics in New York who, with the Irish known to have been there, must have numbered over 1500. The "Catholic Encyclopedia" estimates the number at the outbreak of the War of Independence as about 20,000 and the highest estimate the writer has found is about 24,000 in 1790.

John Gillmary Shea gives some reasons for estimating the Catholic increase as from 244,500 in 1820 to 361,000

[1] Thomas O'Gorman. "A History of the Roman Catholic Church in the United States." 1895. P. 268.
[2] *Ibid.* P. 246.

in 1830; then in 1840 to 1,000,000, in 1850 to 1,726,470, in 1860 to 3,000,000, in 1870 to 4,685,000, in 1880 as 7,067,-000, in 1890 as 10,627,000, and in 1906 as 12,079,142. These estimates are formed on the basis of official returns of various kinds, on the number of churches built, of priests known to have been at work, of immigration statistics, and on reports to the Congregation of the Propaganda as well as material gathered from reports to bishops and other official material.

In the estimates of the Reverend H. K. Carroll for the Census Bureau and published in the "American Year-book" for 1917, the numbers are given as 14,504,492 and in 1926 as 16,193,171. These figures have been challenged by Roman Catholic writers as being an underestimate based upon a too narrow definition of the term Roman Catholic. And no doubt the numbers will vary much as one defines the term strictly or loosely.

Since the World War the Roman Catholic Church has gained much ground in America, and its increase in 1927 is estimated by Doctor Carroll on the basis of his returns as 183,889, bringing up the total numbers to 16,735,691. But P. J. Kennedy and Sons, the official statisticians of the Church, report in the public press the total number as 19,689,049.

Omitting Hebrew congregations, the churches for colored people, and all churches without older historical traditions, like the Mormon and Christian Science, the chief denominations as reported by Doctor Carroll show in round numbers about eighteen millions of the Catholic type, the Protestant Episcopal Church being reckoned as "Catholic" because of both heritage and drift; about five millions and a half of the "Continental" type, including the Calvinistic Presbyterians in this category; and about fifteen millions of the dissenting type.

CHAPTER XX

The Reformation in Europe, under the leadership of Luther and Calvin and their followers, differs in many respects from the earlier English Wyclif-Lollard movement. But the main difference was in the attitude taken toward the historical development of the early Church. For all Christian bodies the Scriptures of the Old and New Testament are the rule of faith and practice, but this literature needs authoritative interpretation, and this the Continental type of Protestantism found in the creeds and patristic writings of the first three centuries. Neither Luther nor Calvin had any intention of revising the Nicene Creed, for instance, and the works of Augustine remain for both a valuable and authoritative though not infallible interpretation of the Scriptures.

This attitude determines also the character of the Church, which was for both Calvin and Luther an historical development, with a history and a continuity, with notes and marks which made it possible to say what bodies belonged to the "true" Church and which had departed therefrom. The pure preaching of the Word and the right administration of the sacraments were such notes, and this involved, as we have seen in another connection, a ministry with authority from the Church of Christ's own founding to preach and to administer the sacraments.

All religions are based upon a belief in the supernatural, and the official dealings with the supernatural are the work of an official priesthood; what is outside this is magic. The Continental type of Protestantism held very firmly to the continuity of the official Church and the official ministry; these formed the guarantee to the immature and the layman that the Word of God was being properly proclaimed and the issues of eternal life were not left to chance and ignorance. The Continental type of Protestantism had two main schools: that of Luther and that of Calvin. There were other shades of opinion struggling for recognition, like that of Zwingli and Erasmus, as well as Anabaptist sects which went further along the road of separation from the historic Church, but although these have never ceased to influence many minds, they have never succeeded in raising up organizations that could challenge the authority of the Roman Communion.

The Continental type of Protestantism has been in contact with American life from the beginning, but not until quite well on in the history of the United States has it played any very great part as a factor in American religious culture. The Calvinistic school influenced the Puritan ministry in Massachusetts, although that influence has been vastly overrated; and later, as we have pointed out, the Scotch-Irish Presbyterians carried this influence into the life of Pennsylvania and spread all over the thirteen States. The early Swedish colonies in what is now New Jersey were Lutheran, and the Dutch Reformed Church was also of the Continental type; nevertheless they could hardly resist the stream of dissenting English tradition, and did not hold their own or remain very pure in type. Presbyterianism was largely merged in Congregationalism even where it seemingly absorbed Congregational churches, and Swedish Lutheranism never laid hold upon the American imagination, and at the most simply maintained a feeble hold on the Swedish-speaking population here and there up to the Revolution. The Dutch Reformed Church never carried on any wide propaganda and acted on American life only through a few strong individuals, and without in any way especially coloring the development.

Lutherans came to America as early as the Dutch settlements, but were not given recognition in Manhattan until the English took possession in 1674, after the second occupation of the island. The first German Lutheran Church in Pennsylvania is generally stated to be that founded by the Reverend Daniel Falckner about 1703. And in 1710 a large number of immigrants from the Rhine country settled in New York and Pennsylvania, although these were not all Lutherans. In Georgia a colony of Salzburgers settled and built up a Lutheran Church. The influence of the Mennonites in Pennsylvania, and of the other German settlements there is too well known to need dwelling upon; yet on the whole this Continental type of Protestant life has had no effect upon American religious life proportionate to the actual numbers of those professing it. In part this is explained by the fact that Lutheranism is much divided, not only by differences in dialect, but also in theology and outlook upon life. Moreover, it is weakened by sectarian dissent, for a very large proportion of the German immigration to America belonged to such sects, within and without the State Churches. The proportion was much larger than in the native land, as such sects had an interest in spiritual freedom and sought it in the New World. The Dunkers, the Seventh Day Baptists, the Mennonites, the Schwenckfeldianer as well as many others less well known, like the Amana Community, cannot be reckoned of the pure Continental type. The same social and political as well as economic circumstances combined to produce in these German sects a spirit and mentality kindred to the English conventicle sect. Nor were there points of actual contact wanting. John Wesley and his friends made missionary trips to Germany, and as already pointed out William Penn headed propaganda in both Germany and Holland; while Germans were at times active in religious work in several parts of England.

Any one who takes the trouble to go a little deeper than the surface will find, it is true, a good deal of fundamental difference between the German and the English sectarianism. Wesley himself soon instinctively felt that his was "another spirit"; nevertheless the likenesses were sufficient to make absorption by the Anglo-American sects of at least the second generation not very difficult, and to obscure various contrasts. The mysticism, for example, that is found in so many of the German sects is not identical with much that is called mysticism in English Dissent. European mysticism is often, if not always, a protest against the excessive intellectualism both of Roman Catholic scholasticism and the dogmatic intellectualism of later Protestantism. It has, therefore, a different character and aim than the simple immediacy, intuitionalism, and reliance upon the Holy Spirit found in the English sects and which is often confused with mysticism. It is not easy to define in a few words the exact difference, which must be more or less experienced by living in the two worlds of thought and feeling; but perhaps it might be indicated by saying that English mysticism is concerned with the *knowledge of* God; while German mysticism *seeks union with* God. There are generally metaphysical interests in German mysticism, as that of Tauler and the "Teutsche Theologie", which are quite strange to English sectarian thought.

Even the organized Lutheran synods were rather

afraid of the tyranny of a strong central organization, and it was some time before the great body of English-speaking Lutherans in New York, Pennsylvania and North Carolina could make up their minds to come together in a general synod. It is chiefly the polity of the various Lutheran bodies that the influence of the dissenting tradition in America by which they have been surrounded may be seen. In lands where the Church was established by law the polity was determined by the facts of taxation for the support of the Church, and the constant danger has always been that a centralized semi-priestly ministry should form a hierarchy supported by the government and be at its disposal for class and political purposes. Naturally the poorer and less influential classes came to America, and these classes valued highly the privilege of self-direction in the affairs of the church which was now their own, and was supported by their voluntary offerings; hence the Lutheran congregations are in general exceedingly jealous of too much interference from the upper church courts, and the individual congregations insist upon a self-government that is very strongly congregational. At the same time, the general feeling is equally strongly churchly; the sacraments are the organizing elements in the cult. The ritual is solemn, the services are orderly and the historic creeds receive an emphasis in all branches of the Lutheran Church such as even those of Calvinistic type hardly give them; for the Calvinistic churches demand for the most part a subscription to a creed from the ordained officers only, while the Lutheran bodies in many ways make the creedal statements, like Luther's Catechism and the Augsburg Confession, the basis of the Christian profession for all members.

There were in 1906 some twenty-four Lutheran bodies,

since reduced by unions between several synods to seventeen, but the differences are often only those of nationality and speech. Danish, Swedish, Slovakian as well as German and English synods stand substantially upon the same dogmatic basis. Doctor H. K. Carroll gives the figures for the year 1927 of the four most important synods, the United Lutheran Synod, the Lutheran Missouri Synod, the Norwegian Lutheran Church and the Lutheran Augustana Synod as 2,054,772. The differences are not in regard to polity in the main, but in regard to dogma, and many times the disputes seem to an outsider relatively unimportant, but these must be judged in the historical significance they have for the contending parties. The doctrine of justification by faith alone with its implications stands always in the foreground, but questions of admission to the sacraments, of the divinity of Christ, etc., have led to much division and discussion.

In all Lutheran communities following the lead of Luther himself, the religious life centers much more about the family life and less about the organized Church than in prevailingly Anglo-American circles. The Catholic Christian year has been retained, and is made the way of approach to a Christian experience; baptism and confirmation are made much of as events in the family life as well as ecclesiastical happenings; the German emphasis upon Christmas Day, for instance, has affected American usage, and the type of piety engendered by this festal usage is very distinctly different from the Anglo-American tradition, even where Episcopacy and High-Church Continental Calvinism has somewhat modified the atmosphere of flight from the world that has deeply marked dissenting piety.

German Pietism was a strong reaction from the excessive scholasticism of official Lutheranism, whether the rather doubtful connection with Calvinism maintained by Ritschl[1] be accepted or not. And there is no doubt that the emotional and personal notes in this school of thought made Lutheranism where Pietism prevailed more accessible in America to Anglo-American influences.

As in all religious bodies the period just before the War of Independence was a time of relative inactivity in the Lutheran churches. The sects like the Labadists and Mennonites grew by natural increase, and received but little addition from Germany. The second and third generations did not always share the religious enthusiasm that brought the original settlers to America. Many became identified with the surrounding population, and mixed marriages often told against the increase of the various churches. Synods were formed among the Lutheran churches; in 1748 Mühlenberg and others formed the Synod or Ministerium of Pennsylvania. In 1786 the Ministerium of New York was formed, but only after the second war with England did the immigration from Germany begin to take on the proportions which it assumed later, and with it began the great increase of the Lutheran churches. The great revival movements that brought such increased activity to the various Protestant churches of dissenting origin were for the most part disliked by the German Lutherans, and they relied upon the steady normal work of the pulpit and the church for the maintenance of the religious life; nevertheless, it was impossible for the churches to do their work in the atmosphere created by the revival without being in some way influenced, either by repulsion or attraction.

The spiritual relationship between German Pietism and the religious life resulting from the Anglo-American Great Awakening was best brought out in the works of

[1] Albrecht Ritschl. "Geschichte des Pietismus." 3 Bde. 1880–1886.

redemptive social helpfulness which mark the two movements, all branches of the Lutheran Church sharing in the
stimulus thus imparted. The necessity was very great in
the United States, where the works of mercy were very
largely left in the beginning of our history to private
enterprise, and the condition of the newly arrived im-
migrant was often very pitiful. Everywhere arose under
the care of the Lutheran churches homes for orphans,
hospitals, schools and rescue houses for the socially
disabled, and the German capacity for effective organization and economical management made these generally very admirable; yet it is hard to say that they directly influenced the philanthropy of the Anglo-American
churches, although there was, no doubt, more or less in-
teraction.

The children of Lutheran parents belonging to churches
in which the services are held in the old mother tongue,
are very apt to drop away from the church altogether or
to join themselves to English-speaking bodies, but there
are no trustworthy statistics as to the preferences of such
children for any special type of English-speaking Protestantism. The English-speaking Lutheran churches seem
to hold their own and are increasing in membership, but
here again it is impossible to say how far they are confined in their increase to European immigration and the
children of immigrants. The emigration from Europe in
the last ten years seems to show a larger proportion of the
Catholic than of the Protestant type, but here again
statistics are not very trustworthy.

In other chapters there has been occasion to deal more
or less at length with the Calvinistic type of Protestantism, which has come to America almost wholly in the
form of English Puritanism or Scotch and Scotch-Irish
Presbyterianism. As we have seen, the influence of

English Puritanism was confined to the clergy and a few of the leaders of Massachusetts, and soon was quite swallowed up in Congregational Dissent. At the same time it stressed again the old Wyclif-Lollard teaching on the authority of the Bible, on the subject of predestination and the pulpit as a substitute for the altar. It was overcome by the emotional individualistic message of conventicle Protestantism, but at the same time compelled the sectarian movement to seek in its own way organization as a means of self-preservation

The direct influence of Calvinism has been greatly overrated, because, as has been noted, it has been overlooked that the central interest of Calvinism was the theocracy, and that this was an impossible ideal in the New World. There is however much in Calvinism that linked it more readily with the dissenting type of Protestantism than with Lutheranism. Calvinism has much more of the spirit of the Old Testament with its desert prophetism in the foreground than Lutheranism. The Old Testament had only meaning for Luther as it foretold and prepared the way for Christ. For Calvin the Old Testament was a civil constitution for the State and still binding as such. It is impossible to think of Calvin rejecting a whole book of the New Testament because it did not commend itself "to his spirit" as Luther did the Apocalypse. [1] And it is equally impossible to think of Luther turning to the law of the Old Testament as the basis of a new ecclesiastical State. The conventicle turned away, it is true, from the theocracy, but it held on firmly to the Old Testament

---

[1] "*Ich sage, was ich fühle. Mir mangelt an diesem Buch nicht einerlei, dass ich's weder apostolisch noch prophetisch halte. . . . Mein Geist kann sich in das Buch nicht schicken, und mir ist die Ursache genug, dass ich sein nicht hoch achte, dass Christus darin weder gelehrt noch erkannt wird, welches doch vor allen Dingen ein Apostel zu tun schuldig ist, wie er sagt Apostelgeschichte I. 'Ihr sollt meine Zeugen sein.' Darum bleibe ich bei den Büchern, die mir Christum hell und rein dargeben.*" Vorrede auf die Offenbarung Johannes im Jahre 1522.*

and had a stern faith in the overthrow of all worldly power to the advantage of the saints and the coming New Age.

Both the Lutheran and the Calvinistic types of Protestantism emphasize an order and feeling for form and reverence, often lacking in the conventicle type of religion, and in this respect they are both profoundly influencing the religious expressions of the more cultivated classes of America. They in this way prepare the way for that reversion to the Catholic tradition so very marked in the architecture both of church buildings and scholastic institutions. American Protestantism has as yet failed to find any architectural expression of its special feeling and outlook, and reverts to the Catholic tradition with its central altar and primitive mystery. Whether combinations of great auditoriums and commercial enterprises will some day voice the inner sense of a dissenting Protestantism is a question only the future can answer.

In the matter of church music, the Continental type of Protestantism has done something for American religious expression and has a still greater future before it. In this art Protestantism has under the leadership of Bach found a mode of expression of marked independence and power. It would be proper perhaps rather to speak of a Northern-Germanic religious music than to try and divide the composers into two schools of Protestant and Catholic, for Mozart, Haydn and their great pupil Beethoven were not Protestant figures, and have given the world a secular as well as a religious music; at the same time, their music and its serious intellectualism has been brought to America, in large part at least, by the Continental type of Protestantism.

Both Lutheran and Calvinistic Protestantism is marked off from Dissent by its much more intense interest in dogmatic theology. Since Jonathan Edwards, America has made no important contribution to systematic theology. The dissenting churches took over uncritically the Catholic theological understructure, and in America have done nothing but ring the changes upon a few of the leading dogmas. No dogmatic theologian of anything more than local importance has come out of the religious life of the various denominations, and under this influence both Lutheranism and Calvinism in America have been in the main content with very unsatisfactory rehashes of the prevailing discussions of Europe. At the same time, they are not inclined to seek a superficial unity, as the dissenting churches are often inclined to do, by simply ignoring the intellectual differences and passing on to ritual or ethical questions. More especially the Lutheran ministry has strongly resisted the temptation, to which American dogmatic theologians have readily yielded, of filling up old and well-defined phrases with new and quite different content.

The great stream of Lutheran immigration came a little too late to influence very greatly the reorganization of Protestantism to which we have referred, but as far as it has influenced the reorganized American church life, its influence has been on the sacramental and churchly side. In fact, both Lutheranism and Calvinism, where untouched by dissenting Congregationalism, stand midway between the Catholic and the radical dissenting traditions. The necessities and new situations in American life have naturally deeply affected the religious culture, and these influences have told upon the two forms of the Continental tradition. The European visitor is struck by the great uniformity of the ordinary worship in American churches, and by the freedom with which they have taken over from one another sometimes quite incongruous features of the rituals of the past. It is now impossible to say what may happen when the national unity has more completely obliterated the lines drawn as a result of various origins. Those elements of world-flight introduced into Dissent in England by its struggle against a pleasure-seeking and oppressive ruling class are being gradually eliminated by contact with both the Catholic tradition as seen in the Roman and Anglican Episcopacy, as well as the Lutheran religious type. Dancing, the theater, novel reading, as well as the opera and secular music have never been condemned by these forms of Christian thinking because these have been the religion of ruling classes. Thus indirectly the Continental types of religions have done much to clear the way for that æsthetic development which is now a marked feature of American life, and which has been delayed by the stunted æsthetic sense of all the sects that came out of English Dissent.

CHAPTER XXI

Into the many vexed questions as to the origin of the
Civil War (1861–1865) we cannot go. It is sufficient for
our purposes to point out that the struggle arose from the
fact that slavery had given rise to a special form of culture,
and that this plantation civilization lay athwart the main
avenue of access to the sea for the rising Northwest. At
that time no railroads crossed the mountains and the
Mississippi River was apparently the given highway for
the great trade of the West and the Northwest with
Europe. A united political life seemed therefore a matter
of life and death to the Northwest, for if the Southern
States broke away from the Union, they were in a position
seemingly to strangle the trade of all the Northern States
depending upon the Mississippi Valley. There floated
upon the Mississippi River a commercial fleet that in
numbers and tonnage is said to have rivalled that between
New York and Liverpool. From 1850 to 1860 were the
most crowded years in which "the River" seemed to have
an unrivalled future before it, for if the railroad had begun
to reach out for the traffic, so also had the improvements in
steam navigation given promise of unlimited usefulness.
The population of the valley had risen to over fourteen
million and the life on the Mississippi was stirring and full
of color. That life has been made immortal in the writings
of "Mark Twain."

Whatever else the Civil War was, it certainly was

mainly a war of the West and Northwest to conserve the Union and thus maintain the uninterrupted navigation of the Mississippi as an indispensable factor in the commercial life of the growing community. The war was the work of the Western Republican party, under the leadership of a Western President, the embodiment of the frontier ideals, one who knew the Mississippi from its source to its mouth. The Western States needed for the most part no draft to send their sons to the front, and it was Western generals, or generals with a long Western experience, who finally won the war by forcing the Mississippi River and holding the Mississippi Valley. Slavery as the fundamental fact in the Southern culture was, of course, the cause of the war, but the struggle was the deadly battle between two quite different types of civilization; two sets of ideals, each claiming with a measure of truth to rest upon historic tradition and to be a justified development.

It looks now to triumphant industrial capitalism as if the struggle had been waged with its fearful sacrifices to secure the freedom of the slave, and for purely ideal ends; and all wars must appeal to some ideals if brave men are to die for the victory. Certainly before the war was over it was regarded on both sides as a battle for freedom and self-determination in the first instance. At the same time the war was not begun to free the slave but to maintain the Union. So in our examination of the attitude of the various religious denominations toward the war, we must constantly remind ourselves that the issues were not as clear-cut as later pulpit utterances would have us believe, and that so far as the churches represent the ethical life of a community, they reveal wild confusion in the attitude of the most moral elements of the community to nearly all the issues the slavery question raised.

In the first place, neither the Bible, the fundamental authority of all the Christian traditions, nor the historical interpretation of that authority in the organized Church takes any dogmatic stand in the matter of human slavery. The attitude of Paul and Thomas Aquinas are too well known to leave any doubt on this point. Some of the last slave owners and serf-holders in Europe were monastic brotherhoods. The Christian Church, however, carried on the work begun by Roman Stoics and others to moderate the hardships attendant upon slavery, thus rendering slavery an increasingly wasteful form of production.

The extreme radical wing of the English dissenting tradition made the first movement to identify abolition with the Christian conception of life. The Quakers in Pennsylvania and then in England protested against the trade in African Negroes, and then in the buying and selling of slaves, and at last against the holding of slaves, and went so far as to try and forbid the recognition of Quakers who held slaves. The grounds were those of Christian humanity, and John Wollman (1720-1772) may be regarded as one of the first absolute Abolitionists on Christian grounds. The Quakers in Pennsylvania had advised against the trade in 1696 and in 1776 all holders of slaves were required to desist, but as a matter of fact Quakers seem in many instances to have held slaves up to a quite late date.

Next to the Quakers we find the Unitarians among the early Christian opponents of slavery, and nearly all the more prominent Abolitionists in New England belonged to this school of thought. Then came generally the Congregational body, to which group belonged some of the most vigorous Abolitionists, particularly just before the war. In 1850 the Northern Presbyterian Church under strong Congregational influences took ground against slavery, although not absolutely condemning it under all circumstances. On the other hand all the denominations in the Southern States were inclined to maintain the legal right of the South to its peculiar culture, including chattel slavery. The Lutheran Church in the Southern States organized in 1862 a separate synod, but not on account of differences about slavery, but because it was supposed that the South would be able to maintain its independence. It has always maintained fraternal relations with the Northern branches. The Episcopal Church refused to permit the war to split its unity, and retained all the churches of the South upon its lists until peace was restored; as did also the Roman Catholic Church.

The three largest Baptist conventions are the Northern, the Southern and the Colored Baptist. There would have been probably some separation in spirit in any case caused by the rise of the slavery question, for the independent form of church polity makes it easy both to split and come together again, but the administration of property made a split almost inevitable, and so there arose for administrative purposes a Southern and a Northern administration of the foreign and domestic mission interests, although the Publication Society, resting as it did on a somewhat different basis, remained the organ of both bodies.

Professor Hiram Mattison is quoted by Helper[1] as dividing the churches into two classes: the anti-slavery churches and the slave-holding churches, and lists as anti-slavery eleven denominations: Friends or Quakers, Free-will Baptists, United Brethren, Associate Presbyterians, Wesleyan Methodists, Orthodox Congregational,

[1] Hinton Rowan Helper. "The Impending Crisis of the South: How to Meet it." London. 1860. pp. 236–237.

General Baptists, Reformed Dutch Church, New School Presbyterians, Unitarians and Universalists. Whereas he counts as "Slave-holding Churches" the Old School Presbyterian, the Protestant Episcopal, the Roman Catholic and the Methodist Episcopal Church.

But the matter is not quite so simple as it now appears to many. There were all sorts of moral judgments on the subject. Slavery had been condemned in the abstract from the time of Jefferson, George Washington and Madison. Nearly all the churches had at one time or another placed themselves on record as wishing that slavery did not exist. That radical Protestantism, which so dominated the minds of the men who gave us the Constitution, was filled with a flaming zeal for individual rights and human freedom in the abstract, and powerfully influenced France along this line through the personal attitude of Benjamin Franklin, Thomas Jefferson and Thomas Paine, but it was no longer in control of the intellectual life of either the North or the South. At the reorganization of Protestantism, other questions were raised; and Unitarianism, which had given to America a new literature and a new outlook upon life, was no longer the leading religious force even in New England, where once it had held almost undisputed sway. Cotton had come in as a staple crop; and the almost universal opinion was that it could not be cultivated without slave labor. A special type of culture had risen on the basis of this economic fact, nor was the Southern population the only one to be interested in and benefited by this culture. In all the seaboard cities were many men and women as much interested in the maintenance of this special form of production as the planters themselves. The Southern States were almost permanently indebted to the Eastern States, and on the other hand the factories and distilleries of the

East were thought to be quite dependent upon the raw material from the South.

Organized Christianity has adapted itself to all manner of political and social arrangements. It has helped to hold the serf to the soil and the slave to his bondage, and has been at home in Roman and Byzantian autocracy, under constitutional monarchy, republicanism, feudalism, capitalism, and it has had both an urban and an agrarian history. When, then, Abolitionists demanded in the name of Christianity that the slaves be freed, all historically minded Christians paused. Radical Protestantism has however never been historically minded; personal experience and the inner light are the final judges in all matters of morals and religion; now radical Protestantism reached in many instances conclusions that the great majority of earnest religious thinkers deliberately or instinctively rejected. William Lloyd Garrison demanded the abolition of slavery in the name of a Christianity which he interpreted as demanding the abandonment of all force. He was opposed to all government built up on anything but moral suasion. He set no value upon the Union of the States to which the great bulk of his countrymen both in the North and South still attached much importance and were no more ready then than the same class would be ready now to think of the Constitution as "a covenant with death and agreement with hell."[1]

On the other hand many sincere men and women were so profoundly under the power of tradition and history that they could not believe that all of a sudden that had become a deadly sin, which Christianity had seen and tolerated for well-nigh nineteen centuries. And even when such wished, as many did, that slavery did not exist,

[1] Adopted by the Massachusetts Anti-Slavery Society, Faneuil Hall. January 27, 1843 at Garrison's suggestion.

there rose such questions as to whether the slave was "ready for freedom"; it is well known that a ruling class seldom thinks that it is ripe for abdication, or that granting that the time for freeing a dependent class has come, the question still remains whether it shall be done at once or gradually. Even the Abolitionists themselves were not agreed at this point. Thus although no sharp line can be drawn, yet on the whole, apart from all economic considerations, radical Protestantism in proportion to its radicalism was opposed to slavery; and ecclesiastical and historical Christianity, again much in proportion to its priestly and sacramentarian character, was in sympathy with the South. Nor was this very strange, for although it is not true that the South was settled by a better class than the New England and Middle States, yet it is true that the South had developed a landed aristocracy and an aristocratic culture that had much in common with that type of mind to which the order, dignity and æsthetic appeal of the historic ritual was congenial.

The Abolitionists violently attacked the churches as a "bulwark of slavery", but in point of fact these only proclaimed the somewhat confused judgments of the average man. Slaves were property before the law, for which money had been paid in good faith, and property had an almost sacred character in the minds of the very class that had settled America, for as over against a landed aristocracy in England the trading classes of the towns and cities had only their property in money and credit, in industry and ships as a source of power. Many a man who deeply regretted slavery still felt that to take away property from unwilling owners was to undermine the whole fabric of society. Wendell Phillips and William Lloyd Garrison could not see that sincere men and women felt that the security of property was as much a moral issue as the freedom of the colored man.

Moreover, property-owning organizations can never afford to be radical, and the churches were all now property-owning corporations; nor has ethical advance ever come through organized religion, but through individual religious prophets; these the churches supplied but generally treated as the prophet is always treated. The churches therefore embodied in the South the moral judgments of the average man to whom they ministered, and were on the side of Southern culture with its attendant slavery, even where the several members were often too poor to own slaves; while in the North and especially in the West and Northwest the feeling grew that the Southern culture was an element that the industrial capitalism of the North could not long endure, and that not only slavery but the whole planting civilization must be abolished.

It is easy now to show that the cost of freeing all the slaves by buying them at twice their market value would have been less than the awful expenditure of the Civil War; but that was not the question, which was whether a type of life and a social organization dear to many if not to most of the dwellers in the South was to be wiped out by the destruction of the cardinal fact of that culture. To the Southern churchman the question was rather whether his pleasures and his prejudices, his social outlook and his mental habits were to be sacrificed that the cultural unity of the United States might be established. And here he soon found that the organized churches about him supported his view, exactly as organized Christianity supported feudalism, long after even the Continental Reformation; as in fact Catholicism still supports it. Whereas in the North the struggle was more or less definitely recognized as a struggle of industrial progress with agrarian backwardness, and here again the member of a Northern church found his views ever more clearly dominating the atmosphere of the organized churches of the North and the West.

It is an interesting question upon which few seem to have pondered: just which type of Protestantism or even which type of religious tradition profited most by the defeat of the South. The old, charming and utterly un-aggressive Roman Catholicism of the South suffered, of course, severely. The leading families lost their property, the hierarchy seemed helpless, the churches were hardly in a position to support themselves, and even the buildings suffered from poverty and neglect. The Church of Rome lost heavily in prestige as the incoming tide of energetic but poverty-stricken Irish immigration took charge of the fortunes of Roman Catholicism. There was no Southern Catholic aristocracy to give the Church social standing in the minds of the multitude. The Episcopal Church, which even in the South bore the stamp of Protestantism, and like the Episcopal Church in the North never had reflected in its purity the Anglo-Catholic outlook, lost property and support but gained again the instant recognition of the Episcopal Church in the North, which had never cut it off from fellowship or dealt harshly with slavery. The Methodist Church in the South had thoroughly absorbed the spirit of its surroundings, and does not seem to have suffered more than all Southern institutions suffered. The same may be said of the Baptist Church, the work of which, together with that of the Methodists, had captured the vast majority of the Negro population. The easy-going emotional type of revival conventicle religion suited not only the impulsive and artistic nature of the Negro, but fitted best into his artificial environment. The Southern Presbyterian Church retained the affections of those who remained in the South, but it lost heavily through the emigration of so many of its members to the North.

In one respect all the churches of the South were strongly affected by the Civil War. The attitude of the radical types of Protestantism in the North was bitterly resented, and traditional orthodoxy gained a strong hold upon the sympathies of the Southern communities; the letter of the Bible became the standard of all faith; all critical and progressive theology is instinctively rejected in the South by both educated and uneducated alike, even to this day, and a deep-rooted suspicion of all progress was implanted in the ecclesiastical mind. The union of the various denominations divided by the war will, no doubt, some time take place, but for the present the drift away from conventional orthodoxy is looked upon with suspicion by those in the South who see the trend of the churches in the North. Even the industrial progress of the South has not yet effected any marked change in this respect, although such a change is bound to come.

Even while the Civil War was being waged, the immigration from Ireland, Germany, Poland and other Continental countries to the Northern States continued and even increased; with the result that relatively the old Anglo-Saxon Protestantism lost ground, although actually gaining in numerical strength. This relative loss set in shortly after 1848 when the Irish and German Catholic as well as German-Lutheran immigration began steadily to increase. The Hebrew immigration also began to increase, due to growing discontent in the lands where orthodox Judaism still holds sway. The close of the war saw also a marked movement in the cities toward a more orderly and æsthetic manner of service. The more churchly types of Protestantism set the pace for the less formal and financially weaker religious bodies. The result was not always happy, for non-sacramental churches took over rituals and customs that had historical associations which the conventicle type of Protestantism had disavowed, and in which they have to this day little interest and of whose inner meaning they are often blissfully ignorant. Nevertheless, the swelling tides of Roman and Anglo-Catholic as well as Continental Protestant tradition could not fail to influence the life of the churches of all shades of opinion, as indeed the non-ritualistic churches also strongly influenced the ecclesiastical types.

Perhaps the fact that the war for the Union, as the half-conscious expression of this demand for cultural unity and deeply affecting all the churches, has had something to do with a growing desire to rather belittle the historic differences between the various types of Protestantism. Certain it is that to-day a stranger might enter a half dozen churches in any of the great cities of North America, and hardly detect in the services that they all represented quite different religious heritages as shown by the different denominational names; and even in the preaching it would only be by an accident that the stranger would detect the particular shade of denominational affiliation. This is partly because, as we have seen, the churches descended from English Dissent have never had a very intelligent interest in theology as a science, and they have profoundly affected the religious bodies dominated by the Continental type of thinking, and so made transition from one body to the other very easy. A kind of free ritual has established itself along the line of least resistance. Universalism has driven the eternal hell of Jonathan Edwards almost completely from the thinking if not from the theory of the pulpit; Unitarianism has made the Athanasian creed a mere historic memory; the emotional appeal of the revival

meeting has become common property, although modified
to meet various degrees of culture and class taste.

The class of workmen which Mr. Dwight L. Moody
used to call the "tin-pail brigade" does not generally go to
any church, not even much to the Catholic Church, which
has still probably the largest hold upon it. This is often
lamented by the clergy as if it were a new phenomenon,
but this is probably not the case. Never in the religious
history of the United States is there much evidence to
show that more than about a third of the population ever
went regularly to any place of worship, and sometimes
the proportion has been probably much less, and it has always been the economically weaker class that has shunned
the expense and the display of social and financial superiority bound up with attendance on church worship.
The enormous industrial development since the Civil
War has, however, greatly increased this class, both
relatively and actually, so that the line between a class
that goes to church and a class that habitually stays away
is now, perhaps, sharper. This is still further emphasized
by the fact that the old intimacy of the conventicle
Protestantism, when the meetinghouse was a social center,
has been regarded as an ideal long after the facts of social
differentiation made such an ideal impossible. The great
cathedral or the crowded service of a Roman Catholic
Mass shut out all invidious comparisons in regard to social
rank; the church was a place where the soul could be alone
with the real presence of God upon the altar, peasant and
prince could kneel together without any further contact or
comparison or claim for mutual recognition. Since the
Civil War the Protestant church buildings have been
greatly improved in appearance, but the relative luxury of
the surroundings bring out in bold relief any poverty
revealed in dress or manners, as is not the case in the

spaces of a cathedral or among the crowds that attend a Mass in a great Roman Catholic church. In the old Protestant meetinghouse it was the right and duty of the members to watch over the dress and conduct of the other members, to condemn excess of dress and rebuke any unseemly conduct. This is no longer possible, but the social implications still remain, and the erection of plainer buildings for the poor, and luxurious pews and surroundings for an economically stronger class has not yet met the needs of the situation from the clerical point of view. Perhaps the emphasis upon the pulpit as the center of united worship instead of the altar will tend to create great church buildings planned to call multitudes together, and ministered to by the few natural preachers able to hold such congregations. In such crowds the economic differences might be swallowed up, and the invidious intimacies of the old conventicle or the primitive Christian assemblies would become impossible.

One evidence of the fact that the Civil War was waged not simply to free the slave but to destroy the culture of which he was the mainstay is seen in the savage way in which the cultured class was eliminated from the political life of the Union in the days of so-called reconstruction. Without question, the churches of the South suffered dreadfully under the strain of both the political incapacity of the "carpet-baggers" from the North and the lawlessness necessary to supplant them and make room for freer institutions. Some of the most serious social questions have arisen from the way this struggle was carried on. The aim of the political party that sent the third-rate politicians to rule the conquered South was not however purely to loot and destroy, but chosen from the very strong and natural instinct for cultural unity. This instinct has led the Anglo-American churches from time to

time to take up somewhat bungling anti-Catholic cru-
sades, which have in point of fact rather tended to drive
the Catholic Church into political activity as a matter of
self-protection, which activity has been on the whole
distracting and unwholesome; at least, so one of the most
high-minded Roman Catholic bishops was inclined to
think. Happily, cooler-minded men have in most cases
refused to accept the wild charges made by fanatic but
sincere opponents of the Roman Catholic Church in
America. At the same time there is no doubt a growing
sense that the old Anglo-American Protestantism, founded
on the faith and hope of the dissenting class in England,
is no longer in a position to guide without serious opposition the fortunes of the New World.

CHAPTER XXII

From the beginning of their history in America the denominations that rose out of the dissenting tradition in England developed in another and very different atmosphere. Whereas in England their life and growth was in a thousand ways affected by the existence of a ruling class, that cherished another religious outlook upon life, they had in America free room to develop along their own lines, with the feeling of being masters in their own house. The element of world-flight in Lollardism and its children was not flight from the world as such, but only flight from the world of the leisured master class. Nor was it a simple matter for the various sects to wind their way amid the temptations of the Scylla of rejection and the Charybdis of an often servile imitation. The Methodism that rose out of the labors of Wesley ran the gamut of various degrees of acceptance of the outward forms of a tradition, whose primary premises it radically rejected.

The reorganization of Protestantism after the War of Independence took place at a time when wealth was increasing and living began to assume new and more luxurious forms. This was still more the case after the Civil War had run its course, and the broad principle had been laid down that only one type of culture would henceforth be tolerated in the United States. There arose among the denominations a common churchly trend. The example of the incoming tides of Roman Catholics and Lutherans, and the rise of a real Anglo-Catholic

Episcopacy, as well as the success of a churchly Presbyterianism had undoubtedly their influence. The Baptist
and Methodist meetinghouses became "churches", and
organs and paid quartets as well as a simple ritual began
to mark the change in the modes of worship. But more
especially the rise of an educated and professional ministry made emphasis upon the churchly type of religious
expression natural, because this contributes to stability
when the emotional appeal for any reason seems to be
losing its effectiveness. Loyalty to one's organization
began to be regarded as a primary virtue, perhaps as an
offset to the indifference to the State, once so characteristic of the dissenting tradition, and indeed still in a
measure characteristic of it in England. Loyalty to the
denomination became a watchword in the assemblies of
the various sects, and this was naturally in the interest of
the professional clergy, whose work was thus made lighter.

The evangelical revival in England had been followed
by an important reawakening of the Anglo-Catholic
feeling in the State Church. The High-Church movement
in England had two sides. Men like Newman and Ward [1]
cared little for the ritual and the æsthetic elements of the
Catholic tradition; what they sought and thought they
found was certainty founded upon a priestly and historic
Church. On the other hand, men like Pusey and to some
extent Manning emphasized the ritual and sacramental
side of Catholicism, as meeting the needs of the starved
religious imagination of a Protestantized England. And
it was this side of High-Churchism that made most
impression upon American Episcopacy. Following upon
the Civil War there was some reaction against the educational ideals introduced by the sharply radical Protestantism of New England. The secularization of education

[1] William George Ward. (1812–1882.) "Ideal of a Christian Church." 1844.

after the manner of the university of Germany and France accorded with the extreme individualism of this radical Protestantism, but the churchly ideals of Oxford and to a lesser degree Cambridge appealed strongly to the awakening longing for organized beauty in American life. Schools sprang up in which the ecclesiastical ideals were again brought to the front, both in the architecture and the worship. The lack of taste and form in the emotional revivalism of the period seemed to many to make all religious worship ramshackle and chaotic. Churchly and academic paraphernalia were introduced into American life to an extent hitherto unknown. Many minds sought order, dignity, harmony and artistic symbolism in the midst of a life but little marked by these things.

In England the conquest of the State Church by the old Anglo-Catholic tradition was in the late Victorian period almost complete. Evangelicalism either fled to Nonconformity or sank into a relatively insignificant minority, which could only hinder the triumphant progress of Anglo-Catholicism with the support of the Protestant party outside the Church. Some of those who had gone over from the High-Church movement to Rome are said to have regretted the hasty retreat in view of the completeness of the victory of the High-Anglican party. Rome also was full of hope in regard to an eventual reunion of Anglican and Roman Catholicism. In the United States only the ritualistic side of the High-Church Anglicanism seems to have made much impression; but this æsthetic note affected not only the Episcopal Church in America, but drew many to the consideration of the whole subject of dignified worship and historical prayers. The hymns sung in the denominational Sunday schools were more particularly the subject of ridicule and of proposals of reform. To many it seemed as if a new and churchly

Protestantism had almost a clear field before it, and that
it was only a matter of time when the old conventicle type
of piety would be well-nigh forgotten.

Those who thought so had forgotten the astonishing
vitality of the old Wyclif-Lollard conventicle type of
religious thinking; and while the upper classes were
engaged in refurbishing the æsthetic ideals of the ancient
and often deeply religious Anglo-Catholic aristocratic
heritage, there was working among the lower English
classes a typical conventicle preacher, alive with the
revival gospel that we have followed down the ages.
William Booth was born in 1829 and had a typical dissenting career, first as local preacher among the Wesleyans,
then as minister among the Methodist New Connection
and at last as founder and leader of an East London
revival mission, called later "Christian Mission" and
then in the summer of 1878 organized as the "Salvation
Army." It was the reëmbodiment of all the central
conceptions of Lollard conventicle Dissent. Its attitude
toward the sacraments was an exact reproduction of
Wyclif's, of whom Booth, of course knew next to nothing.
The Salvation Army has no sacraments, but if any
individual member needs them as a memorial of sacred
antiquity there is no objection. Its theology is the simple
outline of the main positions of the older creeds, but
without any emphasis upon any clear thinking on these
matters. The preaching of an infallible Bible is central.
Christian conduct is the main message, and this can
only be attained through the acceptance of the blood
atonement of a dying Saviour, by which the sinner is
saved from eternal hell and sanctified by the indwelling
of the Holy Spirit, who enlightens every man. The true
Christian life is the life of proclamation of the saving
gospel, and all men and women and even children are

called in conversion to the work of proclamation. The Historic Church has no place in this thinking, and all men and women, so far as they are converted, are kings and priests unto God. The cry is repent and trust to the love of God as seen in Christ Jesus and then go out and proclaim the saving efficiency of this faith, bearing the personal testimony it has saved you and it will save others.

The little centers of the religious life have the old duty of watching over the life and conduct of the members, and of organizing the work of proclamation. The "officers" are purely administrative leaders, but as such have a right to implicit obedience. Nor was the old missionary spirit lacking; in 1880 the "Army" had reached the United States, and flourished there as hardly in England itself. Instinctively the Salvation Army turned away from churches and all sacred places. The saloon, the bar, the public street, even the brothel became a temple of the living God through the preaching of repentance, sin and atonement. Women, of course, were just as welcome as preachers as men, and Catherine Booth was fully as effective as her gaunt eagle-faced husband, and in the Middle Ages would have been enrolled among the favorite saints of the people almost before her death.

It is a striking commentary upon the origin of the class that now governs both England and the United States that even while "General" Booth lived it recognized the Salvation Army as a genuine incarnation of some of its own best religious memories; that it has never suffered serious violence though often criticized in the United States; and that in England "General" Booth was specially invited to the Coronation of Edward VII, it is said at his personal command. The Salvation Army is, of course, the direct opposite of the inter-pretation of Christianity for which High-Churchism has always stood. It omits all emphasis upon a "true Church"; it has no grace-imparting sacraments; no historic priestly ministry to guarantee their right administration; it is essentially individualistic; the Christian life begins practically with individual conversion; it has no authoritative creedal interpretation of the Bible; the sanctifying Holy Spirit is the last authority for each individual; it has no altar, save only the penitent's bench at the preacher's feet.

Moreover, the attitude toward the world is the old dissenting attitude. The theater needs hardly to be condemned, so obvious does it seem to the converted soul that it is of the devil; dancing, worldly music, expensive clothes, are all under the ban. Drinking, smoking and games are also under general condemnation. It is true that music, even instrumental music, may be used, but only to enforce the message and the call to the new life. Preaching stands where Wyclif put it as the central fact of the religious life, and the call is to go out from the world of sin and death and take hold of eternal life. The atonement is preached in its crudest form, and the divinity of Jesus, the Trinity, and heaven and hell are all unquestioned, as if there were no doubt in any Christian mind that these things might have another significance. Even the dress of the "Army" has the same spiritual meaning that Wyclif's "brown russet" had for his lay preachers; it shows forth the life of voluntary poverty and obedience. In respect to organization, the "Army" has learned from Methodism as Methodism learned from the English State Church, the power and secret of a highly developed system and administrative obedience. Nevertheless, the individual "forts" or "barracks" are given immense room for independent action, and are left very much to themselves in the way of providing the needed support.

There have been quarrels and divisions in the "Army ", because it is made up of men and women generally sincere and high-spirited, but it is worthy of note that these differences of opinion do not concern doctrine or even ritual, but matters of administrative detail or of personal competency for given tasks. The attitude toward the State is a most striking reproduction of the attitude of conventicle Protestantism down through all Anglo-Saxon and Anglo-American history. The State is accepted, like the sacraments and creedal Christianity, as an existing fact without much question, but without any real interest in its inner meaning and rather as something belonging to another world of thought and feeling. This seems to have been the pronounced attitude of the Lollards, and has been the general attitude of the dissenters in England, of which Defoe bitterly complained. Whether in England, Germany, the United States or elsewhere, the powers that be are, according to the "Army ", ordained of God and should in general be left to Him. Although Wyclif was personally intensely interested in the question of Church and State, and followed the lead of Fitzralph of Armagh, the later Lollards were far too poor and politically impotent to have even an academic interest in the matter. Like their forbears in England the members of the Salvation Army in the United States have little interest in any social theory, are loyal to the State on general principles, as protecting them and their property. Questions about socialism, communism, anarchy, capitalism or organized labor are as remote to their way of thinking as questions about expressionism, impressionism or cubisms in art. The one thing needful is the inner change of mind brought about by the emotional appeal, and revealed in a life of devotion to the evangelical propaganda. All else is secondary. As we have seen in other connections, this type of religious thinking suffers greatly upon any letting down of the primary enthusiasm, but the "Army" seeks by its organization to maintain this spirit of whole-hearted devotion to the cause.

Two quite unconnected religious appearances deserve a more thorough study than they have as yet received, or than we can here give them. But to omit any reference to them would be to leave the picture of American Protestantism in relation to our culture sadly incomplete. The first of these is that strange religious movement to which we have once before referred known as Mormonism. Professor Eduard Meyer of Berlin is one of the first in Europe to call attention to Mormonism as a most interesting field for investigation by the historian.[1] In highly interesting "Exkursen" he deals with the rise of Islam as compared with Mormonism (pages 67–83) and with that of Christianity (pages 277–300). It would lead us too far from our particular field to pass judgment upon the questions Professor Meyer raises, with an almost unequaled authority, on the historical field. We will only seek to find the setting of Mormonism in American religious history. Out of what religious tradition did it spring? Is it a purely alien product? Why was it among many curious and weird religious beginnings so successful?

It is only necessary to indicate the oft-told story of the rise of the "Church of Jesus Christ of Latterday Saints." How Joseph Smith, an ignorant Vermont boy, born in 1805, apparently with a neurotic heritage, and soon brought by his parents to Manchester, New York, claimed to have visions and to have found a golden book of history and religious instruction, which he then translated by the aid of magic spectacles behind a curtain to

[1] Eduard Meyer. "Ursprung und Geschichte der Mormonen." Halle, 1912.

followers. Thus arose the "Book of Mormon" which was then taken up into heaven by the angel Moroni. There gathered about him a very doubtful company, and he had soon three "witnesses", Oliver Cowdery, David Whitmer and Martin Harris. Soon after he had the "Testimony" of the eight "witnesses", four Whitmers and three Smiths; his father and two brothers. The story of their being driven from place to place is not pleasant reading, and at last the two brothers Smith were foully murdered by a mob, seemingly with the connivance of the guards of the jail where they were confined on charges of impurity. The attempts to found a religious colony in New York, Missouri and Illinois failed because of the generally illegal opposition of the populace. Then at last Brigham Young attempted to escape from the jurisdiction of the United States and took his following to the dreary and salty desert of the Utah Valley in 1847–1848. There some five thousand persons were brought in a masterly way, and kept alive until industry, thrift and irrigation had transformed a seemingly waterless waste into a blooming garden. Then came the long struggle under the leadership of Brigham Young for the right to development and self-determination. The finding of gold in California in 1848 brought at once prosperity and temptation to the little community, as well as the overlordship of the United States. Immigration has brought the numbers up to 558,463 as estimated by Doctor Carroll in 1927.

To try and estimate the controlling forces behind this movement, as do Professor Meyer and I. Woodbridge Riley, [1] involves the consideration of some of the religious history we have tried to sketch. The background of the picture is the collapse of organized Protestantism. Smith

[1] I. Woodbridge Riley. "The Founder of Mormonism, a Psychological Study of Joseph Smith, Jr." New York, 1902.

was born in 1805 when secularism was still triumphant and was still forming the constitutional life of the States. But religious forces were again at work, although the community out of which Mormonism arose had not yet been reached by the reorganizing churches. We must put ourselves back again into a time untouched by the critical rationalism that compelled organized Protestantism to take account of sober history and science. Wild as seem now to us the tales that Joseph Smith made so many believe, they fit in to the learned and unlearned credulity of a precritical Protestantism. We must compare the credulity and nonsense of Cotton Mather's "Magnalia" with that of Joseph Smith rather than with the Protestantism that has had to stand the questionings of generations of trained skepticism.

The moment that we examine Mormon teaching, we see at once that the authority of an elaborately misunderstood Bible is the first pillar of the Church, and that the faith in the revelation by the Holy Spirit to individual souls is the second, and at once we recognize in distorted forms the dissenting tradition. The blood atonement, the saints, adult baptism, the approaching end of the world, preaching, the bodily resurrection, the second coming of Christ among other things all mark plainly the religious type of which Mormonism is a caricature. Nor is it possible for us to separate sharply between the elements of credulity, deception and self-deception. Indeed is there any sharp line? Any one who has had much to do with an imaginative and gifted child should soon see that for such a child there is no sharp line between its daydreaming and the objective happenings round about. In fact these day dreams may assume a concrete reality that the dull commonplaces of every-day life never attain. This world of ignorant credulity was full of longings for some religious hope and knowledge. The former leadership was gone; organized Protestantism had collapsed, but the old longings and the old faith could not be wiped out completely. These shrewd and imaginative Mormon leaders saw "men as trees walking." Elements of sensuality, brutality and violence mingled with their hope and faith, but they were surrounded by sensuality, brutality and violence. On the whole they were themselves temperate, thrifty, free from some of the worst vices of a frontier community, for neither gambling nor prostitution had any place among them. H. H. Bancroft was no Mormon, but no one can read his pages [1] without a sense of shame for the way they were treated. Brigham Young was a great leader, and although crafty, autocratic, sometimes fierce and passionate, with a love for both power and money, it is bad psychology to attempt to explain his power as that of a conscious impostor. He had much good sense, and encouraged harmless amusements like dancing, music and stage acting. His rule was firm and sometimes violent, but tyranny could not be unbridled where ways of escape were so easy, and where critical enemies were ever on the watch.

The opposition to Mormonism was part of that struggle for cultural unity, which as we have seen played such a part in the Civil War. Contrary to the general opinion, the evidence is now overwhelming that the communistic experiments that sprang up about this time seldom went to pieces on economic grounds; on the contrary most of them were an economic success, but they were wrecked on internal divisions or external pressure. The Church of Jesus Christ of the Latterday Saints was a communistic success from the beginning, and the main opposition to it

---

[1] H. H. Bancroft. "History of Utah." San Francisco, 1889. Vol. XXI. History Series.

was not on account of polygamy alone, but because men instinctively realized that it stood for another type of culture, with both primitive as well as very advanced elements. Since the close of the Civil War there has been one long and not wholly unsuccessful struggle to force the Mormon Church to abandon its primitive character and take on the prevalent American social outlook. From the time of the Morrill Act of 1862 to that of the Edmunds-Tucker Act in 1887 the attack has been on polygamy, but the political struggle goes deeper, and probably as the religious fervor of the original " Saints " declines, the unifying force of social arrangement in the United States will make the Mormon divergence simply an interesting memory.

The names of those connected with the rise and progress of Mormonism at once reveals the fact that although there was from the beginning a strong mixture of population from Scandinavian lands, Mormonism was led by Anglo-Americans. It is almost the only communistic experiment begun by Anglo-Americans that has been able to weather the intense individualism implanted by tradition and habit in the Anglo-American population. Nearly all the other more or less successful communistic experiments are either of German or French origin. [1] Nor is it necessary to point out that the communism is of a very limited character. At the same time, no Mormon was ever allowed to starve; the great natural resources of Utah Brigham Young tried to keep for the common use of the Church. The land was held on a tithing system that emphasized the common character of all property. The Church remained the owner and controller of the important monopolies. And in older days the writer has heard a powerful plea from a Mormon "Apostle" for primitive

[1] See note to page 253.

"Christian communism." A very large proportion of the
converts from Europe are lower-class British, but almost
no Irish are included. Next in order would come probably
Scandinavians, for reasons also embedded in the history
of religion and politics in the northern lands. The writer
has attended services in the "Tabernacle" which with
immaterial changes might have been held in many a
dissenting chapel in England. The leaders have given
evidence of intelligence and capacity as well as character,
but the average intelligence is low, although whether
really lower than that of any frontier population it is hard
to say. The general impression made on the traveler
passing through Utah is of thrift and harmlessness.
Polygamy has been given up and is probably disappearing,
save perhaps secretly in a few wealthy families; it was
always expensive and among many families unpopular.

On the whole Mormonism may be regarded as a somewhat degenerate form of the old dissenting tradition, and
among several such forms it has survived on account of
the natural wealth of the valley in which Brigham Young
cast his lot and the rather extrordinary genius and will
power not only of Brigham Young but of many of the
"Apostles." Of this ability the representative of Utah in
the United States Senate is a shining example. The
schools are many and illiteracy among the native-born
is rare. The Church has never yet lacked rather remarkable leadership, and the hearty dislike of the Church by
the intruding "Gentiles" is due in part at least to its success.

Very different in both history and background is another religious form that has entered largely into American present-day culture. To understand the success of Mrs.
Mary Baker Eddy's "Christian Science" it is necessary to examine in some detail the religious atmosphere

out of which it emerged. The closing third of the nineteenth century in the United States was marked by a surge of religious awakening that seemed to the Anglo-American elements of the population perhaps more important than it really was. Its towering personality was Dwight L. Moody who, with Ira D. Sankey as a singing partner, raised the old revival type of appeal to a higher plane. His work was not confined to America only, but the permanent effects of his preaching seem to be confined to that country. Matthew Arnold in his book "God and the Bible", preface xix–xx, summarizes the gospel preached by Mr. Moody, and when this was laid before Mr. Moody, he accepted it, with a few unimportant reservations, as a fair account of his faith. It is substantially the basis of the oldest type of English dissenting Protestantism. At this time the life of America had become much more elaborate than in the days of the Great Awakening. Not only had a great foreign population brought in types of faith to which the emotional revivalism of more primitive time was strange, but other interests had taken a place in American life hitherto little known. Sport had been organized, the theater enormously extended in its influence, travel made cheap and popular, the newspaper and magazine given a new place in the common life. All of these things and others that will occur to the thoughtful, made any religious movement one to be confined largely to a class normally interested in religion, and only slightly affecting the general public. It is true that a hymn like "Hold the Fort for I Am Coming" was sung in cheap boarding houses that seldom heard anything else than music-hall ditties, but large ranges of American life, especially American city life, knew little or nothing about this recrudescence of the oldest revival type of Protestantism. Mr. Moody was only one and the best on the whole of a number of similar revivalists, some of whom tried like Mr. B. Fay Mills to raise the appeal to a higher ethical and intellectual level, and others sank to the low levels described in Mr. Sinclair Lewis' "Elmer Gantry." Deliberately Mr. Moody, under the influence of Henry Drummond of Scotland, the author of "Natural Law in the Spiritual World", turned to the schools and colleges of the country, and with a measure of success. Not all indeed but many of them were swept by a wave of religious emotion out of which came such movements as the "Inter-Collegiate Missionary" effort; the re-organization of the Collegiate Young Men's Christian Association; the reorganization of the religious services of the colleges and some similar movements. It was a fairly prosperous and thoughtful if not very well educated class that felt most the effects of the religious impulse.

But just as Whitefield raised up a Unitarian protest from cultivated ministers like the Reverend Charles Chauncy, and the later awakening called men like Channing into the field to organize what they thought a more rational type of Protestantism, so the revival message of Mr. Moody's era stirred many to seek a less noisy and emotional expression of their religious feeling, and found it often in the ritual of the Episcopal Church or the intellectualism of Unitarianism. At this time the older Anglo-Catholicism was being brought from England into the Episcopal Church, mainly as remarked in its ritualistic form, and was attracting many of the younger men and women. Nevertheless there was still a lack. To a seemingly imperative hunger the work of Mrs. Eddy appealed with a power that seems to the outsider not a little strange. The religion of Christian Science seems to have at first sight little kinship with either the Catholic or the dissenting tradition. It is however an exceedingly self-centered and individualistic gospel, and avowedly based upon the Bible. It offers an antidote to the confusions and vulgarity of an excessive dependence upon material success, and puts the emphasis, in however crude a manner, upon the mind and the need of self-control and peace. Its appeal is neither to the poorer classes nor yet to the intellectually restless. It is easy to ridicule many details of both the administration and the actual practice, but it has brought seeming health and peace to many, and the sincerity of its adherents is built into brick and stone in the rising church buildings on every hand. Neither the well-read reader in German idealism nor the historically minded member of one of the Catholic traditions is likely to find in Christian Science much that will seem fruitful, but it draws its membership from a fairly wide range of both social station and intelligence. It has called increased attention to mental healing and the power of the suggestion in disease, although its contribution at this point can easily be overrated. Healing by faith is a very old religious practice, and was fairly widespread at the time Mrs. Eddy took it up as a central teaching of her new religion. She however organized it and gave it a wider range than it had hitherto had in educated circles.

The facts of Mrs. Eddy's life are now well known. They are set forth with cold historical accuracy in the work of Mr. Dakin.[1] But religions are not built up on biographical facts, but upon mythological explanations of those facts. Christian Science, Thought Healing, and various other very similar trends came to fill up the gap made in the emotional life by a very critical materialism, and that at a time when after the Civil War the life of emotion was singularly starved. Crude German idealism, haunting

[1] Dakin, Edwin Franden. "Mrs. Eddy, The Biography of a Virginal Mind," popular edition. New York. 1930.

memories of evangelical piety, weird psychological mis-conceptions may all be traced in these new movements, but they now are buttressed by spiritual, political and financial vested interests that promise to give them a relative permanence in the religious background of that coming American culture, which will reflect wider ranges of religious thought than the original Dissent of the dominant Anglo-Saxon population.

The world's religious restlessness is revealed in the recent revival of interest in the Occult and in Spiritual-ism. But as we trace the history of the background of American culture we cannot see that it has really played or is likely to play any very great part in building up our outlook upon life. This is a world-wide rather than an Anglo-American phenomenon. Organized religion is al-most committed to regarding it as "unauthorized mirac-ulous intermeddling", and to treat it as "magic", "witch-craft" or fraud. The mental alertness of America's often uneducated but intelligent mixed population makes it an easy field for the prophets of the Occult. Once educated and skeptical criticism counted upon the advance of scientific attainments to make an end to much of this; but when such highly trained men as Sir Oliver Lodge and Baron Schrenck-Notzing lend their names to proceedings that seem to relatively untrained laymen most obvious and transparent fraud, it is plain that both judgments for and against are not the verdicts of "pure reason" but are to some degree at least controlled by temperament and previous prejudices.

This survey of the religious background of American culture can only be an attempt to point out the way which the writer thinks future investigation must take. The difficulties of forming impartial and unbiassed judgments are great but not insuperable, and the present writer hopes that his real sympathy with any and all attempts to look at life *sub specie æternitatis* may have prevented him from doing any serious injustice to the various religious answers to life's most serious questions, with which he has tried as an historian to deal.

GENERAL BIBLIOGRAPHY

A comprehensive bibliography of movements covering five centuries of English and American history is clearly impossible. The list of books here given does not even include all to which the writer gladly acknowledges indebtedness, but is chosen as giving those he has found most useful. No doubt important omissions will be noted by specialists whose fields are touched, but the list furnishes a working introduction to the subject.

Adams, Brooks. "The Emancipation of Massachusetts." Boston. 1887.
Adams, Charles Francis. "Diary and Autobiography of John Adams; Works of John Adams." 10 Vols. Boston. 1853.
"Letters of Mrs. Abigail Adams." 2 Vols. Boston. 1840.
"Three Episodes of Massachusetts History." 2 Vols. Boston. 1892.
"Massachusetts, its Historians and its History." Boston. 1893.
Adams, James Truslow. "The Founding of New England." Boston. 1921.
"Revolutionary New England." Boston. 1923.
"New England in the Republic." Boston. 1927.
"Provincial Society" 1609–1763. (In American Life Series)
Adams, John Quincy. Works. Ed. Worthington C. Ford. 7 Vols. New York. 1913.
The American Church History Series. 12 Vols.
Allison, W. H. "Inventory of Unpublished Materials for American Religious History." Washington. 1911.
Armitage-Smith, S. "John of Gaunt." London. 1904.
Arnold, Thomas. "Select English Works of John Wyclif." 3 Vols. London. 1869.
Asbury, Francis. "Journals." 3 Vols. New York. 1852.
Asbury, Herbert. "A Methodist Saint." (Life of Francis Asbury) New York. 1927.

Bale, J. "Brief Chronicle of Sir John Oldcastle." (Parker Society, Vol. 36)

Bancroft, George. "History of the United States." 10 Vols. Boston. 1834–1874.
  Later edition in 6 Vols. 1883–1885.
Bancroft, H. H. "History of the Pacific States of North America." 34 Vols. San Francisco. 1882–1890.
Beard, Charles A. "An Economic Interpretation of the Constitution of the United States." New York. 1913.
  "Economic Origins of Jeffersonian Democracy." New York. 1915.
  (With Mary R. Beard) "The Rise of American Civilization." 2 Vols. New York. 1927.
Beer, G. L. "The Origins of the British Colonial System." New York. 1908 and "The Old Colonial System," 2 Vols. New York. 1912.
Benton, Thomas H. "Thirty Years' View; A History of the Workings of the American Government from 1820 to 1850." 2 Vols. New York. 1861.
Beveridge, Albert J. "Life of John Marshall." 4 Vols. Boston. 1916–1919.
  "Life of Abraham Lincoln." 2 Vols. 1928.
Bowers, Claude G. "Jefferson and Hamilton, The Struggle for Democracy in America." Boston. Ninth Imprint. 1926.
  "The Party Battles of the Jackson Period." Boston. 1922.
Bradford, William. "History of Plymouth Plantation." Third edition. 1856.
Briggs, Charles A. "American Presbyterianism; Its Origin and Early History." New York. 1885.
Brown, Alexander. "Genesis of the United States." 2 Vols. Boston. 1890.
  "The First Republic in America," Boston. 1898.
Bruce, Philip A. "Economic History of Virginia in XVII. Century." 2 Vols. 1907.
  "Institutional History of Virginia." 2 Vols. New York. 1910.
Burgess, John W. "The Civil War and the Constitution." 2 Vols. New York. 1901.
  "Reconstruction and the Constitution." New York. 1902.
  (Both in the American History Series)
Burrage, Champlin. "The Early English Dissenters, in the Light of Recent Research." 2 Vols. Cambridge University Press. 1912.
  "The True Story of Robert Browne." Oxford. 1906.

"The Church Covenant Idea." 1904.
"New Facts concerning John Robinson." 1910.

Calvin, John. "Institutiones." (Many editions) English translation by J. Allen, 1844.
"Letters." Standard edition in 59 Vols. Strassburg. English translation, Calvin Translation Society, in 48 Vols. Edinburgh.

Cambridge Modern History. 14 Vols. London. 1909–1912. Especially Vol. VII.

Carnegie Institution. "Contributions to American Economic History."

Carlyle, Thomas. "Oliver Cromwell's Letters and Speeches." 3 Vols. 1857.

Catholic Encyclopedia. 16 Vols. New York. 1907–1914.

Channing, Edward. "History of the United States of America." 6 Vols. New York. 1905–1926 (in progress).

Channing, Hart, and Turner. "Guide to the Study and Reading of American History." Boston. 1912.

Channing, William E. "Collected Works." American Unitarian Association. Boston. 1875.

Cheyney, E. P. "Some English Conditions Surrounding the Settlement of Virginia." American Historical Review. 1907.

Clark, Henry W. "History of English Nonconformity." 2 Vols. London. 1911.

Colonial Records of Governor and Company of Massachusetts Bay in New England. Ed. N. B. Shurtleff. 5 Vols. Boston. 1853–1854.

Colonial Records of New Plymouth in New England. Ed. N. B. Shurtleff. 12 Vols. (Especially Vol. XI) Boston. 1855–1861.

Colonial Records of Plantation of New Haven. Ed. C. J. Hoadly. Hartford. 1858.

Cooks, John Esten. "Virginia, A History of the People." Boston. 1883.

Cotton, John. "The Way of the Churches in New England." London. 1645.

Cross, Arthur Lyon. "The Anglican Episcopate and the American Colonies." New York. 1902. (Harvard Historical Studies. No. IX)

Curteis, G. H. "Dissent in its Relations to the Church of England." (Bampton Lectures for 1871)

Dakin, Edwin Franden. "Mrs. Eddy, The Biography of a Virginal Mind." Popular edition. New York. 1930.

Deansley, M. "The Lollard Bible." London. 1920. (With excellent bibliography)

Dexter, Henry Martyn. "As to Roger Williams." Boston. 1876. "Congregationalism as seen in its Literature." New York. 1880.

Doyle, J. A. "The English in America." 5 Vols. London. 1882–1907. (In America under the title "English Colonies in America") *Cf.* contributions to Vol. VII of "Cambridge Modern History."

Earle, Alice Morse. "The Sabbath in Puritan New England." Fifth edition. New York. 1892.
"Margaret Winthrop." New York. 1895.
"Home Life in Colonial Days." New York. 1898.

Eastman, P. M. "Life of Robert Raikes." 1880.

Eddy, Mary Grover Baker. "Science and Health, with Key to the Scriptures." Many editions since 1866.

Edwards, Jonathan. "Complete Works." 2 Vols. London. 1840. (Many other editions)
"Life" by A. V. G. Allan. Boston. 1889. (American Religious Leaders Series)

Eggleston, Edward. "The Beginnings of a Nation." New York. 1896. Especially "The Circuit Rider", "The Hoosier Schoolmaster" and "The Graysons."

Ellis, Sir Henry. "Doomsday Book." Introduction and Abstract. London. 1833.

Emerson, Ralph Waldo. "Complete Works." Riverside Edition. Boston. 1887.

Evans, Charles. "American Bibliography." 9 Vols. 1903–1925. Chicago (in progress).

Farrand, Max. "Records of the Federal Convention of 1787." 2 Vols. New Haven. 1911.

Faust, A. B. "Das Deutschtum in den Vereinigten Staaten." 2 Bände. 1912.

Felt, J. B. "Ecclesiastical History of New England." 2 Vols. Boston. 1855–1862.

Field, T. M. "Unpublished Letters of Charles Carroll of Carrollton." New York. 1902. (U. S. Historical Society Series I)

Fiske, John. "The Beginnings of New England." Boston. 1889. "Old Virginia and Her Neighbors." 2 Vols. 1897.

Fitzralph, Richard (of Armagh). "De Pauperie Salvatoris." Published by Wyclif Society in part in volume containing "De Dominio Divinio." Ed. R. L. Poole.

Forbes, Harriet. "New England Diaries." Mass. 1925.

Force, Peter. "Tracts and Other Papers relating principally to the Colonies in North America." 4 Vols. Washington. 1836–1846.

Ford, Paul Leicester. "The Federalist." New York. 1896.

Ford, Worthington C. "George Washington." 1899. "Writings of George Washington." 14 Vols. 1889.

Franklin, Benjamin. "Complete Works." 10 Vols. Ed. John Bigelow. New York. 1887–1888.

Freeman, Edward A. "History of the Norman Conquest." 6 Vols. 1867–1876. "The Growth of the English Constitution." Fourth edition. 1884.

Froude, James Anthony. "History of England from the Fall of Wolsey to the Death of Elizabeth." 12 Vols. (New York reprint 1872)

Gairdner, James. "Lollardy and the Reformation in England." 2 Vols. London. 1908. (With Brewer). "Fundamental Documents of the Reign of Henry VIII." 21 Vols. Completed in 1910.

Gladstone, William E. "The Church of England and Ritualism", 1874–1875, and "The Courses of Religious Thought." 1876. in "Gleanings of Past Years." Vols. III and VI.

Gobineau, Count Joseph A. "Les Religions at les Philosophies dans l'Asia Central." 1865.

Goodwin, E. L. "The Colonial Church in Virginia." Milwaukee. 1927.

Goodwin, John A. "The Pilgrim Republic." Boston. 1899.

Gordy, J. P. "A History of Political Parties in America." 3 Vols. Ohio. 1895.

Grant, Ulysses S. "Personal Memories." 2 Vols. New York. 1885.

Green, John R. "A Short History of the English People." Third edition by Mrs. Alice R. Green and Miss Kate Norgate. 4 Vols. New York. 1893.

Griffins, A. P. C. "Bibliography of American Historical Societies."
    1905.
    "Index of Articles upon American Local History in Historical
    Collections in the Boston Public Library." Boston. 1890–1895.
Griswold, R. W. "The Poets and Poetry of America." Philadelphia.
    1846.

Hakluyt, Richard. "Discourse on Western Planting." Reprint with
    notes in collection of Maine Historical Society.
    "Principal Navigations." Reprint in Glasgow, 1903, of origi-
    nal edition of 1600.
Hall, Thomas Cuming. "History of Ethics within Organized Chris-
    tianity." New York and London. 1910.
    "The Social Meaning of Modern Religious Movements in
    England." New York. 1900.
Harnack, Adolf von. "Dogmengeschichte." 2te. Aufl. 3 Bde. 1890.
    "Die Mission und Ausbreitung des Christentums." 3te. Aufl.
    2 Bde. 1915.
    "Das Mönchthum, seine Ideale und seine Geschichte." 5te.
    Aufl. 1901.
    "Enststehung und Entwickelung der Kirchenverfassung und
    des Kirchenrechts in den zwei ersten Jahrhunderten. Leipzig.
    1910.
Hart, A. B. "American History Told by Contemporaries", 4 Vols.
    New York. 1897–1901. 5th volume said to be in progress.
Hastings, James. "Encyclopedia of Religion and Ethics." 1908–
    1914.
Hawks, "Contributions to the Ecclesiastical History of the United
    States." 2 Vols. New York. 1836–1839.
Helper, Hinton Rowan. "The Impending Crisis of the South; How to
    Meet it." London. 1860.
Hening, William Walter. "The Statutes-at-Large, being a collection of
    all the Laws of Virginia." (1619–1792) 13 Vols. New York. 1823.
Henry, William Wirt. "Life, Correspondence and Speeches of
    Patrick Henry." 3 Vols. New York. 1891.
Hinds, William A. "American Communities." Chicago. 1902.
Hinton, John Howard. "History and Topography of the United
    States." 2 Vols. London. 1832.
Hodgetts, J. Frederick. "The English of the Middle Ages." London.
    1885.

Holst, Hermann von. "Constitutional and Political History of the United States." English translation in 8 Vols. Chicago. 1899.

Hutchinson, E. M. (With Stedman) "A Library of American Literature." 11 Vols. New York. 1894.

Hutchinson, Thomas. "History of the Province of Massachusetts Bay." 3 Vols. Boston. 1764–1769.

Interchurch World Movement. "Report on the Steel Strike of 1919." By a Commission of Inquiry. New York. 1920.

Jefferson, Thomas. "Notes on Virginia." 1782. "Writings, Autobiography, and other Writings." Congress Ed. H. A. Washington. 9 Vols. 1853–1854.
"Collected Works." 10 Vols. by P. L. Ford. New York. 1892–1899.
"Life." By John T. Morse, Jr. Boston. 1883. James Parton. Boston. 1874. Henry S. Randall. 3 Vols. New York. 1858. Thomas E. Watson. New York. 1903. Sarah N. Randolph. "Domestic Life of Thomas Jefferson." New York. 1872.

Knighton, Henry. "Chronicon." Ed. J. R. Lumly. (Rolls Series) 2 Vols. 1889.

Kropotkin. Peter. "Mutual Aid." New York. 1903.
"Fields, Factories and Workshops." London. 1901.

Larned, J. N. "Literature of American History." Boston. 1902.

Laud, William. "Autobiography." Oxford. 1839.

Lechford, Thomas. "Plain Dealing or Newes from New England." Massachusetts Historical Society Collection III.

Lechler, Gotthard. "Johann von Wiclif und die Vorgeschichte der Reformation." 2 Bde. Leipzig. 1873.

Lecky, W. E. H. "A History of England in the XVIII Century." 8 Vols. New York. 1888.
"History of European Morals." Third edition. 2 Vols. New York. 1900.

Levett, A. E. "The Black Death." Oxford. 1916 (Oxford Studies in Social History)

Lewis, Sinclair. "Elmer Gantry." New York. 1927.

Linn, W. Alexander. "The Story of the Mormons from the Date of their Origin to the Year 1901." New York. 1902.

Long, A. L. "Memories of Robert E. Lee." New York. 1902.

Lowell, James Russell. "Complete Works." Riverside Edition. Boston. 1887.

Luther, Martin. "Werke." Volksausgabe in 8 Bden. Berlin. 1898.

Macaulay, Thomas Babington. "History of England." 8 Vols. 1868.

McMaster, John Bach. "History of the People of the United States." (From the Revolution to the Civil War) 8 Vols. New York. 1883–1910. A ninth volume has just appeared.

McIlwaine, H. R. "The Struggle of Protestant Dissenters for Religious Toleration in Virginia." Johns Hopkins University Studies XII. 1893. No. 4.

Madison, James. "Notes" (on the Federal Convention) in the "Documentary History of the Constitution." 5 Vols. Washington. 1894–1905.

Manning, B. Lord. "The Peoples' Faith in the Time of Wycif." 1919.

Massachusetts Historical Society. "Proceedings and Collections." Boston, 1792. In Series of ten volumes with indices to each series.

Masson, David. "Life of Milton in Connection with the History of His own Times." 6 Vols. London. 1854–1880.

Mather, Cotton. "Magnalia Christi Americana." London. 1702.

Mathew, F. D. "The English Works of Wyclif hitherto Unprinted." Early English Text Society. 1880.

Meade, William (Bishop). "Old Churches, Ministers and Families of Virginia." 2 Vols. Philadelphia. 1857.

Meuller, Karl. "Kirchengeschichte." 2 Bde. (4 Teile) 2te Aufl. 1902–1919. A revision is in progress.

Meuller, Max. "Deutsche Liebe." English Translation and many editions.

Meyer, Arnold Oskar. "England and the Catholic Church under Queen Elizabeth." (English Translation by T. R. McKee) London. 1916.

Meyer, Eduard. "Ursprung und Geschichte der Mormonen." With valuable comparisons with the rise of Christianity and Islam. Halle. 1912.

Meyer, Gustavus. "The History of Great American Fortunes." 3 Vols. 1910.
"The History of the Supreme Court." 1912.
"The History of Tammany Hall." New York. 1917.

Mode, P. G. "Source Book and Bibliography for American Church History." Menasha. 1921.

Morrison, S. E. "The Oxford History of the United States." Oxford.
1927.
"Abraham Lincoln." 2 Vols. Boston. 1893. (Both in American
Statesmen Series)

Morse, John T., Jr. "John Quincy Adams." Tenth edition. Boston.
1886.

Myrck, John. "Instructions for Parish Priests." Early English Text
Society. 1868.

Narragansett Club Publications. (For Writings of Roger Williams)

Neal, Daniel. "History of the Puritans." 1732–1738. (An abridged
edition by Parsons) London. 1811.

Nevins, Allen. "American Social History, recorded by British Trav-
elers." 1923.
"The American During and After the Revolution." 1924.

Newman, Henry. "Apologia pro Vita Sua." London. 1864.

O'Gorman, Thomas. "A History of the Roman Catholic Church
in the United States." 1895. Vol X of American Church
Series.

Oman, C. W. "The Great Revolt of 1381." London. 1906.

Owst, G. R. "Mediæval Preaching in England." 1926.

Palfrey, John G. "History of New England." 5 Vols. Boston,
1859–1890.

Pecock, Reginald. "Repressor of Over-Much Weeting (Blaming)
of the Clergie." Ed. C. Babington, in 2 Vols. (Rolls Series).
1860.

Perry, William S. "Historical Collections relating to the American
Colonial Church." 5 Vols. (Virginia, Pennsylvania, Massachu-
setts, Maryland and Delaware)
"The History of the American Episcopal Church." 2 Vols.
Boston. 1885.
"The Episcopate in America." New York. 1895.

Phillips, U. B. "American Negro Slavery." New York. 1918.
"Life and Labor in the Old South." Boston. 1929.

Pierce, William. "An Historical Introduction to the Marprelate
Tracts." 1909.
"The Marprelate Tracts." (1588–1589) London. 1911.

Powel, E., and G. M. Trevelyan. "The Peasant Rising and the Lollards." 1899.

Rhodes, James Ford. "History of the United States from 1850." 8 Vols. With supplementary volume. New York. 1920.

Riley, J. Woodbridge. "The Founder of Mormonism; a Psychological Study." New York. 1902.

Ritschl, Albrecht. "Geschichte des Pietismus." 3 Bde. 1880–1886.

Robinson, John. "Works." Ed. R. Ashton. 3 Vols. 1851.

Rogers, J. E. Thorold. "Six Centuries of Work and Wages." 1891. "The Economic Interpretation of History." London. 1889.

Rossiter, W. S., and North, D. N. S. "A Century of Population Growth. From 1790–1900." 1909.

Rowe, H. K. "The History of Religion in the United States." New York. 1924.

Rowland, Mary Mason. "Life of Charles Carroll of Carrollton, with his Correspondence and Public Papers." 2 Vols. New York. 1898.

Sainsbury *et al.* Calender of State Papers. Colonial Series. America and West Indies. 27 Vols. 1374–1714. London (in progress).

Seeley, J. R. "The Expansion of England." Tauchintz Edition. 1 Vol. 1884.

Semple, Ellen Churchill. "American History and its Geographical Conditions." London. 1913.

Sewall, Samuel. "Diary." (1674–1729) 3 Vols. Massachusetts Historical Society Collection. Fifth Series. Boston. 1872–1878.

Sharpless, Isaac. "History of Quaker Government in Pennsylvania." 2 Vols. Philadelphia. 1898–1899.

Shea, John Gillmary. "The Catholic Church in Colonial Days." New York. 1886. "Life and Times of Archbishop Carroll." New York. 1888.

Shirley (Cannon), W. W. "Fasciculi Zizaniorum Magister Johannis Wyclif cum Tritico." (Rolls Series) 1858.

Sippell, Theodor. "Zur Vorgeschichte des Quäkertums." Giessen. 1920.

Smith, Joseph. "The Pearl of Great Price." Many reprints.

Smith, Sydney. "Collected Works." 4 Vols. London. 1840.

Smith, William Henry. "A Political History of Slavery." 2 Vols. New York. 1903.

Sohm, Rudolf. "Wesen und Ursprung des Katholicismus." 1909. (Abhandlungen der Philo-Histor. Klasse d, K. Sächs. Gesellsch. d, Wiss. Bd. 27. H 3)

Stearns, Harold E. (Editor). "Civilization in the United States, an Inquiry by Thirty Americans." New York. 1922.

Stedman, E. C. (With Hutchinson). "A Library of American Literature." 11 Vols. New York. 1894.

Steiner, Bernard C. "Beginnings of Maryland." (Johns Hopkins University Studies) XXI, Nos. 8--10.

Stubbs, William (Bishop). "Select Charters and Other Illustrations of English History."
"The Constitutional History of England." 3 Vols. Oxford. 1874. Later edition in 1913.

Swem, E. C. "A Bibliography of Virginia." 2 Vols. Richmond. 1916–1919.

Tatham, G. B. "The Puritans in Power." Cambridge. 1913.

Tawney, R. H. "Religion and the Rise of Capitalism." New York. 1926.

Taylor, Henry Osborn. "The Mediæval Mind." Fourth edition. New York. 1925.
"The Book of Mormon." First edition. 1830. Many reprints.
"The Brut" or "The Chronicle of England." Ed. F. W. D. Brie. Early English Text Society. 1908.

Thompson, A. Hamilton. "A History of English Literature." Thirty-one imprints. 1923.

Tiffany, C. C. "A History of the Protestant Episcopal Church in the United States." Vol. VII of the American Church Series.

Trevelyan, George M. "England in the Age of Wyclif." 1898.
(With Powell). "The Peasant Rising and the Lollards." 1899.

Troeltsch, Ernest. "Gesammelte Schriften." (Especially Band I) Tuebingen. 1912.

Turner, Fred. J. "Significance of the Frontier." American Historical Association Report. 1893.
"Pioneer Ideals." Indiana University Bulletin. VIII: 6.

Tyerman, Luke. "Life of John Wesley." 1870.
"Life of George Whitefield." 2 Vols. 1876–1877.

Ueberweg, Fredrick. "Grundriss der Geschichte der Philosophie." 9te Aufl. umgeabeitet von Dr. Max Heinze. in 4 Bde. Berlin. 1902.

Vinogradoff, Paul. "Villainage in England." Oxford. 1892.
"English Society in the Eleventh Century." Oxford. 1908.

Walker, Williston. "A History of the Congregational Churches in the United States." Sixth edition. New York. 1903. (Vol. III of American Church History Series)

Walsingham, T. "Historia Anglicana." Ed. H. T. Riley. (Rolls Series) 2 Vols. 1863.

Ward, William George. "Ideal of a Christian Church." 1844.

Weber, Max. "Die protestantische Ethik und der Geist des Kapitalismus." in "Archiv für Sozialwissenschaft und Sozialpolitik." Band XX und XXI.

Weeden, W. B. "Economic and Social History of New England." 2 Vols. Boston. 1890.

Weingarten, Hermann. "Die Revolutionskirchen Englands." Leipzig. 1868.

Wendell, Barrett. "A Literary History of America." New York. 1920.

Wertenbaker, Thomas Jefferson. "Patrician and Plebian in Virginia." 1910.
"Virginia under the Stuarts." 1914.
"Planters of Colonial Virginia." 1922.

Wesley, John. "Journal." Published in Standard Edition by N. Curnock. 1910.

White, Andrew D. "A History of the Warfare of Science with Theology in Christendom." 2 Vols. New York. 1897.

Whitefield, George. "Collected Works." 1771–1772. *Cf.* also Tyerman.

Wilkins, David. "Concilia Magnæ Britanniæ et Hiberniæ." 4 Vols. 1737.

Williams, Rogers. "The Publications of the Narragansett Club from 1866 to 1874." 6 Vols.

Winsor, Justin. "Narrative and Critical History of America." 8 Vols. London. 1832.

Winthrop, John. "History of New England from 1630 to 1649." Ed. James Savage. 1832.

Winthrop, R. C. "Life and Letters of John Winthrop." 2 Vols. Second edition. Boston. 1869.

Workman, Herbert B. "John Wyclif." 2 Vols. Oxford. 1926.

Wright, Thomas. "Political Songs of England." Camden Society. 1839.
"Political Poems and Songs." 2 Vols. (Rolls Series)

Wyclif, John. All the publications of the Wyclif Society.

CHAPTER BIBLIOGRAPHIES

CHAPTER I

Ellis, Sir Henry. "Domesday Book." Introduction and Abstract. 1833.

Freeman, Edward A. "History of the Norman Conquest." 6 Vols. 1867–1876.
"The Growth of the English Constitution." Fourth edition. 1884.

Green, J. R. "A Short History of the English People." Illustrated edition by Mrs. J. R. Green and Miss Kate Norgate. 4 Vols. 1893.

Hodgetts, J. Frederick. "The English of the Middle Ages." Edition of 1885.

Levett, A. E. "The Black Death."
"Oxford Studies in Social History." Oxford. 1916.

Myrck, John. "Instructions for Parish Priests." Early English Text Society. 1868.

Rogers, J. E. Thorold. "Six Centuries of Work and Wages." 1891.

Stubbs, Bishop William. "Select Charters and Other Illustrations of English History."
"The Constitutional History of England." 3 Vols. Oxford. 1874. Later edition, 1913.

Vinogradoff, Paul. "Villainage in England." Oxford. 1892.

Walsingham, T. "Historia Anglicana." Ed. H. T. Riley. 2 Vols. 1863.

Wilkins, David S. T. P. "Concilia Magnæ Britanniæ et Hiberniæ." 4 Vols. London. 1737.

CHAPTER II

All the publications of the Wyclif Society, but especially:
De Civili Dominio. Ed. Poole and Losert. Vols. 2–4. 1900 to 1904.
De Dominio Divino. Ed. Poole. 1890.
De Ecclesia. Ed. J. Losert. 1886.
De Eucharistia. Ed. J. Losert. 1892.

De Potestate Papæ. Ed. J. Losert. 1907.
De Veritate Sacræ Scripturæ. R. Buddensieg. 3 Vols. 1902–1905.
Opera Minora. Ed. J. Losert. 1913.
Select English Works of John Wyclif. Ed. Thomas Arnold. 3 Vols. 1869.
Sermones. Ed. J. Losert. 4 Vols. 1887–1890.
The English Works of Wyclif hitherto unprinted. Ed. F. D. Trialogus. Ed. G. Lechler. Oxford. 1869.
Matthew, for the Early English Text Society. 1880.
Armitage-Smith, S. "John of Gaunt." 1904.
Deansley, M. "The Lollard Bible." 1920.
Gairdner, James. "Lollardy and the Reformation in England." 2 Vols. 1908.
Grossetestes. "Epistolæ." Ed. M. Luard. 1862.
Lechler, Gotthard. "Johann von Wiclif und die Vorgeschichte der Reformation." 2 Bde. Leipzig. 1873.
Vinogradoff, Paul. "English Society in the Eleventh Century." Oxford. 1908.
Workman, Herbert B. "John Wyclif." 2 Vols. Oxford. 1926.

CHAPTER III

Bale, J. "Brief Chronicle of Sir John Oldcastle." (Parker Society, Vol. 36)
Knighton, Henry. "Chronicon." Ed. J. R. Lumley. (Rolls Series) 2 Vols. 1889.
Oman, C. W. "The Great Revolt of 1381." 1906.
Owst, G. R. "Medieval Preaching in England." 1926.
Pecock, R. "Repressor of Overmuch Blaming of the Clergy." 2 Vols. 1860.
Powel, E., and Trevelyan, G. M. "The Peasants' Rising and the Lollards." 1899.
Shirley, Canon W. W. "Fasciculi Zizaniorum Magister Johannis Wyclif cum Tritico." (Rolls Series) 1858.
Trevelyan, G. M. "England in the Age of Wyclif." 1898 and later editions.
Walsingham, Thomas. "Historia Anglicana." Ed. H. T. Riley. 1869.
Wright, T. "Political Poems and Songs." 2 Vols. (Rolls Series) "Political Songs of England." Camden Society. 1839.

CHAPTER IV

Same Titles as for Chapters II and III. Also:

Buddensieg, R. "Article in Real Encyclopædia für Protestantische Theologie. 'Lollarden.' "

Froude, James Anthony. "History of England from Fall of Wolsey to the Death of Elizabeth." Vol. I, Chap. 1.

Manning, B. L. "The People's Faith in the Time of Wyclif." 1919.

Rogers, James E. Thorold. "Six Centuries of Work and Wages." New York. Edition undated.

Taylor, H. O. "The Mediæval Mind." 2 Vols. Fourth edition. 1925.

"The Brut, or the Chronicle of England." Ed. F. W. D. Brie. Early English Text Society, 1908.

Thomson, A. Hamilton. "A History of English Literature." Pages 38–70.

CHAPTER V

Calvin, John. "Institutiones." Many editions and "Letters."

Hastings, James. "Encyclopedia of Religion and Ethics." *Cf.* articles under the various heads. 1908–1914.

Luther, Martin. "Werke." Volksausgabe in 8 Bde. 1898.

Sohm, Rudolph. "Wesen und Ursprung des Katholicismus." More especially the Vorwort. III–XXXIII. Leipzig. 1912.

Troeltsch, Ernst. "Die Soziallehren der Christlichen Kirchen und Gruppen." More especially Kap. III. Pages 427–986. Tübingen. 1912.

Von Harnack, Adolf. "Dogmengeschichte." 2 Auf. 1893. Pages 334–370.
"Entstehung und Entwickelung der Kirchenverfassung und Kirchenrechts." Leipzig. 1910.

CHAPTER VI

Froude, James Anthony, "History of England." Vol. II deals with the rising of Protestantism in England. Vols. III and IV with Henry VIII. All must be read with care, as they are full of gross blunders and brilliant misuse of sources.

Gairdner, James, and Brewer. "Fundamental Documents of the Reign of Henry VIII." 21 Vols. Completed in 1910.

Gladstone, William E. "The Church of England and Ritualism." 1874–1875. "Courses of Religious Thought." 1876, in "Gleanings of Past Years." Vols. III and VI.

Newman, Henry. "Apologia pro Vita Sua." London. 1864.

Tract 90. As well as the great Tractarian literature, which is too full to be more than suggested here.

Ward, William George. "Ideal of a Christian Church." 1844. (Still in the writer's judgment one of the most informing books on the Anglican High-Church Movement.)

CHAPTER VII

Masson, David. "Life of Milton in Connection with the History of His Own Time." 6 Vols. 1858–1880.

Meyer, A. O. "England and the Catholic Church." English translation. J. R. McKee. 1916.

Neal, Daniel. "History of the Puritans." 1732–1738. Abridged edition from the four volumes to two. Edward Parsons. London. 1811.

Oliver Cromwell's Letters and Speeches. Ed. Thomas Carlyle. 3 Vols. 1857.

Pierce, William. "An Historical Introduction to the Marprelate Tracts." 1909.
"The Marprelate Tracts." 1588, 1589. London. 1911.

CHAPTER VIII

Adams, Charles Francis. "Massachusetts: Its Historians and its History." 1893.

Adams, James Truslow. "The Founding of New England." Boston. 1921.

Bradford, William. "History of Plymouth Plantation." Third Edition. 1856.

Doyle, J. A. "The English in America." 5 Vols. London. 1882–1907. Published in America under the title "English Colonies in America." Especially II and III. *Cf.* also his contributions to the Cambridge Modern History. Vol. VII.

Fiske, John. "The Beginnings of New England." Boston. 1889.

Goodwin, John A. "The Pilgrim Republic." 1888.

Hinton, John Howard. "History and Topography of the United States." 2 Vols. London. 1832. (Giving some interesting older literature and old maps and pictures)

Hutchinson, Thomas. "History of the Province of Massachusetts Bay." 3 Vols. Boston. 1764–1769.

Mather, Cotton. "Magnalia Christi Americana." London. 1702.

Nevins, Allan. "American Social History Recorded by British Travellers." 1923.

Palfrey, John G. "History of New England." 5 Vols. Boston. 1859–1890.

Robinson, John. "Works." Ed. R. Ashton. 3 Vols. 1851. Especially "Justification of Separation from the Church" and "Apologia Brownistarum."

Sewall, Samuel. "Diary." (1674–1729) 3 Vols. In Massachusetts Historical Society Collection. Fifth Series. Boston. 1872–1878.

The Colonial Records of Plymouth, Massachusetts, Connecticut and New Haven, so far as printed. (Not all were at writer's disposal)

Winsor, Justin. "Narrative and Critical History of America." (Especially Vol. III and more particularly Chapter VIII) 8 Vols. London. 1832.

Winthrop. John. "History of New England from 1630 to 1649. Ed. James Savage. 1853.

CHAPTER IX

Besides the literature already given:

Calvin, John. "Institutes of the Christian Religion." Trans. by Rev. J. Allen. 1844.

Channing, Edward. "History of the United States of America." New York. 1896. From 1765–1865.

Narragansett Club Publications:

Cotton, John. "The Way of the Churches in New England." London. 1645.

Lechford, T. "Plain Dealing or Newes from New England." Massachusetts Historical Society Collection. Vol. III. Series III.

Winthrop, R. C. "Life and Letters of John Winthrop." 2 Vols.

Rossiter and North. "A Century of Population Growth." 1909.

Tatham, G. B. "The Puritans in Power." Cambridge. 1913.

CHAPTER X

Antiquarian, An. "The Blue Laws of New Haven Colony, usually called Blue Laws of Connecticut; Quaker Laws of Plymouth and Massachusetts, etc." Hartford. 1838.

Brown, Alexander. "Genesis of the United States." 2 Vols. Boston. 1890.

Bruce, Philip A. "Economic History of Virginia in XVII century." 2 Vols. 1907.

Cheyney, E. P. "Some English Conditions Surrounding the Settlement of Virginia." American Historical Review. 1907.

Cooke, John Esten. "Virginia, a History of the People." Boston. 1883.

Fiske, John. "Old Virginia and Her Neighbors." 2 Vols. 1897.

Hermann, Weingarten. "The Revolutionskirchen Englands." Leipzig. 1868.

Jefferson, Thomas. "Notes on Virginia." 1782.

Meade, William (Bishop). "Old Churches, Ministers, and Families of Virginia." 2 Vols. Philadelphia. 1857.

Wertenbaker, T. J. "Patrician and Plebeian in Virginia." 1910. "Planters of Colonial Virginia." 1922. "Virginia under the Stuarts." 1914.

Winsor, Justin. "Narrative and Critical History of America." Vol. III.

CHAPTER XI

Adams, Brooks. "The Emancipation of Massachusetts." Boston. 1887.

Adams, C. F. "Three Episodes of Massachusetts History." 2 Vols. 1892.

Adams, James Truslow. "Revolutionary New England. 1691–1776." Especially Chapters III and VIII.

Sharpless, Isaac. "History of Quaker Government in Pennsylvania." 2 Vols. Philadelphia. 1898–1899.

White, Andrew D. "A History of the Warfare of Science with Theology in Christendom." 2 Vols. New York. 1897.

Williams, Roger. The publications of the Narragansett Club from 1866 to 1874, in six volumes.

CHAPTER XII

Edwards, Jonathan. "The Complete Works." 2 Vols. London. 1840. More especially "A Treatise concerning the Religious Affections", Vol. I. Pp. 234–340, and "Narrative of Surprising Conversions", Vol. I. Pp. 344–359. Then also "Thoughts on the Revival of Religion in New England ", Vol. I. Pp. 365–

426. Those interested in his theory of the sacraments will find his position best stated in his "Inquiry concerning Qualifications for Communion", Vol. I. P. 479. His relation to classic English Dissent is best brought out in his "The Christian Pilgrim", Vol. II. Pp. 243–246.

Lecky, W. E. H. "A History of England in the XVIII Century." Vol. II, pp. 593–699. (Dealing however mainly with England)

Wesley, John. His "Journal", published in standard edition by N. Curnock. 1910.
Many "Lives"; best is still by Luke Tyerman. 1870. Various editions of "Works."

Whitefield, George. "Collected Works." 1771–1772.
"Life." Luke Tyerman. 2 Vols. 1876–1877.

CHAPTER XIII

Adams, John, and Mrs. Abigail Adams. "Familiar Letters During the Revolution." New York. 1876

Anderson, J. S. M. "History of the Church of England in the Colonies." 3 Vols. Second edition. 1856.

Bowers, Claude G. "Hamilton and Jefferson." (Especially Chap. V, pp. 92–115)

Cartwright, Peter. "Autobiography."

Cross, Arthur L. "The Anglican Episcopate and the American Colonies." London. 1902. (Harvard Historical Studies, No. IX)

Fisher, Sydney G. "Struggle for American Independence."

Hodges, George. "Three Hundred Years of the Episcopal Church in America." Philadelphia. 1906.

Howard, G. E. "Preliminaries of the Revolution."

Jefferson, Thomas. "Complete Works." Ed. P. L. Ford. 10 Vols. New York. 1892–1899.

Parkman, Francis. "A Half-Century of Conflict." 2 Vols. Boston. 1912.

The American Church History Series. 12 Vols.

Tipple, E. S. "The Heart of Asbury's Journal."

Usher, R. G. "Reconstruction of the English Church." 1910.

CHAPTER XIV

Adams, James Truslow. "Revolutionary New England", especially the last four chapters. Pp. 338–451.

Beard, Charles A. "An Economic Interpretation of the Constitution of the United States." New York. 1913.
Farrand, Max. "Records of the Federal Convention of 1787." 2 Vols. New Haven. 1911.
Ford, Paul Leicester. "The Federalist." New York. 1898.
Ford, Worthington C. "George Washington." 1899.
Madison, James. "Notes" in the "Documentary History of the Constitution." 5 Vols. Washington. 1894–1905.
Nevins, Allan. "The American During and After the Revolution." 1924.
The American Church History Series. 12 Vols. 1895.
Winsor, Justin. "Narrative and Critical History of America." Vol. III. Pp. 215–266.

CHAPTER XV

Asbury, Francis. "Journals." 3 Vols. New York. 1852.
Asbury, Herbert. "A Methodist Saint": a "Life" of Bishop Asbury. New York. 1927.
Carroll, H. K. "The Religious Forces of the United States." Vol. I of the American Church History Series.
Tiffany, C. C. "A History of the Protestant Episcopal Church in the United States." Vol. VII of the American Church History Series.
Walker, W. W. "A History of the Congregational Churches in the United States." Vol. III of the American Church History Series.

CHAPTER XVI

Faust, A. B. "Das Deutschtum in den Vereinigten Staaten." 2 Bände. 1912.
Special Reports of the Bureau of the Census. "Religious Bodies." 1906. Compiled by Mr. William C. Hunt. Part I, Summary and General Tables: Part II, Separate Denominations. Washington. 1910.
Tawney, R. H. "Religion and the Rise of Capitalism." New York. 1926.
Troeltsch, Ernest. "Gesammelte Schriften." 2 Vols. Especially III Kapital "Der Protestantismus."
Weber, Max. "Die protestantische Ethik und der 'Geist' des Kapitalismus." In Archiv für Sozialwissenschaft und Sozial politik. Band XX und XXI.

CHAPTER XVII

Emerson, Ralph Waldo. "Complete Works." Riverside Edition. Boston. 1887.

Franklin, Benjamin. "Complete Works." 10 Vols. Ed. John Bigelow. New York. 1887–1888

Griswold, R. W. "The Poets and Poetry of America." Philadelphia. 1846.

Lowell, James Russell. "Complete Works." Riverside Edition. 10 Vols. Boston. 1891.

Stedman, E. C., and Hutchinson, E. M. "A Library of American Literature." 11 Vols. New York. 1894.

Wendell, Barrett. "A Literary History of America." New York. 1920.

CHAPTER XVIII

The Centenary of the death of Robert Raikes in 1811 brought out a great literature relating to the Sunday school. *Cf.* "Life" by P. M. Eastman. 1880.

The Young Men's Christian Association has also a large literature of its own. There are several good accounts of the work of Sir George Williams.

For the place the layman plays in the various denominations, see the American Church History Series in 12 Vols.

Hinds, William A. "American Communities." Chicago. 1902.

Meyer, Eduard. "Ursprung und Geschichte der Mormonen." Halle. 1912.

CHAPTER XIX

Field, T. M. "Unpublished Letters of Charles Carroll of Carrollton, 1754–1832." New York. 1902. (United States Historical Society Series I)

O'Gorman, Thomas. "A History of the Roman Catholic Church in the United States." 1895. Vol. IX of the American Church History Series.

Rowland, Kate Mason. "Life of Charles Carroll of Carrollton, with his Correspondence and Public Papers." 2 Vols. New York. 1898.

Shea, John Gilmary. "The Catholic Church in Colonial Days." New York. 1886.

"Life and Times of Archbishop Carroll." New York. 1888.

The United States Catholic Historical Magazine.
The admirably edited "Catholic Encyclopedia." 16 Vols. New York.
1907–1914.

CHAPTER XX

Mueller, Max. "Deutsche Liebe" (for sidelight on German mystic
piety).
Special Reports of the Bureau of the Census. "Religious Bodies",
1906; Part II, The Separate Denominations.
Troeltsch, Ernest. "Gesammelte Schriften." 2 Bde., especially Bd. I.
Chap. VII.
The American Church History Series. 12 Vols. (already often cited)
The Yearbooks of the several Denominations.

CHAPTER XXI

Benton, T. H. "Thirty Years' View." 2 Vols. New York. 1854–1856.
Grant, Ulysses S. "Personal Memoirs." 2 Vols. New York. 1885.
Helper, Hinton Rowan. "The Impending Crisis of the South: How
to meet it." London. 1860.
Long, A. L. "Memoirs of Robert E. Lee." New York. 1886.
Rhodes, James Ford. "History of the United States from 1850."
Vols. III, IV and V. New York. 1920.
Semple, Ellen Churchill. "American History and its Geographical
Conditions." London. 1913. Especially Chapters IX and
XIII; more particularly pp. 256–263 and Chap. XIV, par-
ticularly pp. 301–307.
Smith, William Henry. "A Political History of Slavery." 2 Vols.
New York. 1903.
The Abolitionist literature is too large to quote.

CHAPTER XXII

Bancroft, H. H. "History of Utah." 1889. Vol. XXI in his "History
of the Pacific States of North America." (Very full bibliog-
raphy up to 1888)
Dakin, Edwin Franden. "Mrs. Eddy, The Biography of a Virginal
Mind." Popular edition. New York. 1930.
Eddy, Mary Grover Baker. "Science and Health with Key to the
Scriptures." Many editions since 1866.
Linn, W. Alexander. "The Story of the Mormons from the Date of
Their Origin to the Year 1901." New York. 1902.

Meyer, Eduard. "Ursprung und Geschichte der Mormonen." Halle. 1912. (Mit Exkursen über die Anfänge des Islams und des Christentums.)

Riley, I. Woodbridge. "The Founder of Mormonism, a Psychological Study." New York. 1902.

Smith, Joseph. "The Pearl of Great Price." Many reprints.

"The Book of Mormon." First edition, 1830, now rare. Many reprints.

The Christian Science Monitor. Newspaper published in Boston by Christian Science Trustees.

The literature of the Salvation Army is large and easily obtainable. Its organ the *War-Cry* gives details of its publishing activity.

INDEX

ABBEYS, confiscation of, 62, 63
Abolitionists, 285, 288, 289
Acquisitiveness, not a Puritan characteristic, 220, 221, 224
Adams, Charles Francis, reference to, 118
Adams, James Truslow, references to, 69, 84
Adams, John, his religious position, 162, 165; on the trumpery of religion, 174; his appeal, 214
Adams, Samuel, 164, 165
Addison, Joseph, writings of, find an echo in colonies, 140
Agincourt, battle of, 8
Amana Community, 252 n., 273
America, intellectual awakening of, 225, 227; basis of her law, 227
American Baptist Missionary Union, 202
American Board of Commissioners for Foreign Missions, 201, 203
American-Catholicism, negatived by Leo XIII, 265
American literature, 225–239
American Party, 262
American Protestantism, reorganization of, 191–206, 227
"Americanism," 265
Amsterdam, Holland, religious toleration in, 312
Anabaptists, 62, 98, 99, 130, 131, 181, 272
Anglican Catholic Church, evolution of, 30
Anglican Church, Anglo-Catholicism of, 57; as constructed by Cranmer, 58; under Elizabeth, 60. *See also* English Episcopal Church
Anglo-American Protestantism, the Father of, 19; present position of, 296
Anglo-Catholic tradition, not transplanted to the New World, 119–121
Anglo-Catholicism, the Father of, 20; Henry VIII and, 56–65; progress of, 299
Anti-Trinitarianism, 179, 180, 201, 235, 246

Arianism, 102, 108, 167, 199
Arminian Mennonites, 181
Arminian Methodists, 212
Arminianism, 123
Arnold, Matthew, reference to, 310
Articles of Confederation, 164, 169, 177, 184
Asbury, Francis, Methodist Bishop in America, 162, 178, 196, 198
Asceticism, 210, 217, 219
Aston, follower of Wyclif, 41
Astor, John Jacob, 222
Athanasian Creed, 194
"Atheists," 62
Atlantic Monthly, 236
Augustine, visits England, 3
Avignon, removal of Roman *Curia* to, 17

BACH, JOHANN SEBASTIAN, 280
Ball, John, 29
Baltimore, 2d Lord (Cecilius Calvert), 114, 134, 256
Baltimore, 1st Lord (George Calvert), 134, 255
Bancroft, H. H., his "History of Utah," 307
Baptism, 103
Baptists, 181; treatment of, in the colonies, 101, 129, 130; and missions, 200–203; number of, 212; in the Civil War, 286
Barclay, Robert, Quaker, 130
Barrowists, 98
Baxter, Richard, 217
Beard, Prof. Charles A., on the Constitution of the United States, 183
Beethoven, Ludwig van, 280
Beisel, Conrad, founder of Ephrata Community, 252 n.
Bentham, Jeremy, 189
Berkeley, Sir William, Governor of Virginia colony, 111
Bethel-Aurora Communities, 252 n.
Beza, Théodore, 67, 71